Ontology and Oppression

Studies in Feminist Philosophy is designed to showcase cutting-edge monographs and collections that display the full range of feminist approaches to philosophy, that push feminist thought in important new directions, and that display the outstanding quality of feminist philosophical thought.

STUDIES IN FEMINIST PHILOSOPHY

Published in the Series:

Ontology and Oppression

Race, Gender, and Social Reality

KATHARINE JENKINS

OXFORD
UNIVERSITY PRESS

Oxford University Press is a department of the University of Oxford. It furthers
the University's objective of excellence in research, scholarship, and education
by publishing worldwide. Oxford is a registered trade mark of Oxford University
Press in the UK and certain other countries.

Published in the United States of America by Oxford University Press
198 Madison Avenue, New York, NY 10016, United States of America.

© Katharine Jenkins 2023

Library of Congress Control Number: 2023930581

ISBN 978–0–19–766678–4 (pbk.)
ISBN 978–0–19–766677–7 (hbk.)

DOI: 10.1093/oso/9780197666777.001.0001

For James and for Jenny, who, in different ways, made this book possible.

Contents

Contents

Acknowledgements

I gratefully acknowledge the various forms of institutional support that enabled me to work on the project in various stages of its trajectory, including its earlier incarnation as my PhD thesis. My PhD research, at the University of Sheffield, was funded by the Arts and Humanities Research Council. A Junior Research Fellowship at Jesus College, Cambridge, supported me in 2016 as I finished working on the PhD thesis. While working at the University of Nottingham, I benefited from an additional semester of research leave in 2018, supported by the Philosophy Department, which enabled me to make progress on the book manuscript. I am thankful for each of these.

I thank all the people at, and associated with, Oxford University Press USA who worked on this book, including Peter Ohlin, Cheshire Calhoun, Brent Matheny, and Preetham Raj. Wendy Keebler provided expert and sympathetic copyediting, and Susan Monahan did an excellent job compiling the index; I am most grateful to them both.

I have been extremely fortunate to receive outstanding help, advice, and support from very many people as I worked on this research. Without their kindness this book could not have been written, and their suggestions have improved it beyond measure, although naturally all responsibility for its faults rests with me alone.

First, I thank Jenny Saul, who was my primary PhD supervisor—the best anyone could ever hope for—and who has been a wise and generous mentor and friend in the years since. Jenny, I can never thank you enough. Without all you've done for me and for the discipline at large, I probably would not still be in philosophy, much less have written this book (and I certainly wouldn't be having this much fun doing it). I was fortunate to have an excellent secondary PhD supervisor, Miranda Fricker, to whom I am profoundly grateful for her guidance and encouragement. Miranda, thank you so much for helping me not only to complete my PhD but also to learn what kind of philosophy I wanted to write and how to go about writing it. I am very grateful to Rae Langton, who was my external examiner for the PhD and who provided extremely generous and insightful feedback on both that occasion and subsequent occasions, which helped me to improve the project and see how I could take it beyond a PhD thesis. Thank you so much, Rae.

Any work of scholarship owes intellectual debts to the work of others, but I have been incredibly fortunate to receive support and encouragement from other philosophers working in the same area of philosophy that goes far beyond what scholars who share a field owe to one another in general. In particular, I thank Åsa Burman for steadfast friendship and endless encouragement, for reading countless drafts of different sections at numerous stages, and, of course, for our wonderful Social Ontology Road Trip—here's to many more! I thank Ásta for consistent support and advice that helped me figure out crucial steps in transforming the project from a thesis into a book and for giving me such a brilliant example of how feminist analytic metaphysics can be done. I thank Elizabeth Barnes for thorough and lucid comments and warm encouragement, including at critical moments, which helped to improve the manuscript enormously. I thank Robin Dembroff for their comments and camaraderie alike; I am so lucky to have been working on these topics alongside such a brilliant scholar and generous friend. I thank Sally Haslanger for graciously and patiently advising and encouraging me as I struggled to figure out how to situate the project in the philosophical landscape—and, indeed, for doing so much to carve out an area of that landscape in which these topics can be more fruitfully pursued.

My thanks to Lorna Finlayson for an enduring and precious philosophical friendship that spans the lifetime of this project (as well as my philosophical education before it) and generally for putting up with me. In conjunction with Lorna, I thank Rosie Worsdale for an extremely rewarding collaboration on the essay I draw on in Chapter 8. Thanks to Orlando Lazar-Gillard and Tessa Frost, for friendship, encouragement, and extensive feedback over the last two years of this project's life. Over the same period, I also benefited from the constant encouragement and insightful comments of Kate Norlock and Susan Brison—thank you both for being such staunch and splendid feminist philosophy friends.

The kindness that people have shown me as I worked on this book far exceeds my capacity to detail it here given the limitations of space. I must therefore content myself with thanking, very sincerely, the following friends and colleagues who supported the writing of this book in one way or another, such as by commenting on chapters, discussing ideas, and offering suggestions and encouragement: Alejandro Naranjo Sandoval, Alessandra Tanesini, Alexis Davin, Andi Fugard, Aness Webster, Arianne Shahvisi, Arto Laitinen, Asya Passinsky, Ben Colburn, Celia Edell, Chike Jeffers, David Ludwig, David MacDonald, Davina Cooper, Dee Payton, Emmalon Davis,

Esa Diaz-Leon, Filipa Melo Lopes, Fiona Woolard, Florence Ashley, George Pavlakos, Han Edgoose, Hilkje Hänel, J. Adam Carter, Jaana Virta, Jade Fletcher, Jake Beardsley, Jennifer Corns, Johan Brännmark, Kate Ritchie, Katherine O'Donnell, Kathryn Maude, Koshka Duff, Liam Kofi Bright, Lisa Millbank, Luke Roelofs, Lydia Farina, Mari Mikkola, Marta Jorba, Matthew Andler, Matthew Cull, Megan Blomfield, Mike Raven, Naomi Scheman, Neil Williams, Olúfẹ́mi O. Táíwò, Philip Cook, Rachel Fraser, Rebecca Mason, Riki Wilchins, Robin Zheng, Rowan Bell, Ruth Pearce, Sofia Vlaad, Stephanie Kapusta, Stephanie Rennick, and Zoe Playdon. Any omissions here are due to the length of time over which I have been working on the project and my poor record keeping and not lack of gratitude.

I thank audience members and interlocutors at each of the places where I presented material from this book and its precursor papers. These are too numerous to list, but special thanks are due to the members of the Cambridge Feminist Philosophy Reading Group (including Andrew Buskell, Paula Keller, Rae Langton, Lucy McDonald, and Livia von Samson), who very kindly read a complete draft of the manuscript in 2021. I also thank my colleagues at Sheffield, Cambridge, Nottingham, and Glasgow, especially members of the work-in-progress groups who commented on drafts. Comments from all of these sources greatly improved the final book.

My friends and family have been endlessly supportive and patient while I wrestled with this project in its various forms over the years. My heartfelt thanks to all of them. For steadfast friendship spanning the whole lifetime of the project, special thanks are due to Beatrice Balfour, Kathryn Maude, Clare Walker Gore, and Neil Williams. I thank my lovely out-laws, Ian Fraser and Lily Fraser, and my wonderful siblings, Carla Snowball-Hill and Ben Jenkins. My deepest love and gratitude to my parents, Sue Jenkins and Paul Jenkins. I am so lucky that you have all been there for me.

Last but not least, I thank James Fraser, for making everything make sense.

Introduction

I.1. On Not 'Choosing Reality'

On 10 October 2018, a full-page advert ran in the *Metro*, London's free commuter newspaper. The topic of the advert was an imminently closing government consultation on the Gender Recognition Act 2004, the legislation
governing changes of legal gender for trans people in England and Wales.
The government was considering adopting a simplified system in which
trans people would be able to change their legal gender by means of a statutory declaration alone, in contrast to the existing process, which was intrusive, expensive, bureaucratic, and inaccessible to many trans people.[1] This
proposal was strongly supported by trans rights campaigners and LGBT
charities. The advert was run by a group called Fair Play For Women, whose
aim, expressed in the advert and in other materials, was to encourage people
to respond to the consultation with a negative assessment of the proposals,
on the grounds that the proposed reform would put cis women and girls at
risk of harm. The advert posed questions such as 'Do you think fully intact,
male-bodied prisoners should be allowed to live with women in prison?' and
'Do you think someone with a penis is a woman?'. Most of the page was taken
up with large text reading: 'Think about it. #ChooseReality'.

The stark transphobia on display in the advert (a prurient interest in
trans people's genitals, for example) was entirely in keeping with much of
the anti-reform discourse around the consultation. What happened next,
though, was very interesting. The intended implication of the slogan 'Choose
Reality' in its context is that the *reality—the* fact of the matter—is that trans
women who have not undertaken a medical transition (specifically, one that
includes genital surgery) are not women and that for this reason they ought
not to be treated as women socially and politically. However, the hashtag

---

[1] At the time, I argued in support of this reform along with two other philosophers (Finlayson,
Jenkins, and Worsdale 2018).

Ontology and Oppression. Katharine Jenkins, Oxford University Press. © Katharine Jenkins 2023.
DOI: 10.1093/oso/9780197666777.003.0001

was quickly picked up on social media by people *in favour* of reform who turned it on its head to argue that trans people were indeed 'choosing reality' by choosing to live in accordance with their gender identity—something that the proposed legislation would make much easier. One tweet stated, 'When a person transitions and becomes their authentic self rather than live a lie that is them deciding to #choosereality'.[2] Another tweet read, '#ChooseReality and choose to fight for women's rights, because trans women #really are women and trans women's rights #really are women's rights'.[3] This pushback highlights something very important, which is that arguments against trans people using gender-appropriate facilities erase many of the realities of trans people's lives. In this sense, it provides an incisive critique of the claims made in the advert.

However, this way of pushing back at the advert does not challenge an assumption that the slogan 'Choose Reality' implicitly rests upon, which is that the dispute over the legislation *should be settled by establishing what reality is like*. In other words, the responses appear to grant that if someone is "really a man", they should be treated as a man, and if they are "really a woman", they should be treated as a woman. To put this thought another way, we should first establish who 'really is' a member of which gender and then use this to guide our social practices.

The arguments in this book show that in situations of oppression, this is a misguided way to think about reality. The point here is not that facts about gender should not guide our social practices because genders are in some sense "not real". Rather, I, like many philosophers, think of genders as what are called 'social kinds'. In general, 'kinds' are groupings of things that help us explain and predict the world. Chemical elements are good examples of kinds. The term 'kind' is closely related to the term 'category', but whereas categories are usually understood to have at least something to do with our mental representations, or how we conceptualise and classify the world around us, kinds are usually understood as more independent of our classificatory practices. *Social* kinds are kinds that are brought into existence by our social arrangements. *Money*, *monarchs*, and *monuments* are all social kinds. Questions about how things exist fall under the philosophical label of

---

[2] It continued: 'When you fund an [*sic*] run a hate campaign to repress trans* women specifically you're #choosingtransphobia and #choosingmisogyny' (@mumTdumpty, 5.44 a.m., 10.10.2018).
[3] It continued: 'It serves none of us to deny anyone their rights because of their biology or because they don't conform to gender norms' (@LauraC_AI, 9:45 a.m., 10.10.2018).

'ontology'. To give an account of the ontology of social kinds, then, is to say something about how social kinds exist.

I think that social kinds *are* real, and many philosophers agree. This is why I am not claiming that facts about gender should not guide our social practices because genders are in some sense "not real". Rather, the point is that it does not follow from the fact that a social kind exists (which is to say, is real) that it should be reflected in our social practices—for example, in the ways in which we relate to people. Social kinds are brought into being by social arrangements. Since social arrangements are always shaped and suffused by various types of power, the same is true of social kinds. Therefore, to say that we ought always to defer to the social kinds that currently exist is to say that we ought always to defer to the most dominant forms of power in our social setting; this is a moral and political claim that almost everyone would reject.

More precisely, I argue that social kinds can be such that individuals who are socially constructed as members of those kinds can be wronged *by the very fact* of being socially constructed in that way. I term this form of wrong 'ontic injustice': *ontic* because the wrong operates through social ontology, and *injustice* because the wrong is a consequence of our collective social arrangements. Ontic injustice is a wrong at the level of being that affects individuals simply in virtue of their membership in the social kind in question, regardless of their specific experiences. I hope to show that ontic injustice is a distinctive, pervasive, and interesting type of injustice which merits attention from moral, social, and political theorists.

In particular, I will argue that the concept of *ontic injustice* can help us to make sense of certain contestations surrounding gender and race kinds that are extremely important for anti-oppressive, or emancipatory, social movements. This includes the contestation about gender recognition that I started with, but it extends much more broadly as well. The social arrangements by means of which race and gender kinds have been produced have been extremely oppressive. At the same time, however, individuals often identify closely with membership in these kinds: many people feel that their gender or their race is an important and valuable part of who they are. This gives rise to difficulties for social movements seeking to counter race and gender oppression: Should countering oppression be conceived of as involving a project of dismantling or abolishing race and gender kinds? If so, how can this be reconciled with people's experiences of identification with those kinds? And how should we approach the question of categorising people with regard to these kinds? I argue that having the concept of ontic injustice on hand can help us in thinking through each of these difficulties.

Although I do not think that race and gender kinds are uniquely significant social kinds, I have chosen to focus on them for two reasons: first, because I think they offer a particularly clear example of issues concerning ontic injustice; and second, because I believe that certain confusions around these kinds are currently hindering emancipatory social movements and that the concept of ontic injustice can help with this problem. Because of the ways that social kinds which are often thought of as distinct (such as race kinds and gender kinds) are in fact intertwined in complex ways, I consider it crucial to focus on at least two dimensions of oppression in conjunction with each other.[4] I focus on race and gender in order to develop my account of ontic injustice and to explore and illustrate the theoretical power of this concept, aiming at the same time to keep in view the intersection of these dimensions of oppressions with others such as sexual orientation, disability, and class. Moreover, I hope that the theoretical tools I develop here will also be useful to those working more directly on further dimensions of oppression beyond race and gender.

The example of the advert and the pushback it received relates to the question of how people should be socially categorised, and here my main contention is that when kinds are ontically unjust, those who seek to oppose oppression need to be careful how we use these kinds. It may be that they do not serve as a good guide to our social practices and that we need instead to organise our social practices in ways that help to create new, better kinds. Based on this way of thinking, even if it did turn out that some trans women are in some sense "not women", ontologically speaking, this would not automatically justify the claim that those trans women should not be able to access women's spaces and facilities. This is because it might well be an instance of ontic injustice that the kind *women* is constructed in the way that it is. If there *is* a social kind *women* that excludes trans women *but is ontically unjust*, then we may well have good reasons to organise our practices in ways that do not reflect the contours of that kind.[5]

This is the sense in which I take the pushback against Fair Play For Women—though justified and in many ways effective—to come close to granting something that ought not to be granted: that trans women should

---

[4] This idea is termed 'intersectionality', and I will introduce it in more detail in Chapter 2.

[5] I am here in agreement with Robin Dembroff (2018); see §2.5.2 for a comparison of my view with that of Dembroff, and see §8.3.3 for further discussion of Dembroff's arguments.

be treated as women socially and politically *only to the extent that* they are in fact members of the ontological kind *women*. If gender kinds can exist in ways that are wrongful, then finding out about what kind someone belongs to tells us nothing about how they should be treated—and nor do we *need* to know about the nature of the kind that someone belongs to in order to reach a view about how they ought to be treated. To settle that question, we need to think not about ontology but about justice.

To put the point in general terms: we should not assume that our social practices should be guided by the social kinds that currently exist, because those kinds may be ontically unjust. When it comes to social reality, we should not "choose reality" simply because it *is* reality; we should first ask what that reality is like, specifically, whether it is just or unjust. And when it comes to social kinds—such as gender and race—that are bound up with oppression, we have reason to be especially cautious, as I shall show in this book.

I.2. Outline of Chapters

Here, I briefly summarise the chapters that follow. (Readers who are happy to simply begin at Chapter 1 without much in the way of a road map for what will follow may safely skip this section.)

In Chapter 1, I introduce the concept of ontic injustice, considered as a general phenomenon (i.e., without specific attention to race and gender). I aim to show that ontic injustice is a distinctive, pervasive, and interesting type of injustice which merits attention from moral, social, and political theorists. I begin by showing that there is an implicit consensus among different accounts of social ontology that what it is to be a member of a certain social kind is, at least in part, to fall under certain social constraints and enablements. I then argue that the very fact that an individual is a member of a social kind can be wrongful, because the constraints and enablements that partly constitute kind membership can fall short of what is morally owed to the individual who is subjected to them. When this happens, the person suffers ontic injustice. I theorise the wrong involved in ontic injustice as a moral injury, which is a form of damage to the acknowledgement of an individual's moral value. I show how the concept of ontic injustice must be combined with specific accounts of both social ontology and moral value in order to yield judgements about particular cases. Finally, I demonstrate what we stand to gain from incorporating the concept of ontic injustice into our conceptual repertoire, arguing that the concept of ontic injustice is valuable because it helps us to identify and respond to wrongful social constraints and enablements by highlighting their role in social construction and their status as moral injuries.

As I will explain in Chapter 1, in order to apply the concept of ontic injustice to particular cases, it is necessary to combine it with particular normative and ontological commitments concerning the morally relevant properties of the individuals and the precise ontology of the social kinds in question. In developing the concept, I have therefore faced something of a trade-off regarding the extent to which specific normative and ontological commitments should be built into the account. The fewer prior commitments are built into the concept, the greater the number of people who can make use of the concept in different projects they may have, which is clearly a benefit. However, the more open the concept is to being combined with different normative and ontological commitments, the more minimal the concept is. This is a drawback because having a more minimal concept makes it harder to see exactly how it applies to specific cases, and thus harder both to get a firm grasp of the concept and to see why it is useful.

The way I have decided to handle this trade-off is to introduce the concept of ontic injustice itself at a high level of generality, which I do in Chapter 1, and then to go on and model how it can be combined with a specific set of normative and ontological commitments in the context of a particular inquiry, which is what I do in the rest of this book. The particular inquiry that I will focus on concerns race and gender oppression: I want to show how the concept of ontic injustice helps us to understand race and gender kinds in a way that aids us in combating oppression. Chapter 2 supplies the necessary normative commitments, and the necessary ontological commitments follow in Chapters 3 to 7. Although I make a case for these normative and ontological commitments, there is much more to be said, and some readers will, I think, not be persuaded to accept these commitments. However, I hope to offer something that will interest even these readers, namely, a model of *how* the concept of ontic injustice can be combined with specific normative and ontological commitments to yield significant conclusions. I hope that others will take up the concept in the context of different projects and develop it in different ways.

In Chapter 2, I introduce the normative commitments that will guide my application of the concept of ontic injustice to race and gender kinds. I define ontic oppression as a species of ontic injustice in which the constraints and enablements to which the individual is subjected are not only wrongful in a general sense but are specifically *oppressive*. In order to support this definition, I offer an account of oppression as systematic, group-based restraints that steer people towards subordinated social positions, where such positions are characterised by six features: exploitation, marginalisation, powerlessness, cultural domination, violence, and communicative curtailment. On this definition, not everything that is unjust counts as being oppressive, making ontic oppression a particular species of ontic injustice. I also introduce the idea of intersectionality—roughly, the thought that racism and sexism are intermeshed in complex ways that make it impossible to theorise them well in isolation from each other—and I discuss how my understanding of oppression accords with this important insight.

In Chapter 3, I introduce the general ontological commitments that will support my investigation of race and gender kinds, building on the brief sketch given in Chapter 1 to offer a more precise and detailed account of how human social kinds exist. I understand social kinds as *explanatory* kinds, which is to say, kinds that we can use in the process of developing explanations, predictions, and interventions in the social world. I am interested in understanding what these kinds depend on for their existence. My account is intended as a pluralist conceptual framework: an overarching model that allows us to identify many different social kinds that serve different purposes. Since its main claim is that these kinds depend for their existence upon social constraints and enablements, I term it the 'constraints and enablements framework'. This framework includes three variables that we can use to identify social kinds. These variables function like sliders on a sound mixing board: just as by setting the sliders on a mixing board to different settings we can produce different sounds, by setting the sliders of the constraints and enablements framework to different settings, we can identify different social kinds. The three variables are scope, which concerns the context that is taken to be relevant; breadth, which concerns the different varieties of constraints and enablements that are taken into account; and granularity, which concerns the level of detail in which kinds are individuated and relates closely to questions of intersectionality.

In Chapters 4, 5, and 6, I defend a pluralist account of race and gender kinds, by outlining three varieties of race and gender kinds, each of which, I argue, does important explanatory work in relation to emancipatory social aims. These are 'hegemonic kinds', 'interpersonal kinds', and 'identity kinds'. Hegemonic kinds capture large-scale patterns of subordination and privilege that are directly relevant to bringing about emancipatory social change. Interpersonal kinds capture the detailed interactions between people that take place in very specific social contexts, such as a particular workplace. Identity kinds concern people's experienced relationships to categories, which can be understood in two main ways: as a matter of being attuned to the social norms associated with a certain category and as a matter of identifying with a certain social category in terms of one's conception of oneself.

I apply the concept of ontic oppression to each of these three varieties of race and gender kinds, and I argue that we cannot make the blanket statement that race and gender kinds are ontically oppressive; some are, but others are not, and some are even conducive to emancipation. More precisely, I argue that the hegemonic race and gender kinds associated with subordinated groups—which include kinds such as *woman* and *Black*—are ontically oppressive. However, I argue that some interpersonal kinds are ontically oppressive, but many others are not, and some even serve an emancipatory function; the same goes for identity kinds. I also show how attending to identity kinds and the needs to which they can give rise draws our attention to the possibility of a distinctive form of ontic oppression, one that only affects some individuals who are constructed as kind members, in virtue of the interaction between the relevant constraints and enablements and the specific needs of those individuals.

In Chapter 7, I highlight some benefits of my pluralist account of race and gender kinds and respond to some objections. There are three main benefits. First, the account sheds light on the relations between different accounts of race and gender kinds, which have been underexplored in the literature to date. Second, it offers resources for pursuing productive disagreements about the ontology of race and gender kinds. Third, it protects accounts of particular varieties of race and gender kinds from certain objections that lose their force when that variety of race and/or gender kind is not understood as exhausting what race and/or gender is. I then consider and respond to four potential objections to my pluralist account. These concern (1) the proliferation of social kinds, (2) the question of which constraints and enablements are taken to ground race and gender kinds, (3) the direction of explanation between constraints and enablements on the one hand and kinds on the other, and (4) the implications of the account for speech acts that misgender trans people.

My response to this fourth potential objection highlights a specific concern, which is that putting forward a view that acknowledges the existence of some gender kinds that do not align with people's gender identities is likely to have effects that run counter to trans liberation in the current social and political context. Chapter 8 is devoted to addressing this concern by situating my pluralist account of gender kinds and my account of ontic oppression within contemporary discussions about gender recognition. I show how these discussions often exhibit an approach to gender recognition that I term the 'ontology-first approach', which holds that we should first aim to settle questions about the current ontology of gender kinds and then treat this as automatically determining what shape our gendered social practices ought to take. I argue that the ontology-first approach is counterproductive from the perspective of trans liberation: it fuels disagreements about gender recognition and contributes to the perpetuation and amplification of transphobia. I further show how my account entails the rejection of the ontology-first approach. Given the drawbacks of that approach, this is a positive result for my account. I then demonstrate some additional positive effects my account can reasonably be expected to have on discussions of gender recognition: it has the potential to disrupt various problematic framings, and it paves the way for an alternative approach to gender recognition that I believe is more conducive to trans liberation. Overall, I argue that there is cause for optimism about the implications of articulating my account in the current social and political context with respect to trans liberation.

I.3. A Methodological Note

I will end this introduction by saying something about the methodological approach I will take in this book. (Those readers who are not particularly interested in this may safely skip straight to Chapter 1 at this point.)

My approach has two main features. First, it belongs within a philosophical tradition that is usually called 'analytic philosophy', or sometimes 'Anglo-American philosophy'. This is the way of doing philosophy that is most prevalent in anglophone philosophy departments in, for example, the United Kingdom, the United States, Canada, Australia, and New Zealand, although it is by no means confined to these locations and indeed has close ties to some twentieth-century philosophical movements originating in continental Europe. Analytic philosophy is often contrasted with 'continental philosophy', which is more prevalent in German- and French-speaking contexts, though by no means uncommon in anglophone contexts. I won't say any more about the nature of this contrast; those who are familiar with it will already have their own views on the matter, and for those who are *not* familiar with it, I would need to take up a great deal more space than I am able to in order to make sense of the distinction, if indeed any sense can be made of it at all. Merely gesturing at the divide is enough to say what I want to say, which is that this book operates mostly with the conceptual tools and stylistic norms of analytic philosophy and that it is most centrally in dialogue with others working in the analytic tradition, especially analytic feminist philosophy and analytic critical philosophy of race. Naturally, it also draws on work from outside philosophy narrowly conceived, for example, work in gender studies, trans studies, and postcolonial studies, as well as their many intersections.

The questions and topics that this book addresses have, of course, been pursued in both analytic and continental philosophy, as well as in ways that bridge this divide. Indeed, they have more often received sustained attention in the context of continental philosophy than in that of analytic philosophy. I do not propose to try to illuminate the difference in *how* these questions are pursued in these different traditions, still less to defend the idea that it is in any sense 'better' to pursue them via analytic philosophy; my aim here is simply to orient the reader to the work that follows, and especially to head off any puzzlement about why I am or am not engaging with certain thinkers. For anyone wondering why I have chosen the analytic approach that I have, then my first response is simply: it is what I know how to do. If I were to try to go beyond that and say something more principled, I might suggest that analytic philosophy has some potential benefits that are relevant to my aims, most notably an emphasis on directly presenting arguments that proceed in a systematic, step-by-step way without presupposing too much familiarity with a specific textual tradition. I think this means that, done well, analytic philosophy can be profoundly accessible and suited to being adapted for use in many different projects. I also think that the power of analytic philosophy to illuminate oppression remains underexplored, which makes experimentation on this front interesting, at least to me. Ultimately, however, I have written the book I was capable of writing.

The second feature of the method I am using is that it is an instance of an approach to theorising that I will call 'emancipatory theory'. As I understand this approach, aspects of it have been shared by a number of different theorists, including members of the Frankfurt School (where it goes by the label 'critical theory') and various feminist and anti-racist theorists, to name but a few (Horkheimer 1972; Geuss 1981; Dworkin 1974; MacKinnon 1989; Mills 2005).

A discussion of an emancipatory theory approach that is particularly helpful for my purposes can be found in the work of Iris Marion Young, who describes it as involving an effort to undertake 'a normative reflection that is historically and socially contextualized' (2011, 5). Implementing this method, Young does not focus on imagined, abstracted, or simplified societies in order to conduct investigations and build theories but roots her theorising in society as it currently exists, finding the normative resources for that critique primarily within society itself rather than within the realm of abstraction.[6] Young's approach does not rely on an assumed ability to reliably access abstract, universal normative truths and indeed rejects such an ability as illusory—but nor does it eschew norms and ideals altogether by confining itself to merely descriptive claims.

How, then, are these normative insights to be supported? In other words, how are norms and ideals that are developed from a particular society supposed to serve as the basis for criticism of that same society? I find Young's way of answering this question particularly illuminating and will quote it at length:

Normative reflection arises from hearing a cry of suffering or distress, or feeling distress oneself. The philosopher is always socially situated, and if the society is divided by oppressions, she either reinforces or struggles against them. With an emancipatory interest, the philosopher apprehends given social circumstances not merely in contemplation but with passion: the given is experience in relation to desire. Desire, the desire to be happy, creates the distance, the negation, that opens the space for criticism of what is. This critical distance does not occur on the basis of some previously discovered rational ideas of the good and the just. On the contrary, the ideas of the good and the just arise from the desiring negation that action brings to what is given. . . . Each social reality presents its own unrealized possibilities, experienced as lacks and desires. Norms and ideals arise

---

[6] This is also an important feature of 'non-ideal theory' (Mills 2005), an approach in which I have also found much inspiration.

from the yearning that is an expression of freedom: it does not have to be this way, it could be otherwise. (2011, 5–6)

Emancipatory theory, then, relies on the experiences of the members of oppressive societies, their sense that things could and should be different (better, more free) as a touchstone for theorising about what ought to happen. Of course, one feature of oppression is its tendency to shut down this very sense, to make it seem as if things could not have been otherwise; emancipatory theory stakes its viability on the premise that this shutdown is not total.

A key feature of emancipatory theory, on Young's characterisation, is that it is socially situated and does not aspire to 'neutrality'. The emancipatory theorist is aware of their location in a specific social context, and they are invested in the anti-oppressive struggles that are taking place within it. I am situated in the early-twenty-first-century United Kingdom, which overlaps culturally to varying extents with other countries, in many cases due to histories of colonialism and imperialism. Within this context, my own particular social situation includes many aspects. Among other things, I am a woman, white, cis, and bisexual/pansexual/queer (I select different labels from among these depending on who I am talking to or, more mundanely, on what options are in the drop-down menu or tick-box list of the form I must complete). The main way in which I myself have directly experienced 'the yearning that is an expression of freedom', as Young puts it, is in relation to my identity as a woman who has survived sexual violence, experienced at a young age. This yearning manifests as an acute desire for a world in which survivors can speak freely and be perceived as credible and in which the social position of women is not characterised by vulnerability to, and stigmatisation through, sexual violation.

I state these aspects of my identity, experience, and perspective here because I think they are relevant to the situated nature of this writing. While what I say will have been shaped by my identities and experiences, some of which involve oppression or trauma, I do not expect others to accept it *because* of that fact. Similarly, I will discuss experiences of oppression that I have not shared, such as experiences of racism and transphobia, and although I hope I approach these with a significant degree of epistemic humility, I intend also to assume responsibility and accountability in my own right for the ways in which I include these experiences in the theories I seek to develop.

In this sense, I might be described as adopting a modest form of 'standpoint theory' (see, e.g., the papers assembled in Harding 2004a). Standpoint theory is the idea that certain insights are differentially available to those occupying different social positions, and in particular that those subject to oppression can be in an advantageous epistemic position when it comes to gaining knowledge about that oppression.[7] This idea follows very naturally from Young's characterisation of (what I am calling) emancipatory theory, since it is the subjects who are themselves oppressed who are most likely to experience the 'yearning that is an expression of freedom' that prompts critical reflection. In line with this, I will treat attending to what oppressed people have to say about oppression, either individually or collectively, as an especially important route to knowledge. I do not, however, take this commitment to entail adopting an attitude of overriding epistemic deference to members of oppressed groups. This is because, as Olúfẹ́mi O. Táíwò has compellingly argued, such attitudes all too often constitute 'an abdication of responsibility', one that 'places the accountability that is all of ours to bear onto select people—and, more often than not, a hyper-sanitized and thoroughly fictional caricature of them' (2020).

As well as being socially situated and motivated by an emancipatory interest, emancipatory theory is often understood as involving an effort to actually *effect* emancipatory social change. The theoretical contribution is conceived of as an intervention in the particular context in which it is developed, not merely a reflection on it, and this gives the theory its central purpose and a key touchstone for success. As Raymond Geuss puts this point in relation to critical theory, 'a critical theory has as its inherent aim to be the self-consciousness of a successful process of enlightenment and emancipation' (Geuss 1981, 58; see also Horkheimer 1972). This builds in as a success condition of the theory that it should feed back into its social situation in a way that fosters emancipatory social change. The feminist theorist Andrea Dworkin expresses a similar thought in the opening sentences of her first book: 'This book is an action, a political action where revolution is the goal. It has no other purpose' (1974, 17). In a similar vein, Catharine MacKinnon writes, 'It's common for people to say that something is good in theory but

---

[7] Although the combination of emancipatory (or critical) theory and standpoint theory is not uncontroversial, it certainly has its proponents. Sandra Harding, for example, argues that feminist standpoint projects 'must be part of critical theory, revealing the ideological strategies that are used to design and justify the sex-gender system and its intersections with other aspects of oppression' (2004b, 6).

not in practice. I always want to say, then it is not such a good theory, is it?' (2005, 22). I'm very sympathetic to certain aspects of this thought, but I also want to sound a note of caution regarding other aspects.

What I certainly think is true is that there is no hermetic seal between "theory" and "practice". I cannot say things in the philosophy seminar room and treat them as abstract claims that have no relation to what happens "out there in the world", because the philosophy seminar room is *part* of the world. For one thing, it is someone's workplace, someone's place of study, and what they hear there directly affects how their life goes. For another, people can pick up what is said within academic contexts—or what they think was said, or what they can plausibly claim was said—and mobilise it beyond those contexts in the service of particular political projects, for good or ill. So, at minimum, an emancipatory theorist must be alert to the social impacts their theorising may have, both directly and through more diffuse mechanisms, and not seek to wash their hands of these.

Another thing that I think is true relates to Young's idea of 'emancipatory interest'. If a key idea behind emancipatory theory is that one is moved to investigate a topic because of one's socially situated concern to aid emancipatory social struggles, but then one proceeds to theorise in a way that becomes more and more divorced from those struggles—well, something is striking a false note. Either the interest was not so genuine in the first place, or the theorising has taken a wrong turn relative to the aims that prompted it.

In these respects, then, I am sympathetic to the thought articulated by Geuss, Dworkin, MacKinnon, and others. Where I think we should be cautious, though, is in what we claim about *how much difference* theory can make to emancipatory social struggles. While it is true that articulating a theory is an action, it is not, in my view, a type of action that is likely to make a great difference to how emancipatory social struggles actually play out. What really obstructs emancipatory social change is mostly forms of material power, especially the coercive power that is backed by the apparatus of the state. Theory is all well and good, but it won't pay your rent, secure you medical treatment, or protect you from a police truncheon.[8] When it comes to race and gender in particular, it is worth stressing that the fact that these kinds

---

[8] Granted, having a certain sort of *academic job* absolutely can pay your rent. It can also potentially secure you medical treatment, whether in virtue of coming with medical insurance, equipping you with social status and skills that help you to navigate medical bureaucracy, or simply enabling you to pay for treatment privately. It will do a lot less to protect you from state violence, though it may help you get a good lawyer if you're beaten up at a protest. But this is a function of the *job*, not the *theory*, and these ought not to be confused.

are socially produced does not mean that re-description or re-interpretation alone is enough to change them. That requires actually altering the way societies exist and the ways in which specific interactions within them proceed, which is a lot more difficult to do.

This is not to deny the possibility that theoretical innovation can facilitate social change. One general way it can do so is by exposing distortions and obfuscations in prevalent ways of thinking that facilitate the functioning of oppressive social systems.[9] Going beyond this, understanding the onto-logical aspects of race and gender specifically may be useful for emancipatory purposes because understanding exactly how things exist can direct us towards, as Sally Haslanger puts it, the 'levers for change' (Haslanger 2012d, 215). We might, in other words, be able to identify weak points in the material and conceptual systems that underpin oppression, and we might then be able to exploit this knowledge to disrupt those systems more effectively.

Nevertheless, the road between this sort of improved understanding and actually effecting emancipatory social change is a long and hard one, and we should not make the mistake of overestimating the contribution that theory can make to covering this distance. Conceptual resources developed in the pages of a philosophy book may in principle filter through to more accessible venues and wind up in the hands of activists who find them helpful (and I hope the ones in this book will), but they have no power by themselves to enable emancipatory social change. For that, we need the hard work of collectively enacting material resistance to oppressive social systems and structures, to which the main obstacles are not conceptual confusion or lack of precise theoretical apparatus but rather forms of material power.

The combination of analytic philosophy and emancipatory theory that I have described here may strike some readers as surprising. Those who are on comfortable terms with emancipatory theory may wonder why I have not chosen to work within a tradition in which this approach is more prominent than it is within analytic philosophy; I have already spoken to this point. From the direction of analytic philosophy, on the other hand, there are certainly those who are sceptical of emancipatory theory. Such critics typically contend that to attend to the specifics of one's social situation and to be guided in part by political commitments, rather than aiming to articulate timeless and universal truths in a neutral way, is to give up one's claim to be

---

[9] In other words, what is often called 'ideology critique'; see §2.2.

doing analytic philosophy, or indeed philosophy at all (for discussion, see Dotson 2013; Jenkins 2014).

To this, I can only reply that I see no reason to share the vision of what philosophy is and must be that underpins the objection. To recall Young's words quoted earlier, it seems to me that, far from soaring above issues of oppression, an ostensibly detached and neutral approach to philosophy all too often functions to reinforce the specific and concrete oppressions that are present in its particular social context. When it comes to ontology in particular, social kinds—and the theories that aim to capture them—are always situated in social structures characterised by many forms of empowerment and disempowerment. These power dynamics, as we have seen, shape the social kinds that are produced. Given this, we cannot, as theorists, exempt ourselves from the social power that operates in our context; instead, we can and should consciously orient ourselves in relation to that power in ways that are conducive to emancipation.

Thankfully, I am far from alone in adopting a conception of what philosophy, including analytic philosophy, is and can be that is compatible with an emancipatory approach as I have characterised it here. I am grateful for the community of philosophers exploring this and similar approaches—which includes far too many people to list here individually, besides being continually expanding—and I hope that it will continue to grow and flourish. This book is for my fellow travellers in analytic emancipatory theory, and for those of all persuasions who are willing to come along for the ride.

1

Ontic Injustice

1.1. Introduction

In recent years, a number of important contributions to moral, social, and political philosophy have identified distinctive forms of injustice that had not previously been explicitly defined. These have concerned phenomena such as knowledge, as in 'epistemic injustice' (Fricker 2007), and communication, as in 'discursive injustice' (Kukla 2014). In this chapter, I use a similar approach to identify a distinctive form of injustice that concerns social construction. I show that an individual can be wronged by the very fact of being socially constructed as a member of a certain social kind—kinds such as *wife* or *slave*. Since this wrong relates to social ontology, I term it 'ontic injustice'. I hope to show that ontic injustice is a distinctive, pervasive, and interesting type of injustice which merits attention from moral, social, and political theorists. For now, I am considering ontic injustice as a general phenomenon; in later chapters, I will focus on race and gender in particular and explore some specific insights that can be gained by applying the concept of ontic injustice to these kinds.

I will begin by showing that there is an implicit consensus among different accounts of social ontology that what it is to be a member of a certain social kind is, at least in part, to be subject to certain social constraints and enablements. I will then offer a definition of ontic injustice, explain the nature of the wrong it involves, show how the concept can be applied to particular cases, and demonstrate what we stand to gain from incorporating the concept of ontic injustice into our conceptual repertoire.

Ontology and Oppression. Katharine Jenkins, Oxford University Press. © Katharine Jenkins 2023.
DOI: 10.1093/oso/9780197666777.003.0002

1.2. Constraints and Enablements in Accounts
of Social Ontology

1.2.1. The Explicit Role of Constraints and Enablements

Many prominent accounts of the ontology of social kinds explicitly hold
that being a certain sort of social entity is, in some sense, a matter of being
subject to certain social constraints and enablements. Probably the most
well-known example of this is John Searle's account of what he terms 'institutional facts' (Searle 1996; 2011). These are social facts that are the
products of human institutions, such as the facts that certain people are
husbands, judges, and presidents. Searle holds that in order for it to be a
social fact that some individual is, for example, a judge or a president, that
individual must have certain conventional 'deontic powers' (Searle 1996,
100). Deontic powers are socially created permissions, duties, and so on,
and individuals come to have these powers through the shared recognition of other individuals that they have them; this shared recognition is
'collective intentionality' (Searle 1996, 23–26). If members of a society collectively recognise people who have been through a certain ceremony (a
marriage, a swearing in) as having the powers associated with being a husband, a judge, or a president, then this is what makes it the case that certain people are husbands, judges, and presidents. The fact that this is what
makes it the case that someone is a husband, a judge, or a president is what
makes the fact that someone is a husband, a judge, or a president count as
an *institutional* fact in Searle's sense.

Another view that explicitly focuses on constraints and enablements is
Ásta's (2018) account of social properties as conferred properties. Ásta's view
is somewhat different from Searle's, since she is concerned not only with institutional kinds in the fairly narrow sense that he operates with but with
more informal social kinds, which she terms 'communal' kinds. According to
Ásta, to be a particular sort of social entity is to have a certain status conferred
upon you by relevant other social agents, where this status consists of particular constraints and enablements (Ásta 2018, 7–33). For example, you might
have the status 'woman' conferred on you in a cocktail bar, where this means
that you can expect that men will buy you a drink if they wish to make conversation with you and that you are expected to dress in a certain way and
to respond politely to overtures from strange men (unless you are already

talking to a man). Having the status 'woman' conferred on you at a family party, or in a workplace, would involve different constraints and enablements (Ásta 2018, 73). Moreover, when other agents confer the status on you, they typically take themselves to be tracking something about you. This 'base property' can also vary from context to context. In some social locations, it may be genital status, in others, legal sex, and in others, self-identification as a woman (Ásta 2018, 70–92). As should be apparent, on this view, social properties are radically context-dependent: the social property consists in a conferred social status, and the social status in turn consists in constraints and enablements. Thus, being a member of a certain social kind is a matter of being subject to the relevant constraints and enablements.

Searle's account and Ásta's account are alike in that they explicitly hold that social kind membership is at least partly constituted by constraints and enablements. This is the similarity that matters for my present purposes. This similarity can exist alongside a number of differences. For example, Ásta focuses on a broader range of constraints and enablements, rather than only considering conventional deontic powers as Searle does. Searle's account only applies to kinds where there are relatively explicit beliefs about what people are and are not entitled to do, which create conventional deontic powers. For example, in a society in which there are lots of habituated gendered patterns of behaviour but no explicit beliefs about the different rights and responsibilities of men and women, gender kinds would not fall within the scope of Searle's account. By contrast, Ásta allows that a broad range of typical responses to people can be relevant to the construction of social kinds. The response pattern need only makes some actions harder or easier; it need not involve the responders having explicit beliefs about entitlements and obligations. Gender kinds in the society just sketched *would* fall within the scope of Ásta's account.

Another difference between the two accounts is that for Ásta, a person's being a member of a certain social kind is not constituted by their actually instantiating the base property but is conferred by the attitudes of the relevant other social agents who, rightly or wrongly, take them to have it. For Searle, by contrast, what matters is whether or not the person actually instantiates the base property. For example, suppose that a couple is pronounced married by the relevant authorities in a certain state, but the pronouncement ought never to have been made because one of them is secretly already married and the state does not permit marriage under these circumstances. For Ásta, the couple is married, because the status of being married has been conferred on them by the relevant authorities.[1] For Searle, by contrast, they are not married, because they have not been through a genuine marriage ceremony in which all the preconditions were met, and therefore they do not meet the criteria for being married that are collectively recognised in that state.[2]

These differences between Searle's account and Ásta's account illustrate the extent to which accounts of the ontology of social kinds can differ whilst still having in common an explicit claim that social constraints and enablements are at least partly constitutive of social kind membership.

1.2.2. The Implicit Role of Constraints and Enablements

There are other accounts of the ontology of social kinds that, unlike Searle's and Ásta's accounts, do not explicitly equate being a member of a social kind with being subject to social constraints and enablements. Nevertheless, many of these accounts implicitly allocate a similar role to constraints and enablements.

For example, some accounts focus on equilibria in social behaviour (see, e.g., Calvert 1998; Greif and Kingston 2011). David Lewis's (2002) work on convention is an important reference point for accounts of this kind. In such accounts, what matters to social institutions, and hence to the kinds produced by these institutions, is not shared beliefs about how people ought to behave but rather regularities in how people actually do behave. The idea of an equilibrium, in a game-theoretic sense, refers to a situation in which no one can unilaterally deviate from a pattern of behaviour without making themselves worse off. For example, if everyone else drives on the left-hand side of the road, I usually cannot just start driving on the right without making myself (and in this particular case, many others) worse off. Finding oneself in a situation of equilibrium necessarily means being constrained: the available options and outcomes have been altered by the social coordination, and some possibilities (deviating and benefiting from doing so) are ruled out.[3] So equilibria-focused models tacitly allow that constraints and enablements

---

[1] Ásta holds that there are both institutional and communal properties of marriage; the communal properties are conferred informally in particular social contexts by other people treating the couple as married. It is the institutional property of marriage that concerns us in this example.

[2] At least, this appears to be Searle's view in most of his work, although an alternative version of the account seems to be suggested in his discussion of human rights (2011, 174–98).

[3] See Guala and Hindriks 2015 for an interesting model that unifies rules-focused accounts (such as Searle's) and equilibria-focused accounts.

partly constitute institutions and therefore partly constitute membership in the social kinds produced by institutions.

Other accounts of social kinds focus on causal patterns and explanatory and predictive power. Here, too, we find constraints and enablements playing an important, though tacit, role. Consider Ron Mallon's (2016) account of certain social kinds that have human beings as members, which equates these kinds with homeostatic property clusters, described by Mallon as 'clusters of nonaccidentally co-occurring properties that sustain explanatory and practical projects including prediction, explanation, and intervention' (69). These clusters are the result of coordinated behaviours prompted and organised by commonly understood conceptions of social roles. Races and genders are, Mallon argues, kinds of this sort: shared ideas about race and gender prompt people to behave in patterned way, and this make certain outcomes more or less likely for people who have been categorised in a particular way with regard to race or gender. Here, too, constraints and enablements are implicitly in the picture, because in order for there to be patterns of outcomes that can support predictive power, it must be made harder or easier for people to do certain things. For example, if gender serves to predict how much a person earns, then it must be the case that conceptions of gender roles have made it harder for those classified as women to earn a certain wage compared to those classified as men. Although Mallon's focus is on homeostatic property clusters, again we see social constraints and enablements implicitly playing a crucial role.

Thus, the idea that being a member of a certain social kind is at least partly constituted by social constraints and enablements is a tacit feature of many accounts of social ontology. There are, however, some exceptions to this general trend. Katherine Ritchie (2020) equates social kinds of the sort under consideration here with nodes or positions in social structures. Some accounts of social groups that fit Ritchie's template do make constraints and enablements partly constitutive of kind membership. For example, Sally Haslanger has argued that to be a woman is (very roughly) to be subordinated on the basis of presumed female sex ([2000] 2012a).[4] Regardless of how one cashes out the notion of subordination, constraints and enablements are bound to be in the picture, so this version of a social structural model fits the pattern I have identified. However, it is also in principle possible for there to be a social structure, in the sense Ritchie defines, that does not involve

---

[4] I discuss Haslanger's account of gender, as well as her account of race, at length in Chapter 4.

constraints and enablements. The nodes in the structure might be related in ways that do not make it easier or harder for the node occupants to do certain things. Ritchie's model of social kinds as nodes in social structures is therefore compatible with an account on which constraints and enablements do not constitute social kind membership at all.

For this reason, I do not claim that *all* accounts of the ontology of social kinds entail that social constraints and enablements constitute (at least partly) membership in social kinds. Rather, I claim that there is an implicit consensus to this effect: *most* accounts of the ontology of social kinds either directly hold or indirectly imply that social constraints and enablements at least partly constitute social kind membership. In what follows, I will assume a view of the ontology of social kinds that accords with this consensus.[5]

1.3. Defining Ontic Injustice

1.3.1. The Marital Rape Case

The phenomenon that I want to pick out with the label 'ontic injustice' concerns the constraints and enablements that constitute social kind membership. The thought is that in some cases, these constraints and enablements may be wrongful, in the sense that they are in contravention of the individual's moral entitlements.

As an example of this phenomenon, consider the situation of wives in England and Wales prior to 1991, which is when the marital rape exemption was ended in these countries. Prior to 1991, if a husband had sex with his wife without her consent, including by force, this did not constitute rape in the eyes of the law, as it was deemed that in getting married, the wife had consented in perpetuity to sex with her husband. Accordingly, an individual socially constructed as a wife lacked the social entitlement to refuse to have sex with her husband. On an account of social ontology that accords with the implicit consensus identified previously, *what it was* to be a wife in England and Wales prior to 1991 was, in part, to be someone who was not socially entitled to control fully sexual access to their own body.[6] This state of affairs

---

[5] In Chapter 3, I explore the idea that social constraints and enablements constitute social kinds in much more detail.

[6] In focusing on the pre-1991 situation, I do not intend to imply that all is now well. The social attitudes behind the marital rape exemption certainly continue to affect many people in the form of rape myths, including impacting on the justice system. For example, in January 2020, a high court

is clearly morally wrong: everyone is morally entitled to control fully sexual access to their own body. Accordingly, there is a profound mismatch between the moral entitlements of the individuals who were wives and the social constraints and entitlements that constituted the social kind *wife*. It is this mismatch that I think is a distinctive type of moral wrong affecting those socially constructed as wives at that time, and which I aim to capture with the concept of ontic injustice.

It is important to be clear from the beginning about what ontic injustice is *not*. Ontic injustice is not the harm that occurs when individuals actually act in accordance with the relevant constraints and enablements. For instance, in the example of wives in England and Wales prior to 1991, ontic injustice is distinct from the harm of a wife actually being raped by her husband. Furthermore, ontic injustice is not the same as the psychological damage that may arise from a person's being aware of the wrongful constraints and enablements, which is part of what has been termed 'psychological oppression' (see, e.g., Fanon [1952] 2008; Bartky 1991). Staying with the example of wives, we may imagine that a wife who was aware of the fact that she had no legal protection against being raped by her husband might well have found this thought distressing and might also have suffered, for example, damage to her self-esteem. She may even have come to believe that she did not deserve to be able to fully control sexual access to her own body. Any of these psychological effects constitutes a serious harm, but none of these harms is what I am aiming to capture with the idea of ontic injustice.

Rather, the wrong in which I am interested is the mere fact that an individual *is* a certain sort of social being, where what it means to be that sort of social being is to be subject to morally inappropriate constraints and enablements. In the example concerning the marital rape exemption, the

---

appeal found that a family court judge, Robin Tolson, had incorrectly applied the law on rape in a ruling over custody. A woman had contested her former partner's claim for access to their son on the basis that the former partner had been controlling and had raped her. Tolson's ruling went against the woman, finding that no rape occurred because the woman did not attempt to physically resist the penetration. This judgement was overturned by the high court on appeal, in a ruling expressing concern and describing Tolson's approach as 'manifestly at odds with current jurisprudence, concomitant sexual behaviour, and what is currently acceptable socio-sexual conduct' (Guardian 2020). Whilst Tolson's ruling was certainly at odds with the law on rape, and with what is morally acceptable in terms of sexual conduct, it is not, unfortunately, out of line with many widely held mistaken attitudes about rape, or 'rape myths'. In this sense, far from being an anomaly, Tolson's ruling is in fact a paradigm example of how common rape myths affect many people's thinking when it comes to sexual violence. In this sense, the marital rape exemption is still with us. However, social ontologists disagree about the extent to which social attitudes of this sort feed into to constructing social reality. For this reason, I am focusing on the pre-1991 situation as it offers a clearer example for my purposes.

ontic injustice is the mere fact that someone *is* a wife, where being a wife consists, at least in part, of being someone who is not socially entitled to control fully sexual access to their own body. A wife who is not raped by her husband and who suffers no psychological harm from knowing about the marital rape exemption still suffers ontic injustice.[7] Ontic injustice, then, is a wrong at the level of being that affects members of the social kind in question on the basis of their kind membership, rather than on the basis of their specific experiences.

1.3.2. The Definition of Ontic Injustice

Here is my definition of ontic injustice:

> **Ontic injustice:** An individual suffers ontic injustice if and only if they are socially constructed as a member of a certain social kind where that construction consists, at least in part, of their falling under a set of social constraints and enablements that is wrongful to them.

For instance, in England and Wales prior to 1991, the marital rape exemption meant that being a member of the social kind *wife* consisted in part of lacking the social entitlement to control fully sexual access to one's own body. This constraint was wrongful to those individuals who were socially constructed as wives because it removed their social entitlement to do something that they were morally entitled to do (namely, to control fully sexual access to their own body).

First, note that the definition concerns the conditions under which *an individual* suffers ontic injustice. The wrong of ontic injustice, as I define it, occurs on the individual level, even though that wrong is enacted by way of the individual's membership in a certain social group. It is individuals, not groups, who suffer ontic injustice.[8] Where there is a social kind that is such that at least some individuals who are constructed as members of the kind suffer an ontic injustice, I will say that the kind is 'ontically unjust'.

---

[7] There is a parallel here with accounts of freedom as non-domination: a person is dominated if they are vulnerable to the arbitrary interference of another, even if that interference never takes place (Pettit 1996). I explore the relation between ontic injustice and domination in §1.4.3.

[8] This point will become clearer when I discuss the nature of the wrong of ontic injustice in more detail in the next section.

Note, too, that the definition specifies that the set of constraints and enablements must be wrongful *to the individual in question*. This is important, because social constraints and enablements are relational: my being under a certain social constraint (say, not to take your keys from your pocket) means that you have a certain social enablement (in this case, an enablement to retain your keys in your pocket).[9] It follows that a person being subject to a wrongful constraint will mean that others are subject to corresponding enablements that are likewise wrongful. These corresponding enablements are wrongful, but they are wrongful not *to the individual who has them* but rather to other individuals. For example, in England and Wales prior to 1991, a husband had the social enablement to have sex with his wife whenever he wanted regardless of whether she agreed to the sex. The husband's set of constraints and enablements was therefore wrongful, but it was wrongful not *to the husband* but rather *to the wife*. Therefore, the kind *husband*, although it was partly constituted by a wrongful set of constraints and enablements, was not ontically unjust.

One question that might arise about the definition of ontic injustice that I have offered is this: why does the definition refer to constraints *and enablements*, when surely only constraints can prevent people from doing or receiving what they are morally entitled to do or receive?[10] The answer is that I take it that sometimes enablements can indirectly prevent individuals from doing or receiving what they are morally entitled to do or to receive. One way this can happen is if the enablements create a pressure to act in a certain way, depriving the person of choices to which they were entitled.

For example, consider a case in which mothers, but not fathers, are entitled to take time off from paid work to look after children. This might result in mothers feeling obliged to take time off from paid work, because there are no good alternatives, and in their being judged negatively if they do not take time off from paid work. Consequently, mothers' ability to choose how to arrange their lives is compromised, and they may have reduced access to goods associated with paid work.

Now, on some accounts of social ontology, constraints are understood quite broadly, so that this case would count as one in which mothers are under a constraint regarding their careers. If we confined our attention to those views, then we would be able to account for this case purely in terms of

---

[9] Brännmark 2021 offers a helpful account of this relationality in terms of Hohfeldian incidents.
[10] I thank Kate Ritchie for bringing this question to my attention.

wrongful constraints. However, on other views, such as Searle's, constraints are understood more narrowly, such that mothers would not count as being under a constraint, because there is no formal, collectively recognised duty for mothers to take time off from paid work, merely a prerogative to take time off (which is not shared by fathers).

Therefore, the possibility of wrongful enablements must be kept open in order to make the definition of ontic injustice fit with any account of social ontology. Note, too, that the definition refers to a 'wrongful *set* of constraints and enablements'. This allows for the possibility that a certain combination of constraints and enablements may prevent an individual from doing or receiving what they are morally entitled to do or to receive, even if no single constraint or enablement would have this effect by itself.

1.4. The Wrong of Ontic Injustice

1.4.1. Moral Injury

The idea of a wrong that consists of being subject to morally inappropriate constraints and enablements serves to give an initial fix on the phenomenon that I want to identify as ontic injustice, but the question then arises: what *exactly* does this wrong consist of? One thing to note in response to this question is that being under a morally inappropriate set of constraints and enablements, such that other agents are socially licensed to treat one in morally inappropriate ways, will typically raise the *risk* that such treatment, with its attendant material and psychological harms, will occur. For example, the existence of a marital rape exemption will usually mean that wives are at greater risk of being raped by their husbands and also at greater risk of suffering psychological harms as a result of their awareness of this vulnerability. We tend to think that being placed at risk of harm can be wrongful in itself, as when someone is on the receiving end of irresponsible medical practice but, due to sheer luck, does not sustain physical injury. So risk offers one way of understanding the wrong of ontic injustice. Yet I want to suggest that, as well as risk, being placed under a morally inappropriate set of constraints and enablements involves a further harm, one that Jean Hampton has termed 'moral injury' and which is understood roughly as an 'affront to value or dignity' (Hampton 1991, 1666).

The concept of moral injury trades on the fact that the ways in which agents behave towards each other can convey meaning; by turning my back on you when you try to speak, for instance, I convey something about my attitude to you and to your attempt to speak in this context. Sometimes the meaning of a certain behaviour enacts what Hampton terms 'diminishment', which is the appearance that a person's value has been lowered. For example, violence inflicted on a person in a deliberately humiliating way not only harms the person materially and psychologically but also conveys the impression that the person lacks the kind of value that should properly be attributed to people. 'Diminishment', Hampton writes, 'is an "objective" phenomenon, by which I merely mean . . . that it is not something that can be identified with any psychological experience of victimization. Instead, it is something that we "read off" the effects of immoral behaviour' (1991, 1674). Moreover, Hampton stresses that diminishment is not an *actual* reduction in moral worth, which on many accounts of moral worth is not possible, but rather the *appearance* of a reduction in moral worth. The person who is subject to a deliberately humiliating violent attack does not actually come to have lower moral worth as a consequence; rather, the way they are treated gives the false impression that they have lower moral worth than they really have.

Diminishment, in turn, Hampton argues, causes damage to either the *realisation* or the *acknowledgement* of a person's value. Damage to the realisation of value occurs when actual treatment takes place that is contrary to the entitlements someone has in virtue of her moral value. Damage to the acknowledgement of value occurs when someone is represented as having less moral value than she in fact has; for example, an unsuccessful attempt to inflict humiliating violence on someone still conveys the impression that this form of treatment would have been appropriate and hence that she has a lower moral value than she in fact has. If either form of damage to value occurs, the victim has suffered moral injury. Thus, Hampton defines moral injury as '*damage to the realization of a victim's value, or damage to the acknowledgement of the victim's value, accomplished through behaviour whose meaning is such that the victim is diminished in value*' (1991, 1679, emphasis in original).

In articulating the idea of moral injury, Hampton relies on the claim that most of us do in fact operate with some conception of the moral worth of human beings, which is to say, some 'beliefs about how human beings are to be valued, and how to appraise each individual's value' (1991, 1666). For this reason, Hampton contends, we *should* care about the damage to the realisation or acknowledgement of a person's value that is caused by diminishment:

> I cannot explain that offensiveness [of damage to the realisation or acknowledgement of value] by appealing to something else, because it is the foundation of our objection to wrongdoing; it is part of what it means to say that something is valuable that we ought to care about preserving and acknowledging that value. (1991, 1684)

Thus, the concept of moral injury does not supply an account of the moral worth of human beings that we should be concerned to protect from damage—of what such worth is based on, why we should care about it, and so on. Rather, the concept of moral injury identifies a form of injury or wrong that anyone who *already* subscribes to an account of the moral worth of human beings should acknowledge, basing her judgements about putative cases of moral injury on her prior commitments concerning the moral worth of human beings.[11] The concept of moral injury thus relies on a modest metaethical commitment: it will only make sense to someone who holds a conception of the value of different sorts of beings according to which an individual's moral worth is not entirely determined by how they are so-cially represented. This is because a conception on which an individual's moral worth *was* so determined would imply that it is impossible for an individual's moral worth to be *wrongly* represented as lower than it in fact is. There needs to be some gap between actual moral worth and social represen-tation of moral worth in order for the concept of moral injury to get off the ground. Beyond this, however, accepting the concept of moral injury does not commit us to a specific understanding of moral worth.

Important for our purposes is that although moral injury is *related* to the risk of material or psychological harm, it is not *identical* with such risk. For example, noting that books advancing racist and sexist worldviews can cause moral injury, Hampton writes: 'such books morally injure not one individual, but a whole class of individuals, leaving them sitting ducks for treatment lower (perhaps much lower) than that which they deserve' (1991, 1679). Overall, however, she makes it clear that moral injury is defined not merely as risk (being made into a 'sitting duck') but as actual damage ('affront to value or dignity', as Hampton puts it). Moral injury *brings with it a risk of*

---

[11] I will return to this point in §1.5.1.

damage to material and psychological well-being, but what it *consists of* is *actual damage* to the realisation or acknowledgement of value.

The concept of moral injury thus provides the perfect tool for capturing the wrong of ontic injustice. When someone is subject to constraints and enablements that license treatment that falls short of the sort of treatment to which she is morally entitled, she suffers a moral injury, one that takes the form of damage to the acknowledgement of her value. This damage is an additional wrong over and above the wrong of being placed at risk of material and psychological harm. Someone who is socially constructed as a wife in the context of a marital rape exemption has thereby been represented as having less moral value than she in fact has, suffering damage to the acknowledgement of her value that constitutes a moral injury.

So far, I have focused on Hampton's presentation of the concept of moral injury, and I concur with much of it. However, there are two ways in which I need to slightly adapt the notion of moral injury compared to Hampton's presentation in order to make it better fit my purposes. First, Hampton discusses 'behaviour' and seems mostly to be thinking about cases where an agent A behaves a certain way towards another agent B, where the social significance of A's behaviour is such that B suffers diminishment. This makes sense within the context of Hampton's larger project, which concerns theories of punishment.[12] The problem here is that it does not make sense to think of an individual's being socially constructed as a member of a certain kind as something that is enacted through the behaviour of one single other agent. Even in cases where a particular agent plays an important role—the officiant in a marriage ceremony, say—the maintenance of a social ontology requires the participation of many others as well, and this participation is often cashed out in terms of their attitudes rather than specific actions. However, there is nothing in the notion of moral injury itself that necessitates a narrowly interpersonal focus. The wrong that a person suffers when they suffer a moral injury is the actual damage to the realisation or acknowledgement of their value. From the victim's perspective, this damage can be the same, whether it is inflicted directly by one individual or via more diffuse mechanisms.

Given that this is my view, I find the term 'behaviour' potentially misleading since it carries a connotation both of directness and of individuality: person

---

[12] Specifically, she argues that it is because punishable behaviour enacts moral injury that retributive responses can be appropriate: retributive punishment can cancel out the diminishment by affirming the victim's moral worth. I take no stance here on this application of the concept of moral injury.

A behaves in such a way towards person B. In order to signal my inclusion of more diffuse mechanisms that impact on individuals, I will therefore speak of moral injury as accomplished through *treatment*, where direct interpersonal behaviour is just one form of treatment. Someone who has been socially constructed as a member of a certain human kind has been on the receiving end of a form of treatment, even though this treatment cannot usually be equated with the direct behaviour of a specific individual. What matters is that the treatment is the product of human social arrangements and there-fore falls within the scope of considerations of justice, rather than being the product of natural forces. This last point is important. Kinds that are not so-cially constructed cannot be ontically unjust, because they are not the sort of thing that can be appropriately considered to be just or unjust in any sense.

The second adaptation I need to make to Hampton's account of moral in-jury concerns her focus on human beings. Again, this makes sense in the context of a discussion of punishment. But in fact, there is no general reason to limit the scope of moral injury to human beings. The concept of moral injury relies on a prior notion of a conception of the moral worth of human beings, and it is true that such conceptions loom particularly large in our moral landscape. However, it is perfectly possible to have a conception of the moral worth of beings of other sorts—'sentient beings', for example—and many people do seem to hold such conceptions. Such conceptions can func-tion as the basis of a judgement of moral injury just as well as conceptions of human value. I do not claim that everyone in fact holds conceptions of the moral worth of broader classes of beings beyond human beings, nor do I here wish to defend the claim that some such conceptions are warranted. I simply note that such conceptions will serve perfectly well as support for judgements about moral injury, and for this reason, I will not take the notion of moral injury to apply solely to human beings but will treat it as applicable to any sort of being that may be the subject of a conception of value.[13]

1.4.2. Recognition Respect

Although I am defining ontic injustice primarily in terms of moral injury, I find it helpful to consider the close connection between Hampton's account

---

[13] This distinguishes my use of the concept of moral injury from, for example, Mari Mikkola's (2016) use of it in her account of dehumanisation.

of moral injury and Stephen Darwall's account of 'recognition respect' (1977) in order to gain a fuller picture of the wrong involved in ontic injustice.[14] According to Darwall, there are two quite different attitudes that go by the name of 'respect'. On the one hand, 'appraisal respect' is a positive evaluation of a person; this is the sort of respect involved in respecting someone as a sportsperson or as a philosopher. Appraisal respect can be withdrawn, for example, if one learns that one's favourite sportsperson has been taking performance-enhancing drugs or that one's favourite philosopher is a serial plagiarist. Recognition respect, on the other hand, is a matter of recognising certain properties of someone or something and being disposed to respond appropriately to these. This is the attitude involved in respecting someone as a person or in respecting a work of art. We recognise that the person has certain morally relevant properties that mean that we ought not to harm her, exploit her, and so on. Similarly, we recognise that the work of art has aesthetic value, and we ought not to wantonly destroy or damage it. Unlike appraisal respect, recognition respect cannot legitimately be withdrawn; even someone who has forfeited our appraisal respect as a sportsperson still has a claim to our recognition respect as a person.

Darwall further identifies a sub-kind of recognition respect, *moral* recognition respect, in which the properties in question are morally relevant. The case of respecting the person is a case of moral recognition respect, whereas the case of respecting the painting is not. There is a close connection between failures of recognition respect and moral injury.[15] Whenever a failure of moral recognition respect occurs, the individual towards whom the respect was owed suffers a moral injury, because damage has been done to the acknowledgement of their value. But what about the other way around? Does every case of moral injury involve a failure of recognition respect? Not if we stay with Darwall's account of recognition respect. For Darwall, recognition respect seems to be an explicit attitude one person can have towards another. However, I have argued that moral injury can come about as a result of any form of social treatment; it does not result only from directly interpersonal behaviour. Societies, as well as individuals, can send messages about value.

[14] Another related concept is that of a 'dignitary harm' (Waldron 2014), and there are also links to Darwall's work on dignity (2004).

[15] This sometimes comes to the fore in Hampton's presentation, as in the following quote: 'what makes the harm effected by wrongdoing "worse" for us [than the harm inflicted by a natural disaster], and hence the target of a special kind of anger in us, is the way it constitutes a treatment of the victim that violates the entitlement which *that person's value requires other human beings to respect*' (1991, 1678, emphasis added).

Cases of moral injury that do not involve direct interpersonal behaviour do not involve a failure of recognition respect as defined by Darwall. In light of this, it is necessary to ask whether we can expand the notion of recognition respect so that its scope matches that of moral injury.

Elizabeth Anderson (2012) draws a distinction between transactional and structural theories of justice that is helpful in this connection. The former concerns one-off interactions at the individual level, whilst the latter concerns the structural conditions under which such transactions take place. The motivation for looking at the structural aspect of justice is the fact that even if transactions are just at a local level, their cumulative effects may be very bad for some individuals. In such cases, these effects can be avoided through intervening at a structural level. According to Anderson:

> A structural theory [of justice] supplies criteria for assessing global properties of a system of rules that governs transactions, and imposes constraints on permissible rules with an eye toward controlling the cumulative effects of individual transactions that may be innocent from a local point of view. (2012, 164)

I propose to apply this distinction to failures of recognition respect. Darwall is concerned with what I shall call transactional failures of recognition respect, where a particular agent is inattentive to (and unmotivated by) morally relevant properties of some individual. In a parallel fashion to Anderson, I suggest that a structural failure of recognition respect occurs when a structure, such as an institution, is insensitive and unresponsive to morally relevant features of some person or group of people. This insensitivity or unresponsiveness is to be understood counterfactually. For example, consider the fact that if a man raped his wife in England or Wales before 1991, then he would face no legal consequences. This is a matter of the legal system being insensitive to the moral right of women to control sexual access to their own bodies, in the sense that violations of that moral right prompt no legal response.

This structural sense of a failure of recognition respect is importantly different from Darwall's sense, since in the structural case there is not, or at least need not be, an agent who would be capable of 'recognising' anything. Structural failures of recognition respect can therefore be understood by analogy with transactional failures, but they are constituted by the functioning of a structure, rather than by an interpersonal attitude. The important point for my purposes is that in both the transactional and the structural case, there is a systematic failure to respond appropriately to morally relevant properties of some individual or individuals, whether on the part of an agent or on the part of a social structure.[16]

An example of a transactional failure of recognition respect that is implicated in ontic injustice is a person who believes that a wife is not entitled to refuse to have sex with her husband. An example of a structural failure of recognition respect is a legal system that features a marital rape exemption (i.e., that does not classify non-consensual sex between a husband and wife as rape). Structural failures of recognition respect can be overt or subtle; for example, a legal system that lacks effective measures for disrupting the effects of widely held rape myths on trials also counts as a structural failure of recognition respect. This case illustrates that structural and transactional failures of recognition respect can be intertwined. An individual discrediting a victim of rape on the basis of applying rape myths commits a transactional failure of recognition respect; if the individual in question is on a jury in a rape trial and no procedures are in place to prevent their rape-myth acceptance from influencing their verdict on the case, this may be part of a structural failure of recognition respect as well.

To further grasp the distinction, imagine a context in which the legal system features a marital rape exemption, but this exemption is universally believed to be wrong: no one actually thinks that wives are not entitled to refuse to have sex with their husbands. Married women in such a context would not suffer any transactional failures of recognition respect, but they would still suffer a structural failure of recognition respect because the legal system fails to take into account and respond to their moral entitlement to control fully sexual access to their own bodies.

The wrong of ontic injustice, then, involves both a moral injury and a failure of recognition respect.[17] Moral injury is a more direct way of spelling

---

[16] I do not mean to suggest that social structures or institutions are agents or that they can be morally responsible for ontic injustice. The question of moral responsibility for ontic injustice is not something that I seek to address in this book.

[17] The notion of recognition respect has clear connections to more overtly political conceptions of recognition (see, e.g., Honneth 1996; Fraser 2014), and it seems to me that the account of the wrong of ontic injustice that I have offered here could easily be developed in that direction if one were so inclined. This would yield a version of the concept that was suited to use in a certain political framework. Whilst I have no objection to this, I am here seeking to offer a version of the concept that can be incorporated into as many different political and ethical frameworks as possible; I offer my own, more political development in Chapter 2. Thanks to Arto Laitinen for encouraging me to consider this point.

out the wrong of ontic injustice, because it places the focus on what has happened to the individual who has been wronged, not on the attitude by means of which the wrong was enacted. However, the notion of recognition respect enriches our understanding of how moral injury is enacted and, in particular, is useful in that it strengthens the idea of a mismatch between moral entitlements, on the one hand, and social entitlements, on the other. When ontic injustice occurs, there has been a social failure to respond appropriately to the morally relevant properties of the individual in question, and it is this failure that enacts diminishment, the impression that the person's moral value is less than it really is. In identifying cases of ontic injustice, then, we should be on the look-out for instances of mismatch between moral and social entitlements, as highlighted by the idea of recognition respect.

1.4.3. Domination

The wrong of ontic injustice is in many respects similar to a type of unfreedom according to one prominent account of freedom, namely, accounts of freedom as 'non-domination' such as those advanced by Philip Pettit (1996) and others in the neo-republican tradition. Though I am sympathetic to this way of understanding freedom, I shall not here seek to defend it. I shall rather set aside the question of whether freedom should be equated with non-domination and focus on showing that although ontic injustice very often involves domination, it does not always involve domination. This supports my choice to define ontic injustice in terms of moral injury rather than in terms of domination.

On Pettit's view, person A dominates person B when A has the power to interfere on an arbitrary basis with B's choices. 'Interference' here includes both physical and psychological methods of force, coercion, and manipulation aimed at making B's choice situation worse in some way. This must be 'more or less intentional'; accidental worsening of someone's choice situation is not interference. To be able to interfere on an arbitrary basis means that there is no mechanism for holding the dominator accountable for their interferences. The dominator can interfere at will and with impunity, suffering no penalty for their interference (Pettit 1996, 579–80). For an agent to be free from domination, it is not enough that she not be subject to actual interference; it must also be the case that she is protected from potential interference. In other words, she must not be at the mercy of someone who, for the present, is refraining from interfering with her choices but who could easily do so if he chose. A slave whose master is benevolent or disinterested may be in an important sense better off than a slave whose master delights in frequent acts of cruelty, but she is equally subject to domination.

With this definition of domination in mind, let us return to social constraints and enablements. To lack a social enablement to do P usually means that if one tries to do P, one has no assurance that one will not meet with interference and no assurance that such interference would incur penalties or correction. In other words, one has no social protection from arbitrary interferences with one's choices in relation to P. Putting the point this way highlights the close connection between ontic injustice and Pettit's definition of domination as the power to interfere with another's choices on an arbitrary basis. In many—perhaps most—cases, then, ontic injustice constitutes domination: B lacks the social enablement of being protected against arbitrary interference from A, meaning that A has the power to interfere on an arbitrary basis with B's choices, and thus A dominates B.

It is possible, however, for someone to experience ontic injustice without experiencing domination. Suppose, for example, that in virtue of their kind membership, B lacks the social enablement to be protected from A's wrongful interference; however, B is sufficiently physically strong that if A tried to interfere with B, B would simply fight A off and would certainly be successful. In this situation, B suffers an ontic injustice due to being wrongfully deprived of a social enablement. However, B is not dominated by A, for B can use a non-social form of power, brute physical power, to resist A's interference. Cases like this one notwithstanding, structures of social power tend to function in such a way that ontic injustice usually does constitute domination. If A could return with the police, for example, and enlist their support to carry out interference with B, then B would be dominated after all, despite B's physical strength. The same applies if A were able to return with a gang of cronies, or even a mob, confident in the knowledge that the actions of the gang or mob against B would be ignored by the judicial system. Cases like this are common, because those who are deprived of the social enablement of being protected from the arbitrary interference of other individuals are often also deprived of the social enablement of being protected against arbitrary interference more generally, including at the hands of law enforcement agencies and other groups that wield considerable brute physical power. So although not all cases of ontic injustice are cases of domination, the vast majority are.

There can also be cases of domination that are not cases of ontic injustice. For a case of domination to constitute ontic injustice, the domination must be effected via the construction of the dominated individual as a member of a social kind, where that social kind is characterised by a wrongful set of constraints and enablements. Although many familiar cases of domination operate via social kinds (such as the master–slave case), this need not always be the case; for example, one person can be in a position to dominate another due to having superior physical power. Cases of domination that do not constitute ontic injustice are perhaps more common than cases of ontic injustice that do not constitute domination.

1.4.4. The Severity of Ontic Injustice

The severity of an ontic injustice is the severity of the moral injury it involves, which in turn is determined by the strength of the diminishment. The question of what determines the strength of diminishment is a complex issue. I suspect, though, that it is a function of at least three factors. The first factor is the extent to which the social treatment falls short of that to which the individual is entitled. For example, an act of extreme and humiliating violence enacts a greater diminishment than a subtle social slight. The second is the importance of the relevant moral entitlements—how central they are to the conception of value (e.g., of human value) that is in question. Bodily integrity and autonomy are central to many conceptions of human value, so violations of these entitlements enact particularly strong diminishment. The third factor is the interpersonal context in which the diminishment takes place. For example, the meaning that is conveyed by someone being subjected to wrongful constraints and enablements is affected by *who else* is also subjected to those constraints and enablements.[18]

To illustrate this third factor, imagine a society of total surveillance: everyone is constantly monitored, perhaps by some rotating system of mutual monitoring, and no one is exempt. Let us further suppose that this monitoring is justified by reference to some conception of what it is to be a citizen; it is a citizen's duty to submit to monitoring for the collective good. Qua citizen, one loses the social entitlement to maintain privacy; but since everyone is socially constructed as a citizen, everyone loses this entitlement.

---

[18] I am grateful to an anonymous reviewer for encouraging me to develop this point.

Now, assuming that people do have a moral entitlement to greater privacy than they receive in this scenario, there is indeed a moral injury in the picture here, one that is suffered by all citizens. However, the diminishment that is enacted for any given individual is much less severe than it would be if the monitoring only applied to a small group of individuals picked out by some characteristic such as race, religion, or sexual orientation. If that were the case, it seems to me that the impression of lowered value for those individuals would be much more pronounced, and the diminishment would accordingly be stronger.

There may well be further factors relevant to the strength of diminishment beyond the three I have mentioned here, but these seem to stand out as particularly significant.

Not everyone will be friendly to notions such as moral injury and recognition respect. For those who do not accept these notions, the wrong that I seek to pick out with the concept of ontic injustice must be understood more simply as the wrong of being placed at risk of bodily and psychological harms. If a particular wife never suffers marital rape and experiences no distress at knowing that she would have no legal recourse if she were to suffer marital rape, well and good; but she has still been placed at *risk* of these harms in virtue of being socially constructed as a wife, and that is wrong. For someone who rejects the concepts of moral injury and recognition respect, the wrong of ontic injustice will perhaps not seem as deep as it does to one who accepts those notions, but the pragmatic benefits of having the concept of ontic injustice—which will be explored in §1.6 and in the rest of this book—are exactly the same.

1.5. Using the Concept of Ontic Injustice

In order for the concept of ontic injustice to yield detailed judgements about actual cases, it needs to be combined with two further components: first, an account of the moral value of the individual(s) in question and the moral demands to which this value gives rise and, second, an account of the ontology of the social kind in question (which will draw on an account of the ontology of social kinds in general) and in particular of the constraints and enablements that partly constitute it.

1.5.1. Normative Commitments

With regard to the first component, what someone will think about putative cases of ontic injustice will depend on their views about what kinds of moral demands are created by different features of agents. For example, whether or not one thinks that the social kind *non-human animals* is ontically unjust will depend on one's views on the moral entitlements of different sorts of beings.[19] If you hold a conception of the moral value of sentient beings according to which they ought not to be killed simply for the expedience of others, then you will probably think that the social kind *non-human animal* involves a wrongful constraint, because non-human animals are sentient beings and their being killed simply for the expedience of others is socially sanctioned. Recall that the explanation of the wrong of ontic injustice as a moral injury does not purport to supply a general account of moral demands, because applying the concept of moral injury always involves an appeal to some independent conception of the moral value of different sorts of beings and the demands this value generates.

1.5.2. Ontological Commitments

With regard to the second component, making judgments about ontic injustice requires us to know whether or not a certain constraint or enablement is partly constitutive of a social kind in question.[20] This is a point on which people can and do disagree, based in part on the account of social ontology to which they subscribe.

Consider, for example, the phenomenon of bisexual exclusion, whereby bisexual people are often, to varying extents, denied membership in queer communities and denied access to queer spaces and queer cultural resources. This is wrong: bisexual people have a genuine interest in having access to queer communities and cultural resources, and their exclusion

---

[19] The kind *non-human animals* may sound like a biological kind. But consider the different sorts of animals this includes: killer whales, parrots, geckos, ladybirds. I submit that the division of animals into two categories—humans and non-humans—is a social division, even if there is a biological division somewhere in the vicinity. In other words, even if the division of animals into species is a matter of biological kinds, the division of animals into two categories of 'humans' and 'non-humans' is a matter of social kinds.

[20] I am grateful to an anonymous reviewer for pressing me on this point.

is unjustified.[21] Now, is this a case of ontic injustice? Well, that depends on whether there is a wrongful constraint that partly constitutes the social kind *bisexual*.

According to Ásta's conferralist account of social ontology, *bisexual* is here functioning as a communal kind: a social status conferred informally by other social agents in the queer community. When those agents behave towards people whom they understand to be bisexual in ways that convey the impression that those people are unwelcome in queer spaces, then we can say that the social status of *bisexual* includes a constraint that makes it harder to be present in queer spaces. Therefore, a conferralist would say that the social kind *bisexual* is ontically unjust.

However, applying Searle's account to this case would give the opposite result, because Searle holds that conventional deontic powers are the only type of constraint/enablement that contribute to constructing social kinds. Since conventional deontic powers depend on the collective recognition of entitlements, in order for the wrongful constraint generated by bisexual exclusion to partly constitute the social kind *bisexual*, there would need to be an explicit recognition, that is at least widely shared, to the effect that bisexuals are not entitled to access queer communities and cultural resources. Since (I take it) bisexual exclusion typically does not work like this and is usually a much more subtle phenomenon, Searle's account entails that the wrongful constraint generated by bisexual exclusion is not part of what constitutes the social kind *bisexual*, and so this is not a case of ontic injustice.

This shows how judgements about putative cases of ontic injustice depend on one's understanding of the ontology of the social kind in question.

1.5.3. Combatting Ontic Injustice

Because there is no single response that all cases of ontic injustice call for, it is difficult to say very much about combating ontic injustice on a general level. Here my aim is simply to head off at the pass a false impression about what combating ontic injustice involves that some readers may have formed. This false impression is that if a social kind is ontically unjust, that kind must be abolished. To be clear: the fact that a certain social kind is ontically unjust does *not* entail that the best or only response to ontic injustice is to

---

[21] For discussions of bisexual exclusion, see, e.g., Eadie 1993; Serano 2013.

abolish the social kind in question; the best response could equally well be to change social ontology so that the kind is no longer constituted by wrongful constraints and enablements. Whether this is possible in a particular case depends on whether or not the wrongful constraints are a necessary part of the social kind. There is no general answer about whether this is possible; it depends on the kind in question.

For example, the marital rape exemption in England and Wales was ended in 1991; rape within marriage is now legally considered rape. Thus, the institutional kind *wife* has changed. Whether or not all wrongful legal constraints have been removed is another question, but it seems potentially plausible to think that all wrongful constraints *could* be removed without transforming the kind so much that the label 'wife' is no longer appropriate. We may thus think that the social kind *wife* is only contingently ontically unjust. By contrast, consider the social kind *slave*. Although the constraints that constitute the kind *slave* are different in different institutions of slavery that have existed at different times and in different places, all of these institutions involve such a serious limitation of autonomy (besides frequently licensing the most extreme and brutal physical and psychological harms) that it is impossible to imagine a social kind that merited the term 'slave' that did not involve wrongful constraints. Any form of slavery is very seriously wrongful. Therefore, it is natural to think that the social kind *slave* is *necessarily* ontically unjust and that the only appropriate response to this injustice is to abolish the kind completely. Thus, what one thinks about the response that ontic injustice merits will depend on the particular case of ontic injustice, as well as on one's favoured account of social ontology and of the ways in which social kinds persist through time.

1.6. The Theoretical Value of Ontic Injustice

We do not need a concept of ontic injustice to see that some constraints and enablements can be wrongful; what, then, do we gain by having a concept of ontic injustice that draws our attention specifically to the role these constraints and enablements play in social ontology? In other words, we already knew that the marital rape exemption, for example, was an injustice; what do we gain by thinking of it as an *ontic* injustice in particular? The main way I will respond to this question is by discussing particular cases of ontic injustice: in the rest of this book, I will show in detail how the concept of ontic injustice helps us to better understand race and gender oppression. However, remaining at a more general level for the moment, we can still identify three main reasons for incorporating the concept of ontic injustice into our conceptual repertoire.

1.6.1. Understanding the Transmission of Constraints and Enablements

The first reason the concept of ontic injustice is useful is that it helps us to understand the role that wrongful constraints and enablements can play in the construction of social kinds. Simply put, social kinds function to *transmit* constraints and enablements. If I am made into a wife in England prior to 1991, I come under the constraint of not being able to refuse sex with my husband. Nothing specific needs to be done to place me personally under that constraint in particular; indeed, I may not even know about it. Yet, in becoming a wife, I become subject to this constraint, because to be so constrained is part of what it is to be a wife. The operation of social ontology is thus a way by which many people come to be placed under constraints and enablements that are wrongful.

Moreover, because many social kinds involve constraints and enablements that are valuable to people as well as ones that are wrongful, it can be the case that people cannot become members of social kinds that matter to them *without* placing themselves under wrongful constraints and enablements. This is because social kinds "bundle" constraints and enablements, so to speak. Staying with the marriage case, suppose that I want to become a certain person's legal next of kin; under certain social conditions, I can only do this by becoming a wife, hence at the cost of placing myself under an obligation to have sex with my husband whenever he chooses. Although one or both of us might protest at this, nothing can be done about it without changing the nature of the social kind *wife*, which is something that we, as two individuals, are not in a position to do through our own decisions and efforts.

Taking this thought even further, I might value membership in a social kind because of the meaning that kind has to me, independently of any particular constraints and enablements; perhaps I want to be a wife because of the religious significance this kind holds for me. Yet I cannot access this good without placing myself under the wrongful constraint that partly constitutes the kind *wife* in my particular social setting. Thus, noticing how wrongful constraints and enablements can partly constitute membership in a social kind enriches our understanding of the kinds of difficulties they create for actual and potential members of the kind in question.

1.6.2. Capturing Experiences of Diminishment

A second respect in which the concept of ontic injustice is useful is that it can contribute to reflecting in our theories of wrong a type of experience that I take to be fairly common. This is the experience of hurt or distress *relating to one's own status* that can be prompted by events that do not directly impact one but which relate to a group that one is part of. Some examples of this from my own experience include the election of Donald Trump as US president and the confirmation of Brett Kavanaugh as an associate justice of the US Supreme Court, both in the wake of credible allegations of sexual assault against women. In both cases, I felt *personally* harmed, even though I live in a different country, the United Kingdom, and was unlikely to be directly personally impacted by the misogynist acts a person could perform in these offices. Something about the fact that men with the history of these two individuals could nevertheless enter into positions of such power made me feel crushed, vulnerable, *lessened* in some way. It felt as though the recognition of my humanity and my right to be free from sexual violence was on shakier ground than I had previously thought them, or even than they previously had in fact been.

I think such experiences are not uncommon for members of marginalised groups, including those who, like me, occupy relatively socially privileged positions in many respects. What's more, I think various theories already pick up on these experiences; I think that something like this experience is what at least some accounts of hate speech, for example, aim to recognise and guard against. Nevertheless, there is something prima facie puzzling about this experience. The distance between myself and the events that prompted the felt harm calls for some explanation.

I cannot here explore such experiences in great detail. All I want to do here is to suggest that the concept of ontic injustice can serve as one available explanation for such experiences in some cases (and only some—for surely, not all such experiences will admit of the same explanation). The story that we can tell with the concept of ontic injustice is as follows. Sometimes high-profile events can either *reveal* that certain constraints and enablement characterise a certain social group (e.g., that systematic and socially created vulnerability to sexual violence characterises women as a social group) or actually *change* which constraints and enablement characterise that group (e.g., making women *more* vulnerable to sexual assault, perhaps by changing social norms). When this happens, *all* members of the group in question suffer a moral injury, which is to say, damage to the realisation or acknowledgement of their value which takes place via a process of diminishment. Diminishment, as we have seen, is an objective phenomenon that takes place when immoral behaviour gives the impression that someone's moral worth is less than it truly is. So the suggestion is that sometimes these experiences of felt harm are a response to an increased recognition of an ontic injustice that one suffers, a response to an increase in the severity of an ontic injustice that one suffers, or even a response to the imposition upon one of a novel ontic injustice. What is more, they are perfectly natural and reasonable responses in the sense that the felt harm corresponds to the objective harm of diminishment and moral injury.

Now, the question of whether a particular instances of this sort of felt harm is aptly explained in terms of ontic injustice in a given case depends in large part on whether it is plausible to see the events in question as affecting the social kind of which the person is a member. For example, in my case, whether or not ontic injustice is relevant here depends on whether it makes sense to think that there is a social kind *woman* that I belong to and that is constituted by social norms that can be affected by events in the United States, even though, for example, I am not subject to the official constraints and enablement of US laws. I think that it *is* plausible to think this, but that is because I take a fairly wide or permissive view of which constraints and enablements contribute to constituting social kinds.[22] Someone with a narrower view on this point would likely disagree. I am not, therefore, claiming to defend any particular conclusion about this specific example. The point is that ontic injustice offers us one additional *option* for capturing and explaining the felt harm that people may experience in those general sorts of cases—and, I think, a useful one.

---

[22] I will say more about this view in Chapters 3, 4, and 5.

1.6.3. Changing Social Practices

The third and final reason the concept of ontic injustice is useful is that it can help to make the case for intervening to change harmful social practices. By highlighting the wrong of ontic injustice—the moral injury suffered by members of the social kind in question—we show that the social practices that maintain the constraints and enablements that constitute the kind in question are in turn wrongful, and justice requires that they change. Granted, in the case of the marital rape exemption, it was already clear that the wrongful constraint was maintained by a law, and this law was wrongful. But this need not always be so. According to many accounts of social ontology, it is perfectly possible that the constraints and enablements that constitute a social kind can be maintained by diffuse and covert factors. If we accept such an account, then the concept of ontic injustice allows us to say that these diffuse and covert factors are wrongful and must be changed, even if they are not obviously wrongful *aside from* their role in maintaining the construction of a kind that is ontically unjust. The concept of ontic injustice helps us to make a strong case for this sort of intervention by getting a clear fix on the wrong that we are seeking to prevent—ontic injustice—and laying bare its relation to the specific social processes that we are targeting in our efforts to bring about positive social change.

One thing to note here is that the relationship between social practices and harm that is involved in ontic injustice is an immediate one. This can be seen by comparing it to the relationship between discriminatory speech and harm. Consider Mary Kate McGowan's explanation of what it means to say that the latter relationship can be 'constitutive':

> Clearly 'constitution' is here being used in a special technical sense. It does not mean what it means in other philosophical contexts. To say that the employer's ([discriminatory] hiring policy enacting) utterance constitutes the harm of discrimination is not to say that the employer's utterance is cotemporaneous with the discriminatory harms. The harm of discrimination is causally downstream from the utterance that enacts the discriminatory policy. It is not to say that the employer's utterance is sufficient for that harm either. Others need to follow the policy for the discriminatory harms to obtain. Constitution talk here, unlike elsewhere in philosophy, is not akin to an equals sign; it is instead *a distinct norm-driven way of causing*.

In order for an utterance to constitute harm then three conditions are required. The utterance enacts a norm; that norm is followed and harm results
from following that norm. Although, in what follows, the focus is on the
norm enactment part of things, harm constitution requires that the norm
is followed and that following it is harmful. (2019, 24–25, emphasis added)

When an utterance is said to 'constitute' discrimination, then, the harm of the
norm it enacts is causally downstream and is mediated by the behaviour of
other agents. By contrast, if an utterance, or indeed any other action, enacts
a norm that either wrongfully constrains members of some social kind
or socially constructs someone as a member of a social kind that involves
wrongful constraints, then that action has enacted ontic injustice. The harm
of this action—the moral injury that constitutes an ontic injustice—is not
causally downstream and is not mediated by the actions of others.

Suppose, for example, that a legislator introduces a marital rape exemption where previously there was none. The utterance by which this legislation
is enacted perpetrates an ontic injustice: anyone who is socially constructed
as a wife in that context immediately suffers a moral injury. By contrast, for
this utterance to constitute harm in the sense outlined by McGowan, it would
be necessary not only for it to enact a norm but also for people to act in accordance with the norm that non-consensual sex within marriage is not rape
and for this to result in harm. Whilst the third consequence (harm) would
certainly result from the second (the norm being followed), the second
might not result from the first (the norm being enacted). At the very least,
we would have to wait to see how events played out before we could say that
the legislator's utterance constituted harm in McGowan's sense, whereas we
could immediately say that it enacted ontic injustice.

To be clear, ontic injustice is not intended to replace the concept of discriminatory speech. Examining the contrast between discriminatory speech
and ontic injustice simply highlights the greater immediacy of the relationship between social practices and harm that is involved in ontic injustice.
This immediacy has the potential to be useful in making the case that the
social practices that perpetuate ontic injustice must be changed, because it
shows that there is no downstream point at which intervention might prevent harm.

On a general level, then, we can see that the concept of ontic injustice helps
us to identify and respond to wrongful social constraints and enablements
by highlighting their role in social construction and their status as moral

injuries. Further demonstration of the value of the concept of ontic injustice will be given in later chapters in relation to the specific case of race and gender oppression.

1.7. Conclusion

This chapter has set out the concept of ontic injustice as a distinctive type of social wrong. I have argued that the very fact that an individual is a member of a social kind can be wrongful, because the constraints and enablements that partly constitute kind membership can be wrongful to the individual who is subjected to them. I have equated this wrong, ontic injustice, with a moral injury, which is a form of damage to the acknowledgement of an individual's moral value, and with a failure of recognition respect. I have shown how the concept of ontic injustice must be combined with specific accounts of both social ontology and moral value in order to yield judgements about particular cases. Finally, I have argued that the concept of ontic injustice is valuable because it helps us to identify and respond to wrongful social constraints and enablements by highlighting their role in social construction and their status as moral injuries.

2

Ontic Oppression

2.1. Introduction

As we have seen, in order to apply the concept of ontic injustice to particular cases, it is necessary to combine it with particular normative and ontological commitments concerning the morally relevant properties of the individuals and the precise ontology of the social kinds in question. In developing the concept of ontic injustice, I faced something of a trade-off between accessibility and functionality regarding the extent to which specific normative and ontological commitments should be built into the account. The fewer prior commitments are built into the concept, the greater the number of people who can make use of the concept, which is clearly a benefit. However, the more open the concept is to being combined with different normative and ontological commitments, the more minimal the concept is. This is a drawback because having a more minimal concept makes it harder to see exactly how it applies to specific cases, and thus harder both to get a firm grasp of the concept and to see why it is useful.

The way I have decided to handle this trade-off is to introduce the concept of ontic injustice itself at a high level of generality, which I did in Chapter 1, and then to go on and model how it can be combined with a specific set of normative and ontological commitments in the context of a particular inquiry, which is what I shall do in the rest of this book. The particular inquiry that I will focus on concerns race and gender oppression, and it approaches these kinds in the spirit of emancipatory theory, as described in the Introduction. I aim to show how the concept of ontic injustice helps us to understand race and gender kinds in a way that aids in combating oppression.

In this chapter, I introduce the normative commitments that will guide this inquiry, and in Chapter 3, I introduce the ontological commitments. In Chapters 4, 5, and 6, I use the concept of ontic injustice in conjunction with these commitments to assess whether race and gender kinds are ontically oppressive, and in Chapters 7 and 8, I draw out some implications of my conclusions.

Ontology and Oppression. Katharine Jenkins, Oxford University Press. © Katharine Jenkins 2023.
DOI: 10.1093/oso/9780197666777.003.0003

Not everyone will share the normative and ontological commitments I adopt, and although I will endeavour to motivate them, I will not be delivering a comprehensive argument for them. (That would take several books, each quite different from this one.) I hope that at least some readers will already be sympathetic to these commitments. For these readers, the arguments I present in later chapters will be, as it were, live. Other readers are invited to treat the rest of this book as a modelling exercise. For these readers, the value of the ensuing discussion lies in showing, in detail, how the concept of ontic injustice can be combined with specific normative and ontological commitments to yield significant conclusions. I hope that others will take up the concept in the context of different projects and develop it in different ways.

I begin this chapter by giving a preliminary account of the kind of normative commitments that my project calls for. I then supply these commitments in the form of an account of oppression, with reference to its intersectional nature. Finally, I incorporate these commitments into the concept of ontic injustice to give a concept of ontic *oppression* that will guide my investigation into race and gender kinds in the rest of this book.

2.2. The Problem of Naturalising Ideology

The concept of ontic injustice encapsulates an important insight: the mere fact of being made into a member of a social kind can be wrongful in and of itself. In developing the concept of ontic injustice, I sought to make it compatible with a range of different normative commitments by relying on the notion of moral injury, which has to be combined with a substantive account of the moral worth of certain sorts of individuals in order to yield results about specific cases. The result was a concept that many different people can take up and use. From this point on, I take up the concept of ontic injustice in the service of the project outlined in the Introduction, which is to investigate race and gender kinds with an emancipatory interest, which is to say, with a view to contributing to the eradication of racial and gendered oppression. Here I aim to supply some appropriate normative commitments so that the concept of ontic injustice can successfully be applied in the service of this project.

When thinking about ontic injustice from this perspective, a challenge becomes apparent, which concerns the relationship between ontic injustice and what are termed 'ideologies'. Ideologies are here understood as persistent and systematic distortions in collective cultural resources that function to perpetuate oppressive forms of life, the existence of which is at least partly explained by this function. Although ideologies involve beliefs, they are not limited to beliefs in a narrow sense but involve our broader orientation to, and interpretation of, the world. As Rahel Jaeggi puts it, ideologies constitute 'the framework in which we understand both ourselves and the social conditions, and also the way we operate within these conditions' (2009, 64; see also Haslanger 2017b). Where this framework does *not* systematically distort reality in a way that functions to perpetuate oppression, we can think of it as a 'cultural techneë' (Haslanger 2017a, 156–60; 2017b, 16). An ideology is thus a particular and problematic form that a cultural techneë can take; in this sense, 'ideology' is a pejorative term. Identifying and responding to ideologies is an essential part of aiming to counteract oppression, including oppression centred on race and gender.

One common function of ideology is to make wrongful forms of treatment and unjustly structured social orders seem like a natural and appropriate response to putatively pre-existing difference. An example from which we have a little temporal distance is useful here, so consider the belief (widely, though, of course, not universally, held throughout the nineteenth century and beyond) that women ought to receive only a basic education because female biology means that further education is useless at best and physically harmful at worst. Physical factors such as women supposedly having smaller brains and more delicate bodily tissues were cited as support of this. This is an example of ideology, both because it is distorted—female biology is not like this at all!—and because it functions to justify and maintain a social order in which women are subordinated, in part by being denied access to education. One way in which it so functions is by making it seem as though withholding education from women is not really a harm to women, because women could not benefit from it and indeed would actually be harmed by it. There are many things going on here, but one is a presentation of differences with a social origin as though they were a natural difference: the fact of women having, on average, lesser facility with (say) mathematics due to the withholding of education is touted as evidence of women having inferior innate mathematical abilities due to their bodily features. Call ideologies of this sort 'naturalising ideologies'.

Naturalising ideologies regarding race and gender are common and have the potential to interact with the idea of ontic injustice in a very problematic way. This is because the explanation I have given of the wrong of ontic injustice concerns the mismatch between the moral entitlements someone has in virtue of the kind of being that they are and the social constraints and enablements to which they are subject. However, the effect of a naturalising ideology is precisely to give us a false impression of the moral entitlements that someone has in virtue of the kind of being that they are. For example, in the case of women and education, someone in the grip of naturalising ideology would think that in virtue of women's bodily features, they are not morally entitled to any more than basic education. Thus, the effect of naturalising ideology is to make ontic injustice invisible as injustice—to make its wrong vanish into thin air.

A similar point is made by Catharine MacKinnon in relation to theories of equality based on treating similarly those who are similar and differently those who are different, such as when a discrimination law requires a 'similarly situated' person as a comparison point. MacKinnon writes:

> The inequality that is hierarchy, existing [equality] theory builds in as difference, meaning something that can be treated differently—that is, less well, hierarchically as lower—thus making theory systematically unable to identify the one thing it needs to be able to identify and eliminate, in order to do what it has to do. (2007, 53–54)

The existence of naturalising ideologies suggests that although the wrong of ontic injustice *consists in* the mismatch between what an individual is owed (morally speaking) and what they get (socially speaking), nevertheless, under conditions characterised by pervasive ideologies, directly *looking for* such mismatch is not a good way to identify this wrong, because our perceptions are liable to distortion.[1]

In light of this, I plan to cash out the concept of ontic injustice into a more specific concept that incorporates the relevant normative commitments. In doing so, I will focus on the phenomenon of *oppression*. I'll say much more about oppression in subsequent sections; for now, we can make do with a general or pre-theoretical understanding of oppression as having to do with social wrongs that are *severely limiting* and *group-based*. I will define ontic *oppression* as a subspecies of ontic injustice. Simply put, ontic oppression occurs when a case of ontic injustice involves constraints and enablements

---

[1] For more detail on this and other aspects of ideology critique, see Celikates 2006.

that are not only wrongful in a general sense but also specifically oppressive. As with ontic injustice, we can say that a certain social kind is 'ontically oppressive' whenever at least some individuals constructed as kind members suffer ontic oppression.

The concept of ontic oppression that I will go on to define in the rest of this chapter is a particular species or subcategory of ontic injustice: the concept of ontic oppression picks out a subset of the cases picked out by the concept of ontic injustice. I propose to make the concept of ontic oppression, while unfortunately not *proof* against naturalising ideology, then at least *more resistant* to it, by combining it with a detailed and practical understanding of oppression. The thought is that we can give a substantive characterisation of forms of treatment that are taken to be oppressive, and then use the concept of ontic oppression by relying on the premise that oppressive treatment is *always* a morally inappropriate form of treatment of the sort of individuals that all human beings are.[2] This reduces the need to constantly make judgements about the forms of treatment that different human individuals are entitled to in virtue of the sorts of beings that they are, closing down the space for ideological error to enter the picture. As soon as we spot one of the forms of treatment that we have identified as oppressive, we can be confident that it is wrongful without undertaking any further normative investigation.

On this picture, the *wrong* of ontic oppression is the same as the wrong of ontic injustice in general: a moral injury, which is to say, a failure to treat individuals in the way that they are morally entitled to be treated, thereby constituting damage to the realisation or acknowledgement of their value. It is the *mode of identifying this wrong* that is different: rather than directly looking for mismatch, we are relying on an understanding of oppression to help us identify clear cases where things have gone very wrong.

Evidently, the concept of ontic oppression will only be able to do this work if it is combined with a robust and detailed account of oppression, one that can serve to orient us towards the world and help us to identify cases of oppression on a practical level. In other words, the concept of ontic oppression will only be as good as the account of oppression that is used to cash it out. In light of this, I will spend most of the rest of this chapter laying out an account of oppression that can do this work.

---

[2] As a matter of fact, I think it can plausibly be claimed that non-human animals are also individuals of this sort, such that the oppressive treatment of animals is also always morally inappropriate; but I do not undertake to defend this claim here, and it may call for a different account of oppression from the one that I offer in this chapter.

2.3. Defining Oppression

2.3.1. Oppression

I will base my understanding of oppression in this context primarily on two classic works of feminist philosophy: Marilyn Frye's essay 'Oppression' (1983) and Iris Marion Young's chapter 'Five Faces of Oppression' ([1990] 2011).[3] Frye notes that the word 'oppression' derives from the word 'press'. She observes that 'something pressed is something caught between or among barriers which are so related to each other that jointly they restrain, restrict or prevent the thing's motion or mobility' (1983, 2). This observation is the basis of her account of oppression. As she puts it:

> The experience of oppressed people is that the living of one's life is confined and shaped by forces and barriers which are not accidental or occasional and hence avoidable, but are systematically related to each other in such a way as to catch one between and among them and restrict or penalize motion in any direction. (4)

Frye elaborates this conception of oppression using the metaphor of a birdcage. A birdcage is made up of interlocking bars. If you examine just one bar, it will be hard to see how that bar imposes any limitation on the bird, since the bird could just move around it; if, instead, you look at all the bars at once and consider how they interlock, then it will be obvious why the bird is restricted (4–5).

Overall, then, Frye understands oppression to consist of systematically related barriers that serve to restrain, restrict, and immobilise the members of some social group. There are two key features to this account of oppression. First is the claim that oppression consists of systematically interlinked limitations, such that a macroscopic perspective is required to detect

---

[3] I am here aiming to strike a balance: offering an account that is detailed enough to help us make practical judgements, whilst stopping short of the kind of detailed investigation that would need to be a book in its own right (for a book-length treatment, see Cudd 2006). I am also aiming to offer an account that will strike as many people as possible as following fairly familiar lines of thought. For these reason, a focus on these two classic texts suits my purposes. However, there is much more that could be said about oppression, including both the earlier history of the concept and developments subsequent to the publication of these two sources, and for other projects and purposes, a different focus will be called for.

it (1983, 4–7).[4] This can also be expressed as the claim that oppression is a *structural* phenomenon. Second is the claim that oppression is a *group-based* phenomenon: the explanation for why a particular individual is subject to the limitations in question is that they are a member of a certain social group (7–8).

This second requirement could be elaborated in various different ways, depending on what we mean by a 'social group'. For example, Young (2011, 42–48) understands social groups as necessarily having shared ways of life, a propensity for greater or different association with co-members compared to non-members, and a shared sense of identity. This is quite a thick or demanding conception of social groups. I shall here adopt a less demanding conception. When I say that oppression is group-based, I mean that it does not include social limitations that are targeted at individuals qua individuals but only social limitations that apply to all individuals with a particular feature or features, where this feature is fairly widespread. For example, suppose that a society decided, without good reason, that some particular individual was dangerous and should be locked up indefinitely. That individual would be subject to very serious social limitations, and these would be wrongful, but the individual would not count as being *oppressed* because the limitations are not group-based. Even if the case concerned, instead of one individual, half a dozen individuals (perhaps those involved in a particular event), this would still not be sufficiently group-based to qualify as a potential case of oppression.

This way of understanding the 'group-based' requirement for oppression, in contrast to Young's understanding, leaves open the possibility that a form of oppression may target some selection of individuals who do not, in an intuitive sense, have 'a shared way of life'; for example, it is in theory possible, on this view, for left-handed people to be an oppressed group. Of course, oppression produces certain shared social realities and is therefore likely to give rise to shared ways of life and a sense of affinity, but this is not a logical requirement on my view. I take this more permissive understanding to be preferable to Young's because it allows for cases where prima facie oppressive practices actually function to prevent or destroy shared ways of life to count as instances of oppression. For example, if sex between men is illegal, then under at least

---

[4] I take Frye to be here using 'systematic' in a folk or general sense, rather than invoking a specific philosophical sense of systematicity; thanks to J. Adam Carter for encouraging me to clarify this point.

some circumstances, it will be very difficult for queer men to form a community that shares a way of life; the need for secrecy will be liable to stymy the formation of connections between individuals. As another example, practices of compelled residential schooling for Indigenous children, which have been enacted in countries such as Canada, are aimed at the destruction of the shared ways of life of Indigenous communities. Unfortunately, some have succeeded in these aims to at least some degree, and it is not difficult to imagine a situation in which they succeeded completely.

It seems highly counter-intuitive to say that in cases where the criminalisation of sex between men or the compelled residential schooling of Indigenous children is sufficiently effective in preventing or destroying shared ways of living, queer men and Indigenous people, respectively, would no longer count as oppressed groups. Indeed, this seems to get things precisely backwards; the prevention or destruction of shared ways of life seems to me to *constitute part of* the oppression, rather than preventing the case from counting as one of oppression in the first place. That, however, is what Young's understanding of the group-based requirement would commit us to saying. For this reason, I prefer the more permissive understanding.[5] (There is also a further reason for preferring the more permissive understanding of the group-based requirement, which is related to intersectionality, and which I will discuss in §2.4.)

One of Frye's main concerns is to supply tools for showing why certain claims of oppression are false, such as the claim that White people are oppressed because there are certain areas of cities where they cannot easily go (1983, 11–12).[6] Frye grants that the restriction is a genuine limitation but argues that it is part of a broader structure that serves a net enabling function for the group in question. Although, according to Frye, it might be difficult or uncomfortable for a White person to move through certain urban spaces, the flipside of this is that it is often more difficult for people of colour to move outside of these same spaces, and this, in turn, functions to secure and maintain greater access to almost all social goods for White people compared to people of colour. In this case, the limitation *is* part of a systematically linked network of restrictions, but the bulk of these restrictions are imposed on the

---

[5] Thanks to Ben Colburn for encouraging me to explain more fully this advantage of the broader view, as well as helping me to understand it more clearly.

[6] This is the example Frye uses. In reproducing it here, I note that false claims about 'no-go areas for White people' have been cynically used to advance racist agendas and that it is vital to counter these claims.

contrasting group (people of colour, in this case). Therefore, according to Frye, the limitation is not an indication that the group on whom the limitation is imposed (White people, in this case) is oppressed.

I agree with Frye that White people do not constitute an oppressed group. However, I think that Frye's discussion of these cases highlights that thinking of oppression as consisting of networks of social constraints that are (a) systematic and (b) group-based does not yet give us all the tools we need to dismiss some claims about oppression that we might not want to countenance. For example, neither Frye nor I want to say that wealthy White straight cis men are an oppressed group. But our patriarchal social system includes very many restrictions on such men, including that they should refrain from certain activities, not wear certain clothing, and so on. Moreover, these restrictions are certainly systematic. Based on this definition of oppression, we might reasonably ask: just how much does some group need to be systematically constrained before we can say that they are oppressed?

This is as good a point as any to flag the fact that I think oppression is an inherently normative concept, in that to say that some group is oppressed is to make not a merely descriptive claim but rather a morally loaded one (Cudd 1994, 24). Accordingly, I expect to find that oppression is normative 'all the way down', as it were: the criteria for establishing whether something is an instance of oppression will themselves involve normative judgements. We are not, then, looking for criteria that will exempt us from having to make normative judgements in applying them to particular cases. Even so, we do need a certain level of detail about what we are looking for when we seek to establish whether something is an instance of oppression, and I think that Frye's explicit account of oppression stops short of offering this level of detail. However, we can glean some suggestions about how to add in this detail by attending to some of the implicit claims behind the argumentative moves she makes.

In rejecting the claim that men are oppressed, Frye emphasises that the network of restrictions in which the norm 'men don't cry' features is one that overall functions to benefit at least those men who comply with the norms, whereas it functions to the detriment of women whether or not we comply with the norms. Neither women who comply with norms of femininity nor women who depart from them tend to occupy high social positions.[7] This

---

[7] Frye wants to make the blanket claim that men are not oppressed as men. I want to make the weaker claim that some men—wealthy White straight cis men—are not oppressed as men. This is compatible with thinking, for example, that men of colour are oppressed *as men of colour.*

suggests that the definition of oppression needs an additional component that concerns the kind of social position towards which the restrictions tend. Anyone who is subject to significant and systematic restraints is being placed and held in a certain social position. In order to rule out the cases we want to rule out, we need to ask *what sort* of social position that is. In other words, the question is not 'how constraining are the restrictions?', but 'towards what kind of social position do the restrictions tend?'

The criterion we need here, I believe, is something like this: oppressed groups are those who are subject to systematic restrictions *that hold them in a social position characterised by little power and status relative to contrasting groups*; we might say, for shorthand, restrictions that hold them in *subordinated* social positions. So our definition is as follows: oppression consists of networks of social limitations that are (a) systematic, (b) group-based, and (c) subordinating. Some caution is called for here. I have used the concept of 'subordination' to define oppression, but subordination is itself a complex and rich notion and one that is intuitively linked to oppression. Therefore, I need to spell out the concept of subordination as used in the definition of oppression so as not to end up with a problematic circularity. This is where Young's account of oppression enters the picture.

2.3.2. Subordination

Young argues that oppression is not a sufficiently unified phenomenon to give a single set of criteria for identifying it. Rather, she offers what I take to be a cluster analysis, holding that 'oppression names in fact a family of concepts and conditions, which I divide into five kinds: exploitation, marginalization, powerlessness, cultural imperialism, and violence' (2011, 40). Now, I have said that subordinated social positions are characterised by little power and little status relative to contrasting groups. For example, women have less power and less social status, on the whole, than men. I think that Young's cluster account (augmented with a sixth face that I will argue is also needed) offers an excellent way of characterising these social positions.

To be clear, Young offers the 'five faces' as a cluster concept analysis of *oppression itself*. I use them here (along with an additional sixth feature) somewhat differently: to elucidate the notion of *subordination* as it features in a more traditional definition of oppression. My claim is that oppression consists of networks of social limitations that are (a) systematic,

(b) group-based, and (c) subordinating in that they steer individuals towards social positions characterised by one or more of the following features: exploitation, marginalisation, powerlessness, cultural imperialism, violence, and what I shall call 'communicative curtailment'. I find this approach helpful for the purposes of leaving as little room as possible for ideological distortion because the 'faces' of subordination offer us quite specific phenomena and dynamics to be on the alert for. I'll now explain each of these six features of subordination—five from Young's account and a sixth added by me—in turn.

Young's first face of oppression is exploitation, which she defines as 'a steady process of the transfer of the results of the labor of one social group to benefit another' (2011, 49). In other words, one group gains goods at the expense of the other. Although Young draws on Karl Marx, her understanding of exploitation is broader than a traditional Marxist conception. For example, she includes as examples of exploitation the 'transfer of nurturing and sexual energies [from women] to men' (50) and the work of people of colour in service roles, which, she argues, entails 'a transfer of energies whereby the servers enhance the status of the served' (52).

The second face of oppression is closely related to the first. Young notes that whereas members of some oppressed groups are pressed into exploitative work, members of other groups are shut out from work altogether. She describes these people as 'marginals', meaning 'people the system of labor cannot or will not use' (2011, 53). Primary examples that Young offers of groups that are subjected to marginalisation include certain racially marked groups and elderly people; I would add to this many disabled people. Although exploitation has probably received more theoretical attention, Young argues that its relative, marginalisation, 'is perhaps the most dangerous form of oppression' because it tends to result in 'severe material deprivation and even extermination' (53). A group that is 'expelled from useful participation in social life', as Young puts it, is vulnerable to being expelled en masse from society altogether through either murder or forced removal. This risk does not usually face the exploited who are doing essential, if menial, work that benefits the powerful.

Young also emphasises the psychological toll of marginalisation, for even when material deprivation is prevented through welfare provision, marginalised people are typically deprived of rights and freedoms that those not receiving welfare provisions are able to enjoy. For example, they are likely to suffer invasions of their privacy as part of assessments to determine whether they 'deserve' support and they are also likely to suffer losses of dignity due to the stigmatisation of welfare recipients. Moreover, lack of work may prevent people from exercising their capacities in ways that are socially recognised, resulting in feelings of 'uselessness, boredom, and lack of self-respect' (2011, 55). In the current economic context, these points resonate particularly strongly.

The third face of oppression is what Young terms 'powerlessness', which is defined as a lack of ability to 'regularly participate in making decisions that affect the conditions of their lives and actions' (2011, 56). It is important to recognise that Young's conception of powerlessness is intrinsically relational. It is not simply about what outcomes one can or cannot affect but is about the ways in which other people *are* able to affect outcomes in one's life. Thus, 'the powerless are situated so that they must take orders and rarely have the right to give them' (56). The main example that Young uses to illustrate this is that of non-professional workers, who are often required to perform rote tasks and prevented from exercising autonomy, creativity, or judgement in their work. Moreover, non-professionals are seen as less 'respectable' than professionals, which affects their ability to achieve things they may want, such as securing a bank loan.

Updating Young's observations in light of recent developments in the organisation of labour, we can note that powerlessness applies especially strongly to that group of non-professional workers known as 'gig economy workers': Uber drivers, Deliveroo riders, delivery people for various courier firms, and so on. The gig economy model, which relies on presenting workers as self-employed and claiming that the company profiting from their work is merely 'coordinating' or 'providing technology' to facilitate these entrepreneurial efforts, renders workers especially powerless by depriving them of the labour rights, such as paid holidays and sick leave, to which they would be entitled if they were recognised as employees.

Fourth, Young identifies a face of oppression that consist of a phenomenon she labels 'cultural imperialism'. Unlike the first three faces of oppression, cultural imperialism relates more closely to symbolic power than to concrete power. 'To experience cultural imperialism', Young states, 'means to experience how the dominant meanings of a society render the particular perspective of one's own group invisible at the same time as they stereotype one's group and mark it out as the Other' (2011, 59). Like powerlessness, cultural imperialism involves an asymmetry: the dominant culture imposes strongly on the oppressed group, but the oppressed group's culture 'finds little expression that touches the dominant culture' (59). This type of oppression affects, for example, racial, ethnic, national, and religious groups that are marked as inferior or as outsiders; women; and LGBT people. All of these groups have the experiences and norms of dominant groups projected onto them and are often positioned as deviant. Consider stereotypes of gay men as effeminate and as sexually interested in children. The first trope applies a heterosexist logic to those who are not heterosexual ('someone who loves men must be a bit like a woman, so all gay men are feminine'), and the second presents gay men as threatening and perverted. An important aspect of cultural imperialism is the kind of hyper-visibility that this sort of stereotyping brings with it. Groups that are culturally dominated are typically subjected to intense and intrusive scrutiny. Consider, for instance, the popular fascination with Black people's hair, especially Black women's hair, including the frequent uninvited touching of hair by strangers. This hyper-visibility means that the culturally dominated are typically highly conscious of the stereotypes applied to them (for further discussion, see, e.g., DuBois 1997, 38; Collins 2000, 69–96).

The fifth and final face of oppression, according to Young, is violence, which is to say, violence that is 'directed at members of a group simply because they are members of that group' (2011, 62). This includes both widespread actual violence and also the even more pervasive knowledge that one is liable to be a target of violence. Members of oppressed groups often live with the constant fear of hate-fuelled violence, including harassment and ridicule as well as physical assault. Such violence is 'rule-bound, social and often premeditated' and is therefore a social practice (62). Moreover, this violence is often tolerated—it isn't investigated, and/or it goes unpunished (62). Sexual violence committed by men towards women is an example of this face of oppression: it is widespread, it is usually committed with complete impunity, and it is woven into the fabric of women's lives through myriad decisions (what to wear, where to go, how to act) in which the threat of sexual violence is a factor (Card 1991).

The example of sexual violence draws our attention to a phenomenon that often accompanies it: silencing. Survivors of sexual violence often experience various kinds of silencing when they attempt to talk about it (or consider attempting to do so). They may be threatened with bad consequences if they speak, and they may be disbelieved, ridiculed, and harassed when they do. I think that this is a sufficiently marked characteristic of paradigmatically subordinated social positions such as women and people of colour that it warrants inclusion as a sixth 'face of oppression'. I will call this face of oppression 'communicative curtailment' because I take it to include not only silencing as such but also various phenomena that are closely related but do not seem to be aptly captured by the concept of silencing proper.

I take it that a group is subject to communicative curtailment whenever it is the case that group members systematically experience communicative failures, where these failures occur, at least in part, on the basis of group membership. These communicative failures need not be *solely* due to group membership, but group membership must play a part. For example, in the case of the silencing of a woman survivor of sexual violence, the communicative failure is partly due to her group identity as a woman and partly due to the content of what she is attempting to communicate, or contemplating communicating (testimony about sexual violence).

There are various sorts of communicative failures that can constitute communicative curtailment. Here is a non-exhaustive list:

- Locutionary silencing: a person is prevented from making utterances, perhaps physically or by means of threats.
- Lack of platform: a person can make utterances but is prevented from accessing the means of getting those utterances to reach people, such as by being systematically denied access to media channels or (what amounts to much the same thing) being offered access only on the most hostile and degrading terms, as when trans people are invited onto TV shows to 'debate' their fundamental rights such as access to healthcare with an ill-informed and prejudiced opponent.
- Illocutionary silencing (Langton 1993): a person makes an utterance, and it reaches its intended audience, but the audience misinterprets the utterance such that it fails to be the sort of speech act it was intended to be. For example, if a person of colour gives an impassioned critique of a political situation but is interpreted not as making truth-apt assertions but as merely expressing feelings of anger, they have suffered illocutionary silencing.
- Discursive injustice (Kukla 2014): a person makes an utterance, but it is evaluated under inappropriate norms and therefore has a very different discursive effect from the one the speaker intended. For example, if a woman manager gives an order to an employee but this order is interpreted as a request due to the employee's preconception that women are not managers, it may seem like a rudely phrased request even if it was a perfectly politely phrased order.

- Testimonial injustice (Fricker 2007): a person's testimony receives less credibility than it deserves due to prejudices about the person's identity. For example, if a woman who says that she has experienced sexual violence is not believed because the people she is speaking to think that women routinely lie about sexual violence, this is an instance of testimonial injustice.
- Testimonial smothering (Dotson 2011): a person's awareness of the barriers to their testimony being understood and believed leads them to self-limit and either refrain from testifying or reduce the extent of their testimony. An example of this would be a woman who decides to talk about how she has suffered sexual violence committed by a stranger but not about how she has suffered sexual violence committed by a partner, because she (correctly) thinks that her audience will accept her testimony about the former but misunderstand or doubt her testimony about the latter.

One might wonder whether these phenomena already fall under the banner of cultural imperialism. Whilst there are clearly connections between the two, I don't think that all of the examples of communicative curtailment given here fall under cultural imperialism, because the communication that is disrupted need not be culturally specific to the group in question and may not occur because of the asymmetry in how the cultural resources are positioned.[8] Moreover, I think the phenomenon is sufficiently marked that it merits specific attention, as the sizeable feminist literature on silencing and related phenomena attests.

It is important that the concept of communicative curtailment not be too broad. It would defeat the object if anytime anyone experienced any type of communicative failure this was considered subordinating. For example, suppose that someone claims that the Holocaust never took place, but they are in a society in which the occurrence of the Holocaust is considered so firmly established that people struggle to make sense of the idea that anyone could seriously claim that it did not happen. They interpret the Holocaust denier not as making an assertion but as simply issuing a provocation, which is to say, as engaging in some sort of performance that is not meant to be taken literally.

---

[8] I take it that systematic lack of conceptual resources, or hermeneutical injustice (Fricker 2007), is much closer to falling within the category of cultural imperialism.

The Holocaust denier thus experiences illocutionary silencing, because they did not manage to succeed in performing the speech act of assertion.

The concept of communicative curtailment rules out cases like this one, because the communicative failure is not partly due to the individual's membership in a social group but rather is solely based on the content of what they are trying to communicate. By contrast, consider the ways in which women who have suffered sexual violence are silenced: they are discouraged from speaking by threat (both direct interpersonal threats and the implicit threat of the social consequences of making allegations of sexual violence), and they are disbelieved and discredited in myriad ways, via stereotypes that cast women in general as confused and/or vindictive. This happens again and again to woman after woman, such that in any given case, its occurrence can be partly attributed to the fact that the individual *is* a woman. What I am saying here is compatible with acknowledging that, of course, men and non-binary people who have experienced sexual violence are also silenced; the point is that in each case, the silencing has a gendered character, for example, relying on gender stereotypes. Women survivors of sexual violence are silenced *as women*, and men and non-binary people who are survivors are also silenced as members of their respective genders. Thus, the silencing of women who have suffered sexual violence is a genuine case of communicative curtailment because it is based on group membership.

It might be argued that there could be cases like the Holocaust denier case where group membership *does* play a part, the relevant group being 'Holocaust denier'. Here I would appeal to the point I made earlier about how oppression is a fundamentally normative concept, and the criteria for something counting as an instance of oppression will also involve normative judgements. Insofar as this is the case, we can understand communicative curtailment to apply only to cases of *wrongful* curtailment. Although we should approach such judgements with caution, given the potential for naturalising ideology and other distortions to come into the picture, we cannot avoid making such normative judgements altogether.

Indeed, such judgements are also required in order to judge whether the other aspects of subordination—exploitation and so on—are present. For example, we might wonder whether children experience powerlessness. While there is certainly room to think that many of the limitations currently placed on children, especially older children, are wrongful, I think we should allow that there are some instances in which it is appropriate for children, especially young children, not to participate in some of the major decisions that affect the conditions of their lives and actions and to be positioned asymmetrically in this regard vis-à-vis their carers. I want to say that to the extent that this is morally appropriate, it should not be considered an instance of powerlessness. Similarly, administering a life-saving operation to a patient in an unresponsive state (where they have not expressed prior opposition to such procedures) should not be considered violence, even if it results in some forms of bodily harm. As I said at the outset, an account of oppression cannot avoid normative judgements altogether. In the account I am offering here, the primary place in which these judgements enter the picture is via the question of whether or not a form of treatment counts as one of the six faces of subordination.

Let me now sum up the account of oppression that I have arrived at.

Oppression: Oppression consists of networks of social limitations that are:

(a) Systematic: the limitations function in conjunction with one another to restrain, restrict, or immobilise those to whom they apply.

(b) Group-based: the limitations apply to people on the basis of shared features rather than as individuals.

(c) Subordinating: the limitations steer those to whom they apply towards social positions characterised by at least one of the following: exploitation, marginalisation, powerlessness, cultural imperialism, violence, and communicative curtailment.

2.4. Oppression and Intersectionality

In this section, I will discuss in detail how the definition of oppression I have just given relates to the important phenomenon of intersectionality. The concept of intersectionality, roughly speaking, captures the idea that what are usually thought of as different dimensions or axes of oppression, such as racism and sexism, do not act on a person separately and independently; rather, different dimensions of oppression interact in complex ways so that it is often impossible to fully distinguish one dimension from another in a person's experience.[9] The same idea can also be applied to privilege (see, e.g., Collins 2000), though it is oppression that will be my main focus here.

---

[9] Of course, the concept of intersectionality also applies to other axes of oppression besides race and gender, such as class, sexual orientation, trans status, and disability status, to name but a few.

The term 'intersectionality' was coined by Kimberlé W. Crenshaw (1989), although the idea it seeks to capture has a much longer history in women of colour feminist thought (Combahee River Collective 1978; Moraga and Anzaldúa 2015). It can be understood as 'a heuristic term to focus attention on the vexed dynamics of difference and the solidarities of sameness in the context of antidiscrimination and social movement politics' (Cho, Crenshaw, and McCall 2013, 787). The concept of intersectionality encourages us to see racism and sexism as intermeshed, rather than separate, and draws our attention to the dangers of trying to analyse racist and sexist oppressions in isolation from each other. In particular, intersectionality theorists have pointed out that attempts to specify the nature of racial oppression without reference to gender tend to end up focusing on the experiences of men of colour, whilst attempts to specify the nature of gendered oppression without reference to race tend to end up focusing on the experiences of White women (hooks 1982; Hull, Scott, and Smith 1982). The result is an analysis that is empirically inadequate for explaining the way oppression features in the lives of women of colour and other groups situated at the intersections of forms of oppression that are often theorised as distinct.

It will be already clear from what I have said so far that the concept of intersectionality in some form or another must be central to any emancipatory theory that is adequate by its own lights: the commitment to situated social theorising that is capable of contributing to bringing about emancipatory social change calls for an intersectional approach. Moreover, a commitment to standpoint theory makes it imperative to take on board the arguments about the empirical inadequacy of non-intersectional theory for illuminating the situation of women of colour, among others. For these reasons, attending to intersectionality is crucial for my project. There are, however, many different articulations of the general idea of intersectionality, and it is beyond the scope of this project to offer anything like a comprehensive account of the contrasts between them. I will here treat intersectionality as involving three distinct components, each of which has been widely discussed in the literature. I take each component to impose a demand on adequate theories of oppression: a theory of oppression must comply with each component in order to be acceptable. Here I am following Ann Garry in treating intersectionality as a 'framework checker' (2011, 830) for accounts of oppression, social kinds, identity, and so on, rather than as a substantive account of these things. Although I acknowledge the diversity of accounts of intersectionality, and although I'm not offering an argument here for preferring the approach that

I'm taking, I hope it will not strike those who are familiar with the literature as particularly controversial.

The first component is the thought that oppression is *non-additive*, which is to say that we cannot rely on being able to gain knowledge about Black women's oppression, for example, simply by adding together some general claims about race-based oppression and some general claims about gender-based oppression. Experiences of oppression (and indeed privilege) are often "more than the sum of their parts", or, as Crenshaw puts it, 'the intersectional experience is greater than the sum of racism and sexism' (1989, 140). Taking a blanket additive approach is a recipe for building a picture of oppression that *only* does justice to the experiences of the most relatively privileged members of the oppressed group—for example, an account of women's oppression that centres the experiences of white, middle-class, heterosexual women and overlooks or belies the experiences of women of colour, working-class women, and queer women (Spelman 1990, 133–59). This recognition is compatible with allowing that in some specific cases, dimensions of oppression may behave in additive ways; the important point is that we cannot *rely on* or *assume* additivity.[10]

The second, very closely related thought is that oppression is *non-separable*: the oppression experienced by a woman of colour, for example, cannot be neatly separated into the oppression she experiences as a woman and the oppression she experiences as a person of colour (Crenshaw 1989; Spelman 1990). If a Black woman is arrested on suspicion of engaging in sex work by a police officer who then sexually assaults her, does this happen "because she is a woman" or "because she is Black"? If an Asian woman is given appalling medical care when she arrives at a hospital in the middle of what turns out to be a miscarriage, does this happen "because she is a woman" or "because she is Asian"? The concept of intersectionality highlights the fundamentally misguided nature of questions such as these, which assume that the effects of race and gender categorisation are neatly separable. It requires us instead to recognise that the oppression experienced by a Black woman, for example, cannot usually be neatly separated out into oppression experienced "on the basis of race" and oppression experienced "on the basis of gender". Even where there are similarities between the experiences of Black women and White women, or Black women and Black men, race and gender are very often inextricably intertwined and entangled in ways that make neat

---

[10] Thanks to Marta Jorba for encouraging me to clarify my view on this point.

separation impossible whilst rendering attempts to perform such separation unhelpful. As with *non-additivity*, the point is not that oppressions can *never* be separated out in this way but rather that we cannot *count on* their being separable in any given case.

Although *non-additivity* and *non-separability* are conceptually very close—it is natural to think that it is precisely *because* experiences of oppression are non-additive that they cannot be separated into their component parts (Haslanger 2014, 116)—in my view, it is worth including both points in an analysis of intersectionality, because they caution us against different kinds of mistakes. *Non-additivity* cautions us against thinking that we can move smoothly from an analysis of single-axis oppressions to an analysis of the experience of those situated at the intersections of these axes; and *non-separability* cautions us against thinking we can move smoothly in the opposite direction. Since intersectionality is meant to serve as a 'heuristic' (Cho, Crenshaw, and McCall 2013) or 'framework checker' (Garry 2011), I think it is useful to have both *non-additivity* and *non-separability* in the forefront of our minds.

The third thought, which is a rather stronger claim than the first two, is that oppression involves *cross-constitution* or mutual constitution at the level of kinds. It is not just that race and gender kinds interact via forms of oppression that are non-additive and non-separable; rather, race plays a crucial role in constructing the reality of gender, and vice versa (Lugones 2007; Garry 2011; Bernstein 2020; see also discussion in Carastathis 2014; Jorba and Rodó-Zárate 2019). In other words, gender could not be what it is if race did not exist, and race could not be what it is if gender did not exist; race and gender help make each other what they are.

This is a further step to the first two components. Accepting *non-additivity* and *non-separability* means thinking that racism and sexism combine in ways that exceed the sum of their parts, and therefore experiences of oppression cannot be broken down into constituent parts in which race and gender feature as separate. One might think all of this whilst holding that there are race kinds that do not depend for their existence on gender kinds, and vice versa. To accept *cross-constitution* is therefore to accept a further, stronger claim in addition to *non-additivity* and *non-separability*. There are various different ways in which we can understand what *cross-constitution* involves, and I will explore this aspect of intersectionality in more detail in the next chapter (§3.6.2).

There is also a fourth component that may be considered part of intersectionality, which concerns the *explanatory priority* of intersectional kinds over their single-moniker constituents. This is the idea that intersectional kinds have greater explanatory power than the single-moniker kinds that are their apparent 'constituents'—that we can get further with our explanations if we use intersectional kinds such as *Black woman* rather than single-moniker kinds such as *Black* and *woman* (Bernstein 2020, 331). I subscribe only to a qualified version of this component of intersectionality, and I'll explain why in the next chapter (§3.6.2).

As I have said following Garry and others, I understand intersectionality not as a theory or a methodology in and of itself but as what Garry terms a 'framework checker' (2011, 830). Intersectionality as such does not constitute an account of social kinds, power, agency, identity, and so on; rather, it provides a standard that theories purporting to illuminate these phenomena should meet. If we encounter an analysis of how some form of oppression works that treats kinds such as race, gender, disability, and so on as isolated, distinct, or additive, a commitment to intersectionality tells us that this account is inadequate. So how does the account of oppression that I have set out here meet the demands of intersectionality?

The first thing to note here is that the intersectional nature of oppression gives a strong reason for conceiving of the 'group-based' component of the definition of oppression in a less demanding way. A more demanding conception, such as Young's, would mean that oppression can only be understood as targeting groups that have a shared way of life, affinity, and a sense of shared identity. This, in turn, risks ruling out certain intersectional groups as targets of specific oppression. For example, it may well be the case that Black disabled lesbian women encounter specific social limitations that are not shared by White disabled lesbian women, Black non-disabled lesbian women, and so on. If this is so, we want to be able to say that someone is oppressed specifically as a Black disabled lesbian woman. But it may be the case that there is no shared way of life, affinity, or sense of identity that unites Black disabled lesbian women into a distinct group in the sense Young has in mind. Therefore, in order to be sure of fully capturing the intersectional nature of oppression, we need a less demanding understanding of groups. The group-based aspect of the definition that I favour simply requires that the limitations are applied on the basis of some feature or combination of features rather than targeting specific individuals. Limitations that apply to

Black disabled lesbian women easily meet this criterion and therefore can count as constituting a form of oppression on my definition.

I have said that the group-based nature of oppression means that individuals are always oppressed qua group members. Intersectionality raises some questions about how this works. If women are an oppressed group, can someone be oppressed qua woman and also be oppressed qua Black woman? In short, yes. When we consider whether a particular group is oppressed, we can ask: is there a wider group that is subject to the same pattern of limitations and steered towards the same subordinated social positions? If the answer is yes, then we should focus on the broader group and not say the group we started with is oppressed. For example, it's true that left-handed women are subject to systematic limitations and steered towards subordinated social positions, but these limitations and positions are not distinctive compared to the limitations and positions involved in the oppression of women in general. So left-handed women are not oppressed as left-handed women, although they are oppressed as women.[11]

By contrast, Black women are subject to systematic limitations that steer them towards subordinated social positions where these limitations and positions are distinctive when considered in contrast to the limitations and positions involved in the oppression of women in general and also when considered in contrast to the limitations and positions involved in the oppression of Black people in general. We can see intersectionality as cautioning us against saying, 'women are an oppressed group, Black people are an oppressed group, Black women get oppressed twice over because they are members of both oppressed groups (the end)'. Doing so would obscure the distinctive and specific limitations and positions just mentioned. Thinking with the tool or framework checker of intersectionality in mind, on the other hand, draws our attention to the fact that there are specific and distinctive systematic limitations that apply to Black women (and not to all women or to all Black people) and specific and distinctive subordinated social positions into which Black women (and not all women or all Black people) are steered by these limitations. This is compatible with the fact that at a more general and less detailed level of description, we can identify systematic limitations that apply to all women and subordinated social positions towards which all

---

[11] This case is intended to be not a silly or implausible example but a case that might have gone the other way. I take it that left-handed people may well have been an oppressed group in the recent past and that this oppression might plausibly have affected women in different ways from men. Thanks to Koshka Duff for prompting me to clarify this point.

women are steered—and the same, mutatis mutandis, for all Black people. This should lead us to say that Black women are oppressed as Black women, as well as being oppressed as women and oppressed as Black people.

What this means is that there are multiple oppressed groups that overlap, including some that are proper subsets of other oppressed groups. We could try to simplify this picture by saying that only the broadest groups (e.g., women, Black people) are really oppressed. But this would make the account of oppression incompatible with the important insights of intersectionality theorists. Alternatively, we could try to simplify it by going in the other direction and only counting the maximally intersectional oppressions. But making this move would also introduce a major difficulty. In selecting the intersectional groups on which to focus, we would struggle to give a principled reason to stop anywhere short of the level of specific individuals: why stop at 'Black woman' rather than 'Black lesbian women', or 'disabled Black lesbian women', or 'working-class disabled Black lesbian women'? And of course, saying that only individuals are oppressed is a contradiction, given that oppression has been defined as a group-based phenomenon.

Even if we could somehow overcome this difficulty, there would be a further drawback to making this move, which is that theorists of oppression generally agree that single-moniker groups such as women and Black people are oppressed and have developed their theories with this in mind, as we have seen in the work of Frye and Young. Now, of course, this does not mean that we cannot adopt a theory of oppression according to which it is not the case that any single-moniker groups are oppressed. These theorists may simply have been wrong. It does, however, mean that doing so would require a stronger reason than simplicity. For these reasons, then, I will stick with the slightly messier picture on which someone can be a member of multiple oppressed groups, where some of these groups may be proper subsets of others. A person can be oppressed as a Black person, as a woman, as disabled, as a Black woman, and as a disabled Black woman (to name but a few of the intersectional kinds to which she belongs).

This discussion of intersectionality has highlighted the fact that oppression is a fuzzy phenomenon and a matter of degree. There will be some cases in which we are faced with a kind that is so complexly intersectional that there are very few members; does this count as a 'group' for our purposes or simply a collection of individuals? Similarly, there will be some cases where a group is subject to a certain pattern of limitations that steers them towards certain subordinated social positions, and there is a wider group that is subject to a similar pattern of limitations and steered towards similar subordinated social positions—but where the limitations and positions are not exactly the same. Should we say that the first (narrower) group is oppressed as well as the second (broader) group?

In both cases, the answer depends partly on what our explanatory purposes are. Is it useful and illuminating to treat the group as a potential subject of oppression? Does it alert us to some important and perhaps overlooked aspect of the social situation? Or do we gain little insight from it? These questions can only be answered within a certain investigative and political project situated in a particular social context.[12] Although this account of oppressed groups is, I hope, clear enough to guide our thinking, it is not, and is not intended to be, a completely cut-and-dried set of necessary and sufficient conditions for something to count as an oppressed group.

Finally, an important note on terminology: for the rest of this book, whenever I refer to 'race and gender kinds', I intend to refer not only to single-moniker kinds such as *women*, *men*, *Black people*, *Asian people*, or *White people* but also to all the intersectional kinds that include at least one race or gender descriptor, such as *Black women*, *Black gay men*, *disabled women*, *working-class Asian lesbian women*, and so on.

2.5. Defining Ontic Oppression

2.5.1. The Definition of Ontic Oppression

I have now offered an account of oppression, one that is sufficiently detailed to orient us towards the world and guide our practical judgement and that incorporates the important insights of intersectionality theory. Here is the account once more:

(a) Systematic: the limitations function in conjunction with one another to restrain, restrict, or immobilise those to whom they apply.
(b) Group-based: the limitations apply to people on the basis of shared features rather than as individuals.

---

[12] I take my position here to be in line with that of Crenshaw 2010.

(c) Subordinating: the limitations steer those to whom they apply towards social positions characterised by suffering at least one of the following: exploitation, marginalisation, powerlessness, cultural imperialism, violence, and communicative curtailment.

I'm now in a position to use this account to give a definition of ontic oppression. Recall the definition of ontic injustice given in Chapter 1.

Ontic injustice: An individual suffers ontic injustice if and only if they are socially constructed as a member of a certain social kind where that construction consists, at least in part, of their falling under a set of social constraints and enablements that is wrongful to them.

Ontic oppression is defined as a subcategory of ontic injustice as follows.

Ontic oppression: An individual suffers ontic oppression if and only if they are socially constructed as a member of a certain social kind where that construction consists, at least in part, of their being subjected to a set of social constraints and enablements that are systematically interrelated and that steer them towards social positions characterised by suffering at least one of the following: exploitation, marginalisation, powerlessness, cultural imperialism, violence, and communicative curtailment.

This definition of ontic oppression highlights that ontic injustice also constitutes ontic oppression when the wrongful constraints and enablements are *systematic*, that is, interrelated in such a way that they function in conjunction with one another to restrain, restrict, or immobilise those to whom they apply, and *subordinating*, that is, serving to steer those to whom they apply towards social positions characterised by at least one (and typically several) of the following: exploitation, marginalisation, powerlessness, cultural imperialism, violence, and communicative curtailment. Note that constraints and enablements that are partly constitutive of social kind membership are automatically group-based, and therefore it is not necessary to make explicit reference to part (b) of the definition of oppression in defining ontic oppression.

The main benefit of having a concept of ontic oppression for my purposes is that it fares better than the concept of ontic injustice with respect to evading naturalising ideology because it serves to orient us to the world in a particular way. The concept of ontic oppression gives us a list of specific phenomena (exploitation, marginalisation, and so on) with detailed descriptions and directs us to look out for these things as signs that all is not well. Identifying these phenomena does not require us to make as many judgements about what forms of treatment are appropriate for different sorts of people, because we depend on a prior commitment to the claim that each of these forms of treatment is wrongful whenever it occurs as part of a systematic set of limitations applied on the basis of group membership. Thus, when we look out for the six features of subordination, we do not have to rely on our conceptions of what is appropriate for different sorts of people, conceptions that may well be affected by naturalising ideology. In this way, the concept of ontic oppression reduces our reliance on our judgements of what moral entitlements different sorts of human beings have and therefore helps to elide some of the effects of naturalising ideology.

Of course, this approach does not eliminate our reliance on normative judgements completely, because normative considerations will still play a role in our judgements about whether a particular situation counts as exploitation, or marginalisation, and so on. And naturalising ideology can come into the picture here via the potential influence it exerts over our conceptions of what is appropriate for different sorts of people and can affect our perception of the faces of subordination. For example, violence can be made to seem like a natural and justified response to the inherently unruly nature of a certain group of people, cultural imperialism can be made to seem like a natural and justified response to the inherently impoverished nature of a certain culture, and so on. We need to be constantly on our guard against this tendency. Thus, although the concept of ontic oppression does give us much more scaffolding for those judgements, and greatly reduces the room for ideology to influence our thinking, it does not completely insulate our judgements from the distorting effects of naturalising ideology. It does much better in this regard than the concept of ontic injustice, but it is not a silver bullet.

It is important here to distinguish between *what makes something wrong*, on the one hand, and *how we become aware of wrong*, on the other. As I have said, the wrong of ontic injustice—including those cases of ontic injustice that rise to the level of ontic oppression—*consists in* the mismatch between what an individual is owed, morally speaking, and how they are in fact treated in society, and the moral injury that this constitutes; but, as I argued earlier, directly *looking for* mismatch is not a good way to identify the injustice under social conditions pervaded by naturalising ideology. Although we identify ontic oppression by looking for the features of oppression and not by looking for mismatch, the wrong of ontic oppression still ultimately consists in mismatch.

An additional benefit in having the concept of ontic oppression as compared to relying solely on the concept of ontic injustice is that it excludes very weak and minimal cases. Although cases of oppression certainly vary in their severity, in order for a wrong to constitute a case of oppression, it must meet a fairly demanding threshold of severity, in virtue of the requirements for it to be *systematic*. A one-off or incidental wrong cannot, by definition, be oppression. To be clear, I am not saying that oppression as such is more severe than injustice in general, or that any given instance of oppression is more severe than all instances of (non-opppressive) injustice; clearly, there can be instances of injustice that are very severely wrongful without being group-based or systematic in the kind of way that would make them also instances of oppression. The point is rather that the category of *injustice* has, as it were, a long tail, tapering off in very fine gradations until it barely registers; whereas the category of *oppression* also tapers but has a blunter tail with a higher and sharper minimum threshold. Ontic injustice therefore includes many cases that are very trivial, but this is not the case for ontic oppression.[13]

I want to stress the contextuality of the notion of ontic oppression that I have developed here. Ontic oppression, I contend, is a useful sub-kind of ontic injustice to pick out *for my purposes*—for the purposes, that is, of investigating race and gender kinds with a view to bringing about emancipatory social change. For different purposes, different concepts for subtypes of ontic injustice might be called for. For example, for a politics focused on the liberation of non-human animals, it might be that we need to combine the concept of ontic oppression with a different conception of oppression, one that has been crafted to apply to non-human animals. Or we might even need to develop an altogether different concept in place of the concept of ontic oppression in order to pick out a different subcategory of ontic injustice. Crafting a concept that captures the specific type of ontic injustice affecting non-human animals would, in my view, be an excellent project, but it is not the project in which I am engaged here.

[13] Thanks to Ben Colburn for encouraging me to clarify this point.

2.5.2. Dembroff on Ontological Oppression

Shifting from ontic *injustice* to ontic *oppression* brings this concept closer to work by Robin Dembroff on what they term 'ontological oppression'. According to Dembroff, ontological oppression 'occurs when the social kinds (or the lack thereof) unjustly constrain (or enable) persons' behaviours, concepts, or affect due to their group membership' (Dembroff 2018, 26). Although my account of ontic injustice (Jenkins 2016b; 2020b) and Dembroff's account of ontological oppression (Dembroff 2017; 2018) developed independently, I take our convergence on the recognition that social kinds can incorporate injustice to lend weight to the idea that this type of wrong merits attention and investigation. Though the difference in labels ('ontic' vs. 'ontological') that Dembroff and I each selected is convenient, I take it to be theoretically incidental; I don't think there is an interesting philosophical underpinning to the contrast between 'ontic' and 'ontological' in this context.[14] However, there are two differences worth noting between my account of ontic injustice and ontic oppression, on the one hand, and Dembroff's account of ontological oppression, on the other.

The first difference is that I define ontic oppression as a subspecies of ontic injustice, whereas Dembroff does not offer a counterpart notion of 'ontological injustice' along with 'ontological oppression'. Might it be possible to construct one if we so desired? Perhaps, but it is worth noticing that Dembroff's account of ontological *oppression* makes reference to individuals being '*unjustly* constrain[ed] and enable[ed]' (2018, 26, emphasis added). Thus, crafting a counterpart concept of 'ontological injustice' would probably have to involve modifying the definition of ontological oppression in order to enable a clear separation between the two. In a similar vein, Dembroff's definition of ontological oppression includes a requirement that the unjust constraints and enablements be *group-based*, but it does not require that they form or be part of a network of *systematically linked* restrictions, which is the other idea that differentiates oppression from injustice on many accounts. This seems to me to position the type of wrong Dembroff is focused on somewhere in between the ideas of 'injustice' and 'oppression' as I am working with these concepts here, at least in their current formulation. Although I find the differentiation between injustice and oppression useful for my

[14] For my part, I went for 'ontic' over 'ontological' mainly because it is a shorter word.

purposes, given my aspiration to provide a more multipurpose version of the concept as well as a version that incorporates my own more particular normative commitments, I do not claim any blanket advantage to this approach. Rather, I merely note the difference as one distinguishing factor between my account and that of Dembroff.

The second, much more significant difference between Dembroff's account of ontological oppression and my account of ontic injustice and ontic oppression is that ontic injustice/oppression only applies to social kinds that have the potential victims of injustice and oppression as their members. The victim of ontic injustice/oppression must be socially constructed as a member of the kind in question. By contrast, I understand Dembroff's definition of ontological oppression, given previously, to apply more broadly to any social kind that can be understood to constrain or enable an individual. For example, in cases of the racially motivated gerrymandering of electoral districts, the social construction of voting districts might unjustly constrain people's behaviours, preventing them from casting votes that have a fair chance of affecting the outcome of the election, and it might do so on the basis of their racial group membership. Here the socially constructed kind is the kind *voting district*, and this kind does not appear to have the wronged individuals as members. (Individuals do reside within voting districts. But individuals are not members of the kind *voting district*.) This case counts as one of ontological oppression but *not* as one of ontic injustice or ontic oppression.

In this sense, ontic injustice/oppression is essentially about *someone* being *socially constructed as a member of a certain kind*, where *that construction* is wrongful *to them*, whereas ontological oppression is more generally a matter of *the way that some social kind in someone's social context* is constructed being wrongful to them. Both, of course, are interesting, but my focus here is on the narrower phenomenon picked out by the concept of ontic injustice/ oppression. I find this helpful because the narrower focus permits me to say more about the nature of the wrong involved (as I have done in this chapter and in Chapter 1) than if I had focused on the broader phenomenon, which I take to involve a more heterogeneous set of moral considerations.

2.6. Conclusion

In this chapter, I have defined ontic oppression as a subtype of ontic injustice in which the constraints and enablements to which the individual is subjected are not only wrongful but oppressive. In order to construct this definition, drawing on accounts by Frye and Young, I have offered an account of oppression as systematic, group-based restraints that steer people towards subordinated social positions, where such positions are characterised by six features: exploitation, marginalisation, powerlessness, cultural domination, violence, and communicative curtailment. The concept of ontic oppression incorporates the normative commitments that motivate the investigation into race and gender kinds that will be my focus in later chapters. But first, in Chapter 3, I must outline the ontological commitments on which I will rely in that investigation.

3

The Constraints and Enablements Framework

3.1. Introduction

As we saw in Chapter 1, the concept of ontic injustice needs to be combined with some normative and ontological commitments in order to yield conclusions about particular cases. The concept of ontic oppression that I set out in Chapter 2 incorporates some normative commitments that are suitable for the investigation that concerns me here, which is an investigation into race and gender kinds in the spirit of emancipatory theory. Accordingly, my next task is to supply the necessary *ontological* commitments by giving an account of the ontology of social categories that is suitable for applying to race and gender categories.

In order to do this, I will build on the brief sketch given in Chapter 1 of facts about individuals' membership in social kinds. As explained there, in line with many social ontologists, I take such facts to be at least partly constituted by the individual's falling under certain constraints and enablements. What is needed now is a more detailed account of what this involves. This is because until we know *which* constraints and enablements constitute membership in a given race and/or gender kind, we cannot say whether or not it is a site of ontic oppression. What is more, the account needs to be suitable for theorists approaching social kinds with an emancipatory interest, as was described in the final section of the Introduction.[1]

In this chapter, I develop a pluralist framework for theorising human social kinds in general which meets these requirements. I term it the 'constraints and enablements framework (CEF), because it treats human social kinds as being at least partly constituted by constraints and enablements. Then, in the

---

[1] For some other approaches to social ontology explicitly informed by emancipatory theory or critical theory, see Groff 2012; Renault 2016; Thompson 2017; Harris 2021. Another prominent example of this kind of approach, namely, work by Sally Haslanger (e.g., Haslanger 2012c), will be discussed in detail in the sections that follow.

Ontology and Oppression. Katharine Jenkins, Oxford University Press. © Katharine Jenkins 2023.
DOI: 10.1093/oso/9780197666777.003.0004

next three chapters, I apply the CEF to race and gender kinds in order to assess whether those kinds are ontically oppressive. I will argue that there are various different types of race and gender kinds and that some are ontically oppressive whilst others are not.

I'll begin this chapter by giving some general background to the idea of a *social kind*. This will place me in a position to set out the CEF as a pluralist conceptual framework: an overarching model that allows us to theorise various different social kinds. I'll then introduce and explain each of the three main components of the framework—'scope', 'breadth', and 'granularity'— and show how these enable a range of different sorts of social kinds to be theorised. Finally, I will illustrate some of the benefits of the CEF.

3.2. Social Kinds and Social Construction

3.2.1. Social Kinds as Explanatory Kinds

I take social kinds to be a particular variety of explanatory kinds, which is to say, kinds—groupings of things in the world—that can figure in successful explanations. The nature of explanation is a complex philosophical topic in its own right, and here I can do no more than gesture at a view on this issue. I understand explanations as answers to 'why' questions posed in contexts. For example, suppose I am testing samples of substances in a chemistry laboratory; most of the samples burn yellow, but one of them burns green, and I ask, 'Why does this sample burn green?' My chemist companion replies that the sample contains boric acid in ethyl alcohol, that boric acid forms complex esters with alcohol, and that these esters burn with a green flame. In offering this explanation, she is making an assumption about the sort of information I am asking for: she assumes that I already understand combustion in general, and she assumes that I have a particular contrast class of alternatives in mind, namely, I want to know why the sample burned green *instead of burning yellow.*

These assumptions are very reasonable ones based on the context of my question. If the chemist was wrong about them, however, her explanation might not be a good one for my purposes. For example, suppose I don't understand combustion well and I want to know why the sample burned green instead of, say, freezing solid. In this case, a better explanation would involve telling me about combustion. What the chemist has to say about boric acid

is still *true*, but in this case, it would not be a good explanation. Thus, explanation is, as Bas Van Fraassen puts it, 'a three-term relation, between theory,
fact, and context' (1980, 156). When a theory is offered as an explanation,
it must fit with the facts, but it must also fit with the request for information that has been issued in the relevant context. Thus, it doesn't make sense
on this view to talk about theories being explanatory, or having 'explanatory
power', *in general* or *as such*. Instead, we must always have in mind a certain context, and a certain need for information located within that context,
which gives us the criteria for assessing whether an explanation is successful
or not.[2]

Explanatory kinds are groupings of things that can figure in successful
explanations. For instance, in the chemistry example, *boric acid* is an explanatory kind. The concept of an explanatory kind as I am deploying it here
is, like the concept of explanation, context-relative: kinds are explanatory
or not explanatory relative to the context of a particular explanatory purpose or project (see, e.g., Haslanger 2016a). Whether or not a kind plays a
role in good explanations depends on what sort of explanations are being
considered.[3] For example, the fact that some object is a member of the kind
holy statue may be very important when it comes to explaining how people
interact with it, for example, why they place flowers and candles in front of it.
However, this fact would be totally irrelevant to an investigation into certain
physical properties of the object, for example, why it does or does not tarnish
when exposed to the air. Conversely, whether the material from which the
statue is made belongs to the kind *bronze* or the kind *gold* may be irrelevant
to how worshippers engage with it but highly relevant to explaining why it
does or does not tarnish. Explanatory value is a matter of degree; a kind can
be more or less explanatory, in the sense that it can feature more or less prominently in more or fewer explanations.

A background view to this understanding of explanatory kinds is a promiscuous pluralism with regard to kinds simpliciter: any set of things unified
by some property or some specific combination of properties is a kind in a

---

[2] In this sense, the pluralist account of kinds that I will go on to offer is based on a pluralism about explanation.

[3] My understanding of social kinds has some features in common with Dupré's (1995) 'promis-cuous realism' about natural kinds. However, I am here only discussing social kinds; I make no claim either way about whether social kinds are natural kinds, and I make no claims at all about natural kinds that are not social kinds. On the issue of whether social kinds are natural kinds, see Sundstrom 2002a; 2002b. For an argument for the claim that the general notion of 'natural kind' is unhelpfully coarse-grained, to which I am sympathetic, see Ludwig 2017.

thin sense.[4] It follows that only a small subset of kinds are explanatory. For example, I take it that *object currently on my desk* is a kind in the thin sense, as is *organism with a mass of one kilogram or greater*, though neither of these kinds is very explanatory relative to most purposes. Most (thin) kinds are not explanatory kinds. All kinds have some property or properties that unify the kind members, and in the case of explanatory kinds, there are also some further reasons for the kind's having explanatory value in relation to a particular inquiry. These reasons can relate to the context in which the kind is situated. For example, the reason the kind *holy statue* has explanatory value in relation to understanding people's behaviour has to do with the social practices that are in place in the relevant society.[5]

The explanatory projects that concern me in this book are those projects motivated by an emancipatory interest, as described in the final section of the Introduction; roughly, these are attempts to understand the world so as to change it in ways that combat oppression. In a sense, then, there is an overarching meta-project in the picture here, which is to understand all oppression in ways that enable us to combat it. However, this project is extremely general—far too general to point us in the direction of kinds that would be helpful for our explanations. We cannot engage in such general reflection on oppression and emancipation and hope to discover anything much of value. Instead, what's needed is to engage in more specific emancipatory projects.

These projects can be 'more specific' in a number of different senses. They may be concerned with oppression targeted at a particular group or groups in a particular place and time (e.g., racial oppression in the twenty-first-century United Kingdom), they may be concerned with oppressive acts that takes a particular form (e.g., sexual violence), and they may be concerned with oppression in a particular context or area of life (e.g., employment). Our ability to identify the kinds that are explanatory relative to a certain emancipatory project depends on our practical understanding of that project. We cannot tell in advance, simply from knowing the project, what kinds will help us in our explanations, predictions, and interventions. Rather, we need a practical understanding developed on the basis of empirical research and direct involvement.

---

[4] Nothing substantive hangs on this; the reader who finds this talk of thin kinds objectionable can simply interpret any talk of non-explanatory or thin kinds as a shortcut for talking about sets of things that share a certain property or combination of properties.

[5] I will discuss social practices in more detail in §3.3.1.

Emancipatory projects form an overlapping patchwork. For example, it is not possible to adequately investigate racial oppression without considering sexual violence—both sexual violence perpetrated against people of colour and narratives that inaccurately portray people of colour, especially men of colour, as disproportionately likely to be perpetrators of sexual violence. Within this overlapping patchwork, there is no guarantee of harmony; what seems like a reasonable way of proceeding with respect to one project may turn out to generate serious difficulties if applied in the context of another project. This possibility for conflict applies equally to social kinds. Social kinds that are explanatory with respect to one project may be unhelpful with respect to another project. I do not see any way of avoiding such conflicts in advance or any prospect for laying down general rules for how such conflicts may be resolved.

In responding to such conflicts, we must never lose sight of the fact that our ultimate goal is to end *all* oppression. However, an awareness of this goal is not, by itself, enough to lead us to suitable resolutions. We need to proceed on a case-by-case basis, cultivating epistemic and ethical sensibilities that help us to identify and skilfully manage these conflicts and treating our attempts at resolution as conditional and subject to revision and development as circumstances change and our own understanding develops. In other words, the nature of explanation and the nature of emancipatory struggle jointly mean that we need to adopt a pluralist view of explanatory kinds; there is no single, streamlined set of kinds that can do all of the explanatory work we need to do. Rather, we need to work with a range of different explanatory kinds that are suited to different specific purposes, where figuring out which kind we need for a particular explanatory endeavour is recognised as a substantive task.[6]

3.2.2. Varieties of Social Construction

As I have said, by 'social kinds' I mean those explanatory kinds that are dependent on social factors.[7] In this subsection, I consider the nature of this dependence in more detail. There are two main ways in which an explanatory kind

---

[6] I take my position here to be in harmony with recent work that insightfully explores the connection between ontology and Indigenous knowledge (see, e.g., Ludwig 2016; Ludwig and Weiskopf 2019).

[7] I grant that there are also *thin* kinds that are dependent on social factors, but I shall here narrow my focus only to explanatory kinds; thin kinds dependent on social factors are not included with 'social kinds' as I shall use the term here.

can depend on social factors. In *causal construction*, social factors contribute causally to bringing a kind into existence, and in *constitutive construction*, social factors at least partly constitute the kind in question, which is to say, they will feature in an account of what it is for the kind to exist (Haslanger 2012b, 87).[8]

As an example of a kind that is causally socially constructed, consider the species *Gallus gallus domesticus*, the domestic chicken. Through various social practices (farming and selective breeding), which in turn are driven by other social practices (the consumption of chicken meat and eggs), human beings have caused domestic chickens to have certain significant features that they have, such as laying eggs frequently. However, these social practices are not part of what it *is* to be a domestic chicken. To put the point another way, we can define a domestic chicken with reference to biology alone: if someone did not know what a domestic chicken was, I could explain this to them without referring to social factors. I could describe to them the biological features that define the species, including, if necessary, its genome. I would only need to refer to social practices if the person went on to ask me *why* there are such things as domestic chickens or *how* domestic chickens *came to be* the way they are (for instance, how they came to produce eggs at the rate that they do).

By contrast, as an example of a kind that is constitutively socially constructed, consider landlords. To be a landlord is to stand in complicated social relations to other individuals (such as tenants and bailiffs), to social institutions (such as estate agents and courts), and to material resources (such as buildings and land). Standing in such social relations is just *what it is* to be a landlord; or, to put the point another way, if we took away those social relations, there would be nothing left that could be said to make someone a landlord. If I tried to explain what makes some person a landlord but I could not say that they are someone who *owns* a certain *property* and *rents* it to a *tenant*, thereby creating certain *entitlements* and *obligations*—all of which are social factors—then I would be quite at a loss for how to respond. Unlike with domestic chickens, there is simply no way to spell out what it *is* to be a landlord without referring to social factors. The kind *landlord* is constitutively socially constructed.

---

[8] I use the same definition of causal construction as Haslanger, but I depart very slightly from her phrasing of constitutive construction: she describes it in terms of needing to make reference to social factors in *defining* the kind. I depart from Haslanger in this way because it seems to me that there can be lots of different ways of defining something, not all of which are closely connected to constitution. Focusing directly on existence in the definition of constitutive construction avoids having to tackle the complexities of different kinds of definitions. I take this to be a superficial difference only.

In what follows, I will be concerned with social kinds that can be ontically unjust or ontically oppressive, in the senses defined in the previous two chapters. This narrows the field in two ways. First, the kind must have as its members individuals who can appropriately be considered subjects of moral value. This is because the wrong of ontic injustice (including ontic oppression) consists in a moral injury, and only beings that are subjects of moral value can experience moral injury.[9] For simplicity, and given my interest in race and gender kinds, here I am going to focus on kinds that have human beings as their members, although, as I have said, I also think that non-human animals can suffer ontic injustice. This means that I am restricting my focus to what are usually called 'human social kinds'—kinds such as *priest*, *celebrity*, and *woman*. Although I do not rule out expanding the CEF to other social kinds that are not human social kinds—kinds such as *dollar bill* and *holy statue*—I do not try to do this work here.

Second, the kind must be constitutively socially constructed. This follows from my definition of ontic injustice, which makes reference to kinds being constituted by constraints and enablements that are wrongful or oppressive. Thus, only kinds that are constituted by social factors—constitutively socially constructed kinds—can be sites of ontic injustice. Kinds that are merely causally socially constructed can be *produced by* wrongful social factors, but they cannot be sites of ontic injustice because they are not *constituted* by (social) constraints and enablements, and it is this constitution that is the basis for ontic injustice or oppression. So the framework I am going to offer applies only to *human* social kinds and only to those human social kinds that are *constitutively* socially constructed.

3.3. Overview of the Constraints and Enablements Framework

3.3.1. Constraints, Enablements, and Social Structures

Let us briefly take stock of the ground covered so far. Explanatory kinds are groupings of things unified by a shared property or properties, and they have explanatory value relative to specific explanatory projects. The specific

---

[9] This is in contrast to Dembroff's concept of 'ontological oppression', which applies to social kinds more broadly; see §2.5.2.

explanatory projects that concern me here are emancipatory ones; I am interested in the kinds that have explanatory value relative to emancipatory aims. Social kinds are a particular type of explanatory kind: those explanatory kinds that depend on social factors. My focus here is on a particular type of social kind: *human* social kinds (social kinds that have human beings as their members) that are *constitutively* socially constructed (social factors make the kind what it is), since only these kinds can be ontically unjust or ontically oppressive. My aim in the rest of this chapter is to offer a framework for theorising these kinds.

There are two main desiderata for this framework. First, it must enable us to identify the property or properties that unify the members of such kinds, since this is necessary for making judgements about whether a kind is a site of ontic injustice (or ontic oppression). Second, it must offer resources for systematising a pluralist account of kinds, helping us to keep in good conceptual order an ontology that includes a range of different explanatory kinds that are suited to different specific emancipatory purposes. This is needed because the nature of explanation and the nature of emancipatory social endeavours jointly mean that there is no single, streamlined set of kinds that can do all of the explanatory work we need to do.

The central claim of the framework I will offer, the constraints and enablements framework (CEF), is that what unifies the members of such kinds is the fact of being subject to similar social constraints and enablements— or, to put it differently, the kinds are unified by the property of *falling under such-and-such constraints and enablements*.[10] This suggestion is in line with the fairly broad consensus in social ontology, discussed in Chapter 1, on the prominent role of constraints and enablements in constituting social kinds. Perhaps less obviously, it is also in line with a body of work that emphasises the importance of social structures for explaining important social facts (for an overview, see Soon 2021), as I shall now show.

Proponents of structural explanation emphasise that not all social facts can be explained in terms of facts about individuals; rather, it is sometimes necessary to appeal to social structures, since these unify the apparently

---

[10] Recall that I am excluding thin kinds from my talk of 'social kinds', so that I should not here be understood as claiming that all *thin* (non-explanatory) kinds that depend on social factors and have humans as their members are unified by shared constraints and enablements. In fact, I think that thin kinds can be unified by all sorts of different properties. My claim about constraints and enablements only applies to human social kinds, which I take to be a particular type of explanatory kind. Thanks to Esa Diaz-Leon for encouraging me to clarify this point.

disparate actions and events that take place at an individual level under a pattern. Accordingly, structural explanations enable us to make sense of why such patterns hold and are causally robust (Haslanger 2016b, 121–25). As Haslanger points out, structural explanation is crucial for understanding oppression in ways that enable us to oppose it, because often structural change is a necessary part of emancipatory social change: 'changing structures is often a precondition for changing patterns of thought and action and is certainly required for durable change' (Haslanger 2015, 1; see also Haslanger 2016b, 124).

How, then, do social structures relate to constraints and enablements? Structures in general are 'complexes, networks, or "latticeworks" of relations' (Ritchie 2020, 405). I follow Haslanger in thinking of social structures in particular as involving social relations (a) among people and (b) between people and material objects, where these relations are in turn constituted through social practices. Social practices are, roughly, the coordinated and thus patterned actions of social agents in a material context, and they are made up of two interdependent elements: resources, and schemas (Haslanger 2016b, 126). Resources are material things taken to have value, including negative value.[11] Schemas are sets of conceptual resources that serve to organise access to material resources. In a typical case, practices arise in response to the need to coordinate access to resources; they thus offer solutions to collective action problems. To participate in a practice is to engage with resources in accordance with schemas; as Haslanger puts it, 'Our practices relate us to each other and to the material world' (2016b, 125).

The important point for our purposes is that these relations function to constrain and enable us in patterned ways, depending on the position, or 'node', that we occupy in a social structure. A node in a structure is defined by its relations to other nodes in the structure together with any restrictions or requirements on the objects that can occupy the node (Ritchie 2020, 405). A node in a *social* structure—also sometimes called an 'office' or a 'position' (Haslanger 2016b, 125) – is therefore defined by the social relations in which occupants of the node stand to other people and to material resources. The node *landlord*, for example, is defined by the ways

---

[11] The fact that resources can have negative value leads to some slightly counter-intuitive results given that it has positive connotations in ordinary usage. Sewage, for example, is a resource (in the sense Haslanger has in mind) because it is something that is, in general, negatively valued—people usually want to be far away from it and wish there was less of it.

in which occupants of this node are related to other people (e.g., tenants, bailiffs) and to material resources (e.g., buildings, land). Accordingly, the co-occupants of nodes in social structures fall under similar constraints and enablements to one another.

This intimate relationship between social structures, on the one hand, and constraints and enablements, on the other, is illustrated in Ritchie's (2020) discussion of Ásta's conferralist account of social kinds (which we encountered in Chapter 1). Ritchie holds that some social groups (which she terms 'feature social groups') are aptly thought of as nodes in social structures (2020, 415). She offers a reading of Ásta's conferralism about gender kinds as being compatible with this account of groups:

> A proponent of a conferralist view could hold that women is a social kind that is defined in terms of constraints and enablements which are relations between people and other entities. Further, membership in the kind in a context (i.e., occupying a node in a context) requires that one be conferred the status through persistent judgments. (2020, 417)

The fit is certainly a neat one. Ásta's conferralist account states that social kinds are social statuses, and social statuses are constituted by constraints and enablements, which are clearly to be understood as relational. It is then a small further step to say that these relations form a structure and that the relevant social kinds are nodes in social structures. Thus, Ritchie's point here helpfully illustrates the relationship between social structures, on the one hand, and social constraints and enablements, on the other.

Important for our purposes is that this relationship is, in fact, the reason social structures can play such an important role in explaining social facts (Haslanger 2016b, 125). Because occupants of nodes in social structures fall under similar constraints and enablements, we can capture significant regularities in the behaviour and experiences of people by recognising that they occupy the same node in a social structure and appealing to the social structure in our explanations. To borrow the example that Haslanger uses, if we want to know why a certain woman quits her job after having a child (deciding to stay at home, care for her child, and rely on her husband's earnings), a good explanation will appeal to the fact that she occupies the node *wife/mother* in a gendered social structure that provides a 'choice architecture' for decisions that individuals make within it, shaping the available options and the social meanings (affirmation, stigma) attaching to those options (Haslanger 2016b, 121–25). Such an explanation will be applicable to different individuals with different histories and psychologies providing that they occupy the same node, because in virtue of occupying that node, they are similarly constrained and enabled and thus likely to make similar choices. Thus, it is constraints and enablements, attaching to nodes, that enable social structures to be so useful in explanations of social facts. Therefore, the kinds unified by those constraints and enablements have explanatory value. This is why my claim that what unifies the members of constitutively constructed human social kinds is the fact of being subject to similar social constraints and enablements fits so well with a commitment to structural explanation.[12]

It is often very important to focus our attention directly on social structures and the many different ways in which they can generate explanatorily interesting kinds. Social structures play an underpinning role that supports the existence of patterned social constraints and enablements. In developing a framework for theorising constitutively constructed human social kinds, however, my primary focus will be on the constraints and enablements themselves, rather than on the social structures. This is because the concepts of ontic injustice and ontic oppression direct our focus more towards the *impact* that an individual's positioning in a social structure has on them (and the normative significance of this impact)—which is captured by the constraints and enablements that they fall under. A framework focused directly on the constraints and enablements is therefore more helpful for my purposes. It important, however, to be clear that there is no tension between this framework and a commitment to the explanatory value of social structures, as I have shown in this section. Moreover, in the ensuing discussion, it will be helpful to keep in mind that all of the constraints and

---

[12] I have previously phrased the relevant claim as being that social kinds are 'at least partly constituted' by social constraints and enablements. I am now able to swap out this phrase for the more precise claim that constraints and enablements are what unify constitutively constructed human social kinds, in the way described in this section and the last section. I intend to leave open the question of whether the fact that social constraints and enablements play this role in unifying these social kinds amounts to their *fully* constituting such social kinds or to their *partly* constituting such social kinds (the phrase 'at least partly constituted' is, of course, compatible with either of these alternatives). It surely amounts to the latter, but one might think that it does not amount to the former because other factors also play a constitutive role alongside constraints and enablements—for example, the existence of a social structure, or social practices, or other mechanisms that underpin explanatory value. Although this is an interesting question, pursuing it is beyond the scope of this chapter.

enablements that I will discuss attach to nodes in social structures that are maintained by social practices.

3.3.2. Components of the Constraints and Enablements Framework

Having adopted a focus on constraints and enablements, the crucial question is *which* constraints and enablements constitutively construct kinds with explanatory value. Or, more precisely, we need to ask: once we know what our explanatory project is, how can we figure out which constraints and enablements unify the kinds that will serve our explanatory purposes? According to the background picture presented in the previous section, identifying a social kind will always involve an act of generalisation or abstraction. Faced with a plethora of thin kinds that are not useful to us, we need to figure out which kinds are caught up in patterns and regularities that make them suitable for use in explanation, given our interests and purposes. Thus, the task is to identify or pick out certain bundles of constraints and enablements under which individuals fall, where the kinds unified by *these* bundles are the kinds that have explanatory value. I will suggest that identifying these bundles of constraints and enablements involves three acts of specification.

First, we need to specify the *context* in which the constraints and enablements apply. Are we considering how individuals are constrained and enabled in the context of a certain social space or institution, such as a family, workplace, or university? Or are we considering how individuals are constrained and enabled across the whole range of social spaces that they traverse as part of their lives? Or something in between? I think of this decision as determining the 'scope' of the constraints and enablements that unify the kind.

Second, we need to consider which *types* of constraints and enablements are included in the bundle that characterises the kind. As we will see, constraints and enablements come in different forms; for example, some relate to how others treat us, and others relate to our own psychological capabilities. Including different combinations of these varieties of constraints and enablements will lead us to specify different social kinds, which may be more or less useful for different purposes. I think of this as determining the 'breadth' of the constraints and enablements that unify the kind, because it concerns how broad or narrow a focus we take in considering the constraints and enablements that are candidates for inclusion in our specification of the kind.

Finally, we need to decide *how general or specific* we should be in our understanding of what the relevant constraints or enablements are. I think of this as determining the 'granularity' of the constraints and enablements, because it relates to how fine-grained or coarse-grained our understanding of the constraints or enablements is. Are we describing the constraints and enablements at a highly specific level of detail? Or are we painting with broader brushstrokes? As I shall explain, this is important for how the CEF handles intersectionality.

These three variables—scope, breadth, and granularity—give us the basic shape of the CEF. They can be thought of analogously with sliders on a sound mixing board: different combinations of settings will give us different outputs. The CEF offers a way of theorising constitutively constructed human social kinds that can be used to identify many different kinds, according to our different emancipatory purposes. It does this by picking out scope, breadth, and granularity as the important variables, against a background picture of human social kinds as explanatory kinds. A given human social kind is to be understood as an explanatory kind that is unified by a particular bundle of constraints and enablements, and such bundles are to be understood as being individuated by having a certain scope, breadth, and granularity.

This is a very bare outline of the framework. To fill it out, I'll now explain each of these variables in more detail, starting in the next section with scope and then moving on to breadth and granularity in the following two sections. In each case, I'll argue that as emancipatory theorists, we cannot pick a single 'setting' for the variable that will *always* best serve our explanatory purposes, but rather we need a model that allows for flexibility.

Before fleshing out the CEF in more detail, it is worth noting explicitly that I do not intend it to answer all of the questions we might have about the ontology of the social kinds in question. The CEF, together with the background view of social kinds on which it depends, does not constitute a full account of the ontology of social kinds. Questions remain about what depends on what and how—for example, about the precise dependence relations among social structures, social practices, and individual events and actions. Some readers may also have questions about whether the picture I am giving is one on which human social kinds qualify as 'real' or merely 'nominal', although

I must confess that I find this distinction somewhat elusive. The purpose of the CEF, and of my discussion in this chapter more broadly, is not to settle all such questions.[13] Rather, the aim is to illuminate *enough* about the ontology of these kinds that we can apply the concepts of ontic injustice and ontic oppression to them, which requires understanding which social constraints and enablements unify a given kind so that we can normatively assess those constraints and enablements.

3.4. Scope

In seeking to pick out a social kind, we can adopt a wider or a narrower focus in terms of the context in which we are looking for the constraints and enablements. I'll refer to this as *scope*. For example, we might choose to look just at constraints that are operating in a specific time and place, such a particular meeting in a workplace. This would be a very narrow scope. Alternatively, we may choose to look at the constraints and enablements that are in place across a large area over a lengthy period of time—Europe since the Middle Ages, perhaps. This would be a much wider scope.

An emancipatory approach may seem to direct us towards prioritising kinds that come into view when we adopt a very wide scope. Since, as we saw in Chapter 2, oppression is a structural phenomenon, it may seem that we primarily need to attend to social kinds that are broad-brushstroke and large-scale. It's certainly the case that such kinds have a great deal of explanatory power with regard to the maintenance of oppressive social orders. For example, in Chapter 4, I'll look at some accounts of race and gender kinds that aim to capture these kinds on a global context across many centuries. Such accounts have much to recommend them, and the social kinds they capture do important explanatory work.

However, it is also a key insight of emancipatory approaches that social change requires, among other things, that people come to understand the

---

[13] Although I don't think the CEF is compatible with *all* ways of filling in the deeper ontological picture, I think it is compatible with a range of such ways. To give just two examples, I think it is compatible with both Dupré's (1995) 'promiscuous realism' and Massimi's (2022) 'perspectival realism'. On the other hand, I don't think it is compatible with Hacking's (1990) 'dynamic nominalism' (despite harmonising well with some of Hacking's insights), because that view allocates a central role to human practices of labelling and categorising, and, as we shall see, the CEF allows for the existence of constitutively constructed kinds that are not the focus of labelling or categorising by human beings. While further exploration of this point would be interesting, it is beyond the scope of this chapter.

texture of their own lives in different ways, leading to affective shifts as well as changes in beliefs. As we saw in Chapter 2, the ideologies that support oppression involve not only false beliefs but also false or distorted orientations to the world or relations to social practices (Jaeggi 2009; Haslanger 2017b). It follows that loosening the grip an ideology has on us involves changing the way we experience and relate to the world.

Building on this observation, it's significant that the way we experience and relate to the social world is not 'all at once', as it were. We never have a direct or immediate experience of society as a structural whole; rather, we experience it piecemeal, as specific situations in which we find ourselves. It follows that these specific situations are where a lot of the action is in terms of unmasking ideologies. This thought is expressed in feminist understandings of consciousness raising (MacKinnon 1989, 83–105). For example, through considering kinds of treatment and responses directed at people who are perceived as women in a certain context, an individual may come to realise that treatment she thought was specifically targeted at—or even caused by—her as an individual is, in fact, part of a pattern of treatment systematically directed at those perceived as women in that context. This in turn may direct her towards other constraints and enablements in other contexts, enabling her to build up a picture of gender-based oppression as a broader structural phenomenon based on an initial understanding that is quite context-specific.

It follows that an emancipatory approach also calls for us to make reference to narrower, more context-specific social kinds as well as ones with wider scope; because this is the scale in which people mostly experience their lives, engaging on this scale is crucial for loosening the grip of ideologies. Of course, it may well be the case that *for a specific sub-project* within emancipatory social theory, either a very wide or a very narrow scope gives us human social kinds that can do all of the explanatory work. However, in general, human social kinds with explanatory value for emancipatory purposes can have a range of scopes, narrower as well as wider.

3.5. Breadth

Many different sorts of constraints and enablements can play a role in constituting human social kinds, and these different constraints and enablements interact in complex ways. The CEF allows for human social kinds to be based on different varieties, or combinations of varieties, of constraints and enablements. This is the aspect of the model that I have termed *breadth*. Here I'll divide constraints and enablements into four sorts: those based on the interpersonal behaviour of individuals other than the individual who is constrained and/or enabled, those based on socially shaped psychological factors internal to the constrained individual, those based on the individual's socially shaped body, and those based on the socially shaped material environment in which the individual is situated. In offering this taxonomy, I am not claiming to be identifying sharp dividing lines; as we shall see, these different varieties of constraints and enablements are intimately interconnected. Rather, I am offering a heuristic device in order to help us impose a rough conceptual order on a messy tangle of phenomena. I'll explain each variety of constraints and enablements in turn and then explain how they factor into the CEF.

3.5.1. Interpersonal Constraints and Enablements

What I will call *interpersonal* constraints and enablements are constraints and enablements directly based on the interpersonal behaviour of individuals in a specific social context. An example of a constraint of this sort is a person not being able to vote because they are not a citizen. An example of an enablement of this sort is someone being able to park their car in a place where parking is usually not permitted because they are disabled. Although these constraints and enablements are backed up by broader systems of power, their impact on individuals operates through the specific behaviour of other social individuals in particular contexts. If the non-citizen goes to a polling station on voting day, they will be turned away. If a parking warden is looking at the disabled person's parked car and sees the badge indicating that the driver is disabled, they will refrain from issuing a ticket when they otherwise would have done so. Both of these examples are quite formalised and explicit, but interpersonal constraints and enablements can also be tacit and subtle. For example, an Asian woman may find that when she tries to speak in a work meeting, she is frequently interrupted and ignored, whereas this does not happen to her other colleagues who are not Asian women. Her colleagues' behaviour means that she is constrained from contributing fully to the discussion.

I have chosen to begin with interpersonal constraints and enablements be-cause they have received the most discussion in social ontology. For example, they are central to Ásta's (2018) account of social construction. Ásta argues that for a feature F to be socially constructed is for it to be the social signif-icance of some other feature (or set of features) B, which serves as the basis for conferrals of social status (2018, 44). In this account, instantiating a cer-tain social property is equated with having a certain social status, and having a certain social status is equated with falling under certain constraints and enablements. Social status, according to Ásta, is *conferred* upon an agent A in a social context by the actions and attitudes of other agents in the context, which are typically a response to some perceived feature or features of A and which serve to place A under constraints and enablements. Some conferrals of social status are more official, resulting in 'institutional' properties (e.g., *being a citizen);* some are more informal, resulting in 'communal' properties (e.g., *being cool).*

In most conferrals, the behaviour of the conferring agents is aimed at tracking some property or properties of the agent upon whom the social status is being conferred, which Ásta terms the 'base property'. For example, the institutional status of *being disabled,* as encountered in the parking case, is conferred upon individuals based on a perception of their bodily capabilities. The institutional status of *being a citizen* is conferred on the basis of the perception that a person meets a complex disjunctive set of criteria, such as having been born in the state in question, or having parents who were born in the state in question, or having lived in the state in question for a cer-tain length of time, and so on. The social status an individual has in a context is determined not by whether or not they really instantiate the base property in question but by whether they are perceived to instantiate it. Someone who has lost their paperwork may lack the social status *citizen* in a certain context even though, in fact, they do instantiate the base property for conferrals of citizenship.

Some interpersonal constraints and enablements fall into a subset that is termed deontic constraints and enablements. Deontic constraints and enablements relate to social perceptions of people's entitlements, obligations, rights, prerogatives, and so on. For example, based on the disabled badge, the parking warden judges that the driver of the car is *entitled* to park in that location, so this is a deontic enablement. From the perspective of emanci-patory theory, deontic constraints and enablements need to be understood in a way that allows that the way in which entitlements, obligations, and so on operate in practice is often very different from the way in which people explicitly believe them to operate, and it is the former, rather than the latter, that has the most impact on people's lives. This is necessary in order to account for the distorting effects of ideology on people's perceptions of deontic normativity; often in oppressive situations, some rights, for example, will be widely thought to be universal when, in fact, it is only the privileged who are meaningfully able to exercise them. As emancipatory theorists, we need to be able to account for the gap between how people *think* deontic normativity operates and how it *actually* operates.

Johan Brännmark's (2019; 2021) account of deontic constraints and enablements is helpful in this respect. Brännmark understands deontic constraints and enablements in terms of patterns of deontic incidents—incidents such as being treated as having a duty to do P or being felt to have overstepped the mark in doing Q. In other words, he conceives of deontic constraints and enablements in terms of the social moves that are effectively 'open' to an individual, where this is determined by how people actually respond to one another in various situations rather than by their explicit beliefs. Conceiving of deontic constraints and enablements in this way means that we can allow for deontic constraints and enablements to be generated by, for example, racist and sexist implicit attitudes on the part of people who would disavow explicitly racist and sexist beliefs.

As Brännmark puts it:

> People can identify types of responses as sexist and racist in the abstract and think that *being a woman* or *being a person of color* does not really warrant having fewer moves open to one; but they can still, in a patterned way, regard specific actions by a concrete person occupying these social positions as overstepping boundaries—it is just that *being a woman* and *being a person of color* will not be consciously recognized as the cues to which they are responding. (2019, 1055)

For example, a person might not explicitly believe that women should speak less than men, but (due to unconscious sexist bias) they might regularly perceive a woman who speaks for 50 percent of the time in a two-person conversation as dominating that conversation, where they would not have that perception if a man did the same (Brännmark 2021, 517). The point also applies equally well to the question of which actions are perceived as *not* overstepping boundaries. For instance, a person might consciously believe that Black people deserve as much respect for their bodily boundaries as White people but might not perceive touching a Black person's hair without invitation as a disrespectful thing to do, although they would consider it disrespectful to do the same to a White person. To return to the example given earlier of the Asian woman who is interrupted by her White male colleagues, one thing that could be happening in that scenario is that the colleagues do not perceive these interruptions as overstepping a boundary, although they would perceive similar interruptions directed at one another as doing so. If this is the case, then the Asian woman in that scenario is under a deontic constraint. These are all examples of people being under different deontic interpersonal constraints and enablements based on their race and/or gender. Brännmark's account allows us to recognise them as such despite the fact that the people involved do not explicitly believe that others have different entitlements and obligations based on their race or gender.

Brännmark's discussion of deontic constraints and enablements also highlights the need to be attentive to the role played by the presence or absence of negative or corrective responses (Brännmark 2021, 517). For example, if a woman could manage to speak for an equal amount of time to her interlocutors if she tried hard but in doing so she would be perceived as having hogged an unfair amount of time and would suffer a drop in the esteem of her interlocutors, this is a deontic constraint. What matters is not only how hard she must try in order to speak but also the fact that even if she succeeds, she will face a negative consequence. Thus, being under a deontic interpersonal constraint concerning B may mean that one is likely to suffer penalties for doing B that others would not suffer, even though one is no more likely than others actually to be prevented from doing B if one attempts it. This can be understood as a constraint because it is made more difficult for one to both do B *and* avoid the penalty.

Although Brännmark makes these two points—about the possibility of unconscious constraints and enablements and about the importance of corrective responses—in relation to *deontic* constraints and enablements, specifically, both points can profitably be applied to *non-deontic* interpersonal constraints and enablements. Interpersonal constraints and enablements are non-deontic when they do not involve social perceptions of people's entitlements, obligations, rights, prerogatives, and so on. For example, it might be the case in a particular region that tall people are more likely to be promoted into managerial roles, based on unconscious attitudes that position tall people as authoritative, as good leaders, and so on. In this context, tall people have a social enablement, but this is not a deontic one, because a person making a decision about promotions would not feel under any kind of obligation, whether explicit or subtle, to promote the tall person. Like deontic constraints and enablements, non-deontic interpersonal constraints and enablements need not be explicitly recognised by the agents who participate in them, since they can be constituted by patterns of incidents. Moreover, when it comes to constraints, these patterns can include negative consequences as well as outright mechanisms of prevention.

3.5.2. Psychological Constraints and Enablements

Our experience of having interpersonal constraints and enablements (deontic and otherwise) imposed on us and witnessing them being imposed on others shapes our dispositions, attitudes, and beliefs. These in turn affect what we attempt to do. For example, over time, someone who is regularly interrupted and ignored in work meetings or in an educational setting may as a result develop a lower confidence in their abilities or the worth of their ideas, making them reluctant even to attempt to speak up in those contexts (see, e.g., Tanesini 2016; 2018). This reluctance constitutes a *psychological* constraint.

It is vital to recognise that psychological constraints and enablements, in the sense I have in mind, are typically formed in response to experiencing or witnessing coercively imposed interpersonal constraints and enablements or coming up against other manifestations of social structures, such as being exposed to certain cultural representations. Thus, although there is a sense in which psychological constraints involve an individual engaging in self-limiting behaviour, it would be wrong to view them as 'self-imposed' in a way that locates their ultimate causal origin within the individual's own mental states. For this reason, I view them as a type of social constraint or enablement.

Although psychological constraints and enablements have been discussed a great deal by philosophers interested in racial and gender oppression, they have not played a central role in many accounts of social ontology (one exception is Burman 2007). I include them among the constraints and enablements that can constitute membership in a social kind because they play a significant role in many accounts of oppression. Frantz Fanon, for example, discusses the psychological effects of colonial oppression in *Black*

Skin, White Masks, describing it as 'psychic alienation.' 'My blackness was there,' he writes, 'dark and unarguable. And it tormented me, pursued me, disturbed me, angered me' (2008, 88). Drawing on Fanon, Sandra Bartky argues:

> To be psychologically oppressed is to be weighed down in your mind; it is to have a harsh dominion exercised over your self-esteem. The psychologically oppressed become their own oppressors; they come to exercise harsh dominion over their own self-esteem. Differently put, psychological oppression can be regarded as the 'internalization of intimations of inferiority'. (1991, 22, citing Joyce Mitchell Cook, unpublished talk)

According to Bartky, psychological oppression can operate in a number of ways. One of these is stereotyping: the oppressed are subject to stereotypes that are usually negative and always limiting. For example, all women and people of colour of all genders are stereotyped as irrational. White women, specifically, have been stereotyped as incompetent and passive. Black women, specifically, have been stereotyped as strong and domineering. And so on. Stereotyping is harmful not only because of its effects on the way others typically treat members of the stereotyped group but also because it may be internalised by the stereotyped individual and lead to difficulty in developing a sense of an authentic or unified self, thereby limiting self-determination.

Another way in which psychological oppression can operate is through denigrating the culture of the oppressed or even blocking the conditions for the oppressed to develop cultural expressions that reflect their life experiences insofar as these are different from those of members of the dominant group. I am inclined to equate this with Young's account of 'cultural imperialism', which we encountered in Chapter 2 as an aspect of subordination.[14]

Finally, psychological oppression can operate via objectification, including sexual objectification. For Bartky, being sexually objectified involves having one's sexual functions separated off from the rest of one's person and instrumentalised or being reduced to one's sexual functions. Catcalling on the street, for example, forces a woman to become aware of the sexual aspects of her being and of how these are being perceived by the catcaller. Her own experience of herself in that moment is subordinated to his external

---

[14] That is, I treat it as an aspect of subordination, which I then use to help define oppression; Young instead considers it to be a face of oppression. See §2.3.2.

perception of her body. As Bartky expressively puts it, 'There is an element of compulsion in this encounter, in this being-made-to-be-aware-of-one's-flesh; like being made to apologize, it is humiliating' (1991, 27).

Or consider Fanon's vivid description of racist objectification:

> I move slowly in the world, accustomed now to seek no longer for upheaval. I progress by crawling. And already I am being dissected under white eyes, the only real eyes. I am *fixed*. Having adjusted their microtomes, they objectively cut away slices of my reality. I am laid bare. I feel, I see in those white faces that it is not a new man who has come in, but a new kind of man, a new genus. Why, it's a Negro! (2008, 87)

Here Fanon is reduced to his racial classification, again in a way that is humiliating ('crawling', 'laid bare'), his understanding of himself as 'a man' subordinated to others' perception of him as 'a Negro'.[15]

The flipside of the psychological constraints that are present in psychological oppression are psychological enablements, where additional options feel open to one. A person with many psychological enablements is able to move through the world with confidence, perceiving plentiful opportunities for action and feeling unhindered by aspects of their social being such as gender and race. The flipside of psychological oppression is psychological privilege, where psychological enablements are present to an excessive degree that amounts to an unjustified sense of entitlement, perhaps including an inappropriately inflated sense of one's own importance or capabilities.

As I propose to use the terminology, psychological constraints and enablements are not inherently laden with value. It may be prudentially good for one to have some psychological constraints, such as feeling constrained from intruding on others' personal space without permission, and conversely, it may be prudentially bad to have some psychological enablements, such as feeling enabled to drive at high speed on the roads. The terms 'psychological oppression' and 'psychological privilege', by contrast, are inherently evaluative: to say that someone experiences psychological oppression is not only to say that they experience very many psychological constraints; it is also to engage in a negative normative evaluation of this state of affairs in a way that situates these constraints within a broader social structure that subordinates some social groups. The same goes, mutatis mutandis, for

---

[15] See Yancy 2016 for a contemporary account of racist objectification.

psychological privilege. Thus, two observers may agree that some individual has very many psychological enablements but disagree about whether they experience psychological privilege; perhaps observer A holds that the individual in question merely has a healthy sense of confidence, whilst observer B holds that the enablements exceed what is normatively appropriate in the context and contribute to reproducing the systemic social subordination of others, therefore tipping over into psychological privilege.

Despite the fact that psychological constraints and enablements are in general produced by experiencing or witnessing interpersonal constraints and enablements, the two sorts of constraints and enablements can come apart from each other in particular cases. For example, consider a trans man in a social context in which he is consistently perceived as a cis man. He is viewed by others as being entitled to use men's bathrooms. However, his knowledge that the bathroom is a situation in which people are more likely to realise that he is trans and his knowledge that if this happened it could put him at risk of serious physical violence may give rise to a fear that results in him refraining from using men's bathrooms. This can apply even in situations where others would still consider him entitled to use the men's bathrooms if they became aware that he was trans.[16] This reluctance on his part constitutes a psychological constraint, one that may directly contradict the interpersonal constraints and enablements in a particular context (i.e., the fact that others around him consistently view him as entitled to use the men's bathroom) and which constitutes a significant difference in his situation compared with that of other men around him who are cis.

Another example of psychological constraints and enablements coming apart from interpersonal constraints and enablements is described by the academic Christina Sharpe:

> It is a big leap from working class, to Ivy League schools, to being a tenured professor. And *a part of* that leap and *apart from* its specificities are the sense and awareness of precarity; the precarities of the afterlives of slavery. . . . They texture my reading practices, my ways of being in and of the world, my relations with and to others. (2016, 5)

Here Sharpe highlights a contrast between, on the one hand, the psychological constraints she experiences in the form of a sense of precarity, which she

---

[16] Thanks to Robin Dembroff for suggesting this example.

relates both to her working-class background and to her racial and gender identity as a Black woman in the United States more broadly, and, on the other hand, the actual security of her social position as a tenured professor at a prestigious university, a social position that involves many interpersonal enablements. Someone in Sharpe's position may experience some psychological constraints that are out of line with the interpersonal constraints they are under at the present time.

Similarly, psychological enablements can come apart from interpersonal enablements. A person with prior experience of privilege may feel entitled to take up more than an equal share of conversational space, to proffer opinions with great confidence on topics about which they know very little, and so on, even in a context where this kind of behaviour is frowned upon by everyone else and will generate pushback. On an interpersonal level, an individual in this situation is under the same constraints as everyone else, but they experience distinctive psychological enablements. Of course, regularly receiving such pushback is likely to lead to a change in a person's psychological enablements—or, to put the same point differently, it will be difficult for someone to maintain the unwarranted psychological enablements unless they are spending significant amounts of time in environments where the interpersonal interactions reinforce their sense of entitlement.

Because of the intimate causal connections between interpersonal constraints and enablements, it is important to recognise that there is no sharp line between these two sorts of constraints or enablements. This is illustrated well by Patricia Hill Collins's work on 'controlling images' of Black femininity: ideologically constructed figures or tropes that function to stereotype and oppress Black women (2000, 69–96). These controlling images include the 'mammy', a desexualised maternal figure who loyally serves a white family; the 'matriarch', a domineering figure whose financial independence is understood as emasculating to Black men; and the 'jezebel', a sexually aggressive and hyperavailable figure who features prominently in Black popular culture. These figures constrain the behaviour of the Black women who have no choice but to negotiate them; as Collins puts it, 'Because controlling images are hegemonic and taken for granted, they become virtually impossible to escape' (2000, 90).

However, Collins also argues that although controlling images of Black femininity *can* be internalised or actively taken up by Black women, their extreme negativity tends to prevent this; they are so derogatory that they 'almost necessitate resistance' (2000, 100). To the extent that a Black woman does not internalise controlling images, these images function as interpersonal constraints on her (affecting the kinds of responses she can expect from others) rather than as psychological constraints (affecting her own sense of what she can and cannot do). If she does internalise them, however, they also become psychological constraints, which can limit her ability to do certain things even in contexts where the other agents do not subscribe to the controlling images. Thus, controlling images can function as either interpersonal or psychological constraints or as both at once, illustrating the intimate connection between these two sorts of constraints and enablements.

3.5.3. Bodily and Environmental Constraints and Enablements

The final two sorts of constraints and enablements that are included in this framework, and which I shall discuss together in this section, are *bodily* constraints and enablements and *environmental* constraints and enablements. These concern the ways in which people's physical bodies and material environments, respectively, are shaped by social factors. Although these material varieties of constraints and enablements are comparatively neglected in accounts of social ontology (Sundstrom 2003), one place in which they are both brought into clear focus is Mallon's (2016) account of social kinds in terms of social roles. According to Mallon, a social role exists if the following conditions are met:

SR1. *Representation*: There is a term, label, or mental representation that picks out a category of persons C, and that representation is associated with—and figures in the expression of—a set of beliefs and evaluations—or a conception—of the persons so picked out.

SR2. *Social Conditions*: Many or all of the beliefs and evaluations in the conception of the role are common knowledge in the community. (2016, 58)

Mallon further argues that some social roles are what he terms 'entrenched': they have a causal significance so great that we need to make reference to it in order to understand the social world. Social roles can become entrenched by influencing behaviour, either consciously or unconsciously, and by affecting the cultural and material environment (2016, 82–89). For example, social roles corresponding to racial groups can affect people's behaviour, as they respond both strategically and non-strategically to the representations that make up the roles, including in their treatment of others, both explicitly and implicitly.

Mallon understands social roles as *homeostatic property clusters* (Boyd 1999): 'clusters of nonaccidentally co-occurring properties that sustain explanatory and practical projects including prediction, explanation, and intervention' (Mallon 2016, 69). The properties in a homeostatic property cluster non-accidentally and regularly co-occur, either because the presence of some properties tends to causally contribute to the presence of other properties or because some common underlying mechanism causes each property. As a result, homeostatic property clusters support explanation, induction, and prediction. Homeostatic property clusters can be understood in terms of complex combinations of constraints and enablements: the way a homeostatic property cluster works is that having one property in the cluster makes you more likely to have the other properties as well.

The property clusters with which Mallon is concerned involve both interpersonal and psychological constraints and enablements. However, Mallon also—rightly, in my view—picks up on the ways in which social roles shape individuals' physical bodies and the ways in which they can produce material and cultural environments that constrain and enable individuals. For example, he discusses the ways in which racist interpersonal treatment can affect health outcomes via effects on blood pressure (Kaplan 2010, cited in Mallon 2016, 87) and the way in which racial residential segregation can come about through mechanisms such as 'White flight' and 'redlining'.[17] These dynamics are important, and we can capture them within the CEF as part of what constitutes the reality of human social kinds such as race by including bodily and environmental varieties of constraints and enablements within the taxonomy.

A person experiences a bodily constraint or enablement when their body is shaped by social factors in a way that constraints what they can or cannot do. This could be by affecting their health outcomes, which is to say constraining or enabling their pursuit of health and the activities that require certain forms of health. The example discussed by Mallon of greater levels of ill health suffered by people of colour, due to the stress of racism, is one example of a bodily constraint of this sort. Not all bodily constraints and

---

[17] 'White flight' refers to the migration of White urban residents away from racially diverse areas. 'Redlining' refers to the systematic withholding of mortgages and other financial services from non-White racial groups and/or residents of racially diverse areas. For discussion, see Rothstein 2017.

enablements relate to health as such, however. For example, the way in which women are socially discouraged from developing muscular physiques and from participating in exercise and sport can also be understood as generating bodily constraints, since those targeted for this discouragement are less likely, in fact, to develop a muscular physique and in turn less likely to be able to lift a heavy object, say, where this last difference can be traced in part to social factors.

Bodily constraints and enablements are heavily intertwined with both interpersonal and psychological constraints and enablements. For example, factors in racial disparities in health outcomes include the stress caused by interpersonal racist treatment and racial bias in medical care, both of which are interpersonal constraints. Moreover, psychological constraints and enablements affect how people hold and move their bodies, as Young explores in her paper 'Throwing Like a Girl' (1980). As Young vividly describes, women are socialised in ways that can lead to a feeling of being inhibited from involving all of the body in a movement, from adopting an open stance, and so on, which in turn can make it more difficult to perform certain actions such as throwing a ball hard and far. In Young's view, there *is* a sense in which we can meaningfully talk about a characteristically feminine way of throwing, for example, but only insofar as this is understood to be produced by social factors that originate in the way people respond to young girls and operate through embodied psychological experiences of felt limitation and inhibition. This is another example of a bodily constraint, on my account.

A person experiences an environmental constraint or enablement when their material environment is shaped by social factors in ways that constrain what they can or cannot do. Ronald Sundstrom captures the sense of environmental constraint that I have in mind with reference to the organisation of urban and rural spaces:

> those who, because of their race, ethnicity, or class, are given little choice but to live in ghettos, barrios, under-developed rural areas, or other sites of concentrated poverty are systematically denied the benefits of society and must shoulder a disproportionate amount of its burdens. The result is that their life chances suffer. (2003, 91)

Of course, we could also make the accompanying point about racial, ethnic, and class *privilege* in terms of disproportionate *access to* benefits and *distance from* burdens. Another example of what I am thinking of as an environmental enablement is a building that has individual, self-contained, single-user bathrooms. This enables people to use the bathroom without having to choose one of two communal spaces that are usually marked with gender signifiers. A building with just two gender-marked bathroom spaces correspondingly constrains people: in such a building, one cannot use the bathroom without making a statement about one's gender.

Without suggesting that the material and conceptual aspects of our experiences should be understood in sharp separation from each other—indeed, the bathroom case serves to illustrate how they are inextricably intertwined—it is this material dimension of socially produced space that I am aiming to capture with the notion of environmental constraints and enablements. As Sundstrom puts it, 'Remove the iron bars, concrete slabs, and rails that demarcate and police categories, and the category itself will change' (2003, 93). My presentation of environmental constraints and enablements contrasts slightly in this regard with that of Mallon, whose social role account of human social kinds treats these constraints and enablements together with those arising from the ways in which social roles shape the *cultural* environment, for example, by affecting the relative epistemic credibility of differently racialised individuals (2016, 82–89). However, in my account, constraints and enablements arising from *cultural* environments can be cashed out in terms of interpersonal constraints and enablements. If a cultural environment is characterised by widespread attitudes of distrust towards the testimony of people of colour, say, then this must be a matter of individuals tending to respond in certain ways to one another and perhaps having internalised these constraints and enablements psychologically. Thus, although treating the cultural and material environments together makes sense within Mallon's framework, within my framework, it would give rise to a double-counting of some constraints and enablements. It is the constraints and enablements produced by *material* environments that I do not think can be cashed out in terms of interpersonal or psychological constraints and enablements, and, therefore, it is these constraints and enablements that I seek to capture in the further category of *environmental* constraints and enablements.

To see how constraints and enablements arising from the material environment exceed the interpersonal and psychological constraints and enablements, suppose that a Black person with tech qualifications is looking for work in a city that is home to a tech company with many well-paying jobs. If their application to work at the tech company would be treated less favourably because they are Black, this would be an interpersonal constraint. If they would be hesitant to apply because of racialised stereotypes they have internalised, this would be a psychological constraint. But suppose that they live in an area of the city that is far from where the tech company is based, that is predominantly populated by people of colour, and that has very poor public transport links making it extremely difficult for them to physically travel to and from the tech company each day. The positioning of the tech company and the lack of public transport are environmental factors that constrain the person's actions. What is more, these constraints are not equivalent to interpersonal or psychological constraints, although, of course, interpersonal and psychological constraints will have played a *causal* role in the shaping of the material environment. This example highlights why it is useful to have a category of constraints and enablements that captures those constraints and enablements that are generated by the *material* social environment: unlike constraints and enablements arising from the cultural environment, these constraints are not covered by the categories of interpersonal constraints and enablements and psychological constraints and enablements.

As well as both being connected to interpersonal and psychological constraints and enablements in the ways that I have already described, bodily and environmental constraints and enablements are intimately interconnected with each other. An especially important way in which environmental constraints and enablements can contribute to oppression is through their effects on people's health. For example, a person's physical proximity to amenities such as parks and swimming pools, facilities such as hospitals and clinics, and hazards such as waste disposal sites has obvious implications for their likelihood of positive or negative health outcomes.

3.5.4. Pluralism about Constraints and Enablements

Each of the four types of constraints and enablements that I have discussed here—interpersonal, psychological, bodily, and environmental—has already been theorised in detail by other philosophers. What is distinctive about my approach to constraints and enablements in relation to social kinds, however, is a focus that includes all four types of constraints and enablements in one framework. Many accounts of social kinds focus on one particular variety of constraints and enablements and posit social kinds that are constituted exclusively by those constraints and enablements.

However, I think in each case, there are limits to what the account can do for us.

For example, Brännmark focuses on deontic constraints and enablements, understood as a subset of interpersonal constraints and enablements, and terms the kinds that are constituted by these constraints and enablements 'institutional kinds'. However, this account leaves unaddressed the ontology of non-institutional social kinds. Ásta's account of social kinds focuses on kinds that are constituted by interpersonal constraints and enablements more broadly construed but excluding psychological, bodily, and environmental constraints and enablements. Focusing on interpersonal constraints and enablements in this way, however, makes it difficult to account for the ways in which people are constrained and enabled through social relations that are not directly manifested in interpersonal interactions, including bodily and environmental constraints and enablements (Burman 2019; Griffith 2019; Barnes and Andler 2020). My account is different from both Brännmark's and Ásta's in virtue of positing a wider variety of constraints and enablements as playing a role in constituting social kinds.

My account is also broader than Mallon's, though in a different respect. Mallon's account includes interpersonal, psychological, bodily, and environmental constraints and enablements, making it broader in this respect than many other accounts of social kinds. The account is very helpful for understanding how these constraints and enablements interact. However, Mallon restricts his focus in a different way, by attending only to those constraints and enablements that are associated with a common-knowledge conception of a social role. I agree with Ritchie's (2017) argument that, contra Mallon, it is crucial for an account of social kinds to recognise that there can be causal mechanisms that produce homeostatic property clusters even where there is no explicit representation of the social role and no associated conception and accordingly no common knowledge of the role and conception (see also Àsta 2018, 52–53).[18] For example, a society could have a social class system that includes effects on people's bodies, such as health outcomes, and on the material environment, such as the positioning of amenities, even if class was not explicitly represented

---

[18] For some key discussions of the broader topic of the ways in which different social kinds do or do not depend for their existence on our having attitudes towards them, see Thomasson 2003 and Khalidi 2015. Like both Thomasson and Khalidi, as well as Ritchie, I hold that many social kinds can exist without our having any attitudes towards them.

or consciously acknowledged and accordingly failed to generate social role kinds as understood by Mallon (Burman 2019). This may be especially important for intersectional kinds, which I shall discuss in the next section. This is because, as Ritchie (2017, 482) notes, there may not be common-knowledge conceptions for complexly intersectional social roles, such as *non-disabled bisexual Asian woman*, but where we nevertheless may find homeostatic clusters of constraints and enablements. Since the CEF allows for there to be social kinds that do not involve a common-knowledge role and conception, the CEF allows for a broader range of human social kinds than Mallon's social role account of human social kinds does.

Each of the approaches taken by Brännmark, Ásta, and Mallon yields social kinds that have genuine explanatory power, including for emancipatory projects. However, focusing on any of these varieties of social kind without an analysis of how it relates to the other varieties places some important explanations out of reach, explanations that matter from the perspective of emancipatory projects. I do not intend this as a criticism of those accounts; it is perfectly legitimate to set out to look for social kinds that do a good job of explaining a certain sort of phenomenon or capturing a certain conception of social construction, and this can lead us to focus only on a certain variety of constraints and enablements for the purposes of the project at hand. However, adopting an exclusive narrow focus on a specific variety of constraints and enablements is not productive for my purposes here—which is to say, for emancipatory purposes broadly conceived. As I have shown, the different sorts of constraints and enablements are intimately related, and each is helpful for understanding some aspects of oppression. This is why the CEF includes all four varieties of constraints and enablements under the variable of breadth.

At this point, it is worth briefly mentioning the role of *non-social* constraints and enablements. For example, I am unable to lift something weighing one metric ton, but intuitively, this does not seem to be caused by social factors, such as my diet or the way I have been socialised to relate to my body or what kind of exercise it is considered appropriate for me to take part in. Accordingly, this limitation does not meet the criteria for being a bodily constraint as defined previously. This highlights two things. First, the taxonomy that I provide is only for *social* constraints and enablements; I do not attempt to provide any taxonomy of non-social constraints and enablements. Second, non-social constraints and enablements can play a role in constituting social kinds. In order for a kind to be a social kind on my view, it is not necessary for social constraints and enablements to be the *only* shared properties that unify the members of the kind. Non-social constraints and enablements can be in the mix and can interact with social constraints and enablements to produce the patterned outcomes that support explanation. It's just that there must be *some* shared social constraints and enablements present for the kind to count as a social kind. Often, we might think of the non-social constraints and enablements as forming a background against which social factors make a difference to what we can do. Building a new bridge across a ravine can change the environmental constraints and enablements that someone falls under partly *because* the person couldn't simply fly across the ravine before the bridge was built.

To sum up this section, the CEF allows for human social kinds to be based on different varieties, or combinations of varieties, of social constraints and enablements, according to what will serve our explanatory purposes. This is the aspect of the model that I have termed 'breadth'. The appropriate level of breadth for a human social kind varies significantly with our explanatory purposes. For example, if one wants to examine the contribution that practices within a particular institution make to oppression, one might find it helpful to focus solely on interpersonal constraints and enablements. If we wanted to know about the internal culture of a particular police force in relation to racism, for instance, we might find it useful to focus solely on interpersonal constraints and enablements, considering how people directly respond to one another in racialised ways. However, if we wanted to know about the broader role that policing plays in a White supremacist society, we would need to adopt a broader focus and consider, for example, how environmental constraints and enablements factor into things like the over-policing of communities racialised as other than White and the criminalisation of activities necessary to the survival of the racially marginalised (for a study along these lines in the UK context, see White 2020). These broader questions are also very important.

Just as we saw in the discussion of scope, when it comes to breadth, it can sometimes be helpful to focus on a specific variety (or set of varieties) of constraints and enablements for particular emancipatory purposes. We should not always assume that the broader we go in terms of constraints and enablements, the more useful the kinds we arrive at. We need to look at the specific explanatory project we are pursuing and consider which variety or varieties of constraints and enablements help us to make the sort of explanations we need to make.

3.6. Granularity

3.6.1. Defining Granularity

The third decision that we need to make when specifying a social kind is how fine-grained or coarse-grained our specification of the constraints and enablements ought to be. By this I mean how much variation is to be subsumed within 'the same' constraint or enablement. For example, consider a workplace in which women are more frequently interrupted in meetings than men, and women of colour are more frequently interrupted than White women. If we focus on the constraint *less able to speak without interruption*, this applies to all the women in the workplace. But if we instead think of the relevant constraint *interrupted about half of the time*, this might only apply to White women, with women of colour being subject to the constraint *interrupted about three-quarters of the time*. And this in turn is less fine-grained than if we were to also separate women by more specific racial group, by age, by class, by their job role in the organisation, and so on. Thus, whatever constraints and enablements we settle on, we will have to select an appropriate level of *granularity* for our explanatory purposes, making this the third component of the framework.

In this picture of constraints and enablements that I have given, it is the existence of patterns in the actual actions and experiences of individuals that allows us to articulate constraints and enablements for multiply intersectional kinds (e.g., *disabled Black lesbian woman*). We can then take a more and more coarse-grained approach to describing these patterns that will give us simpler intersectional kinds (e.g., *Black woman*), until finally we arrive at single-moniker kinds (e.g., *woman*). These single-moniker kinds are the farthest away from the actual actions and experiences of individuals. Nevertheless, single-moniker kinds still exist, according to the framework, because they can also have explanatory value, alongside more intersectional kinds.[19]

It is worth noting that there may be *specific* cases in which there are *no* patterns that unite the different intersectional kinds that constitute a

---

[19] It is tempting to think that these individual actions and experiences are what is most ontologically basic, though I will not attempt to defend this claim here. If this is right, then the CEF attributes greater ontological priority to intersectional kinds compared with single-moniker kinds. Other discussions of intersectionality that give a somewhat similar picture of the ontological priority of intersectional kinds include Brännmark 2021, 523; Bernstein 2020.

single-moniker kind. In such cases, on my account, there *is* no single-moniker kind but only intersectional kinds. Imagine that we wanted to specify kinds in the context of a particular bar (scope) and based on interpersonal constraints and enablements only (breadth). Let us suppose that this bar is both extremely racist and extremely sexist. Black women work as waitresses. Black men work as bartenders. White men are customers who order and pay for drinks. White women are patrons but not customers—they only frequent the bar as the guests of White men, who order and pay for drinks on their behalf.

If a White woman arrived at the bar, she would be assumed to be there to meet a White man, rather than being a customer in her own right. If a Black woman arrived, she would be assumed to be a waitress or someone seeking work as a waitress, rather than a patron of any sort. In this case, the constraints and enablements that characterise the status of the White women and the constraints and enablements that characterise the status of the Black women have very little, if anything, in common.

The social dynamics of the bar can be best explained by way of intersectional kinds such as *Black woman* and *White woman*, not single-moniker kinds such as *woman*. Suppose Anne, a Black woman, enters the bar by herself and tries, unsuccessfully, to order a drink. Why can't Anne manage to order a drink? Because Anne is a Black woman, and everyone assumes she is a waitress or perhaps is looking for work as a waitress. Now, we could answer the question by saying instead: because Anne is a woman, and women don't order drinks here. But this is much less explanatory. For one thing, it doesn't tell us what people expect Anne to do instead of ordering drinks. For another, it obscures the difference between Anne's situation and the situation of Betty, a White woman, who also cannot order a drink. Betty's inability to order a drink is due to the fact that she is assumed to be the guest of a White man, who will order (and, crucially, pay) on her behalf; whereas Anne's inability to order a drink is due to the fact that she is not considered to be a patron at all. Single-moniker race or gender kinds do little, if any, explanatory work in this social context; all the important social dynamics are captured by the intersectional kinds *Black woman* and so on. Accordingly, in this case, we might want to say that if we are looking to specify kinds based on interpersonal constraints and enablements in the context of this bar, there is no such social kind as *woman* simpliciter.[20]

---

[20] Whether we ultimately ought to say this will depend on the other constraints and enablements that are in play in the context. I have only focused on one constraint (not being able to order a drink).

3.6.2. Granularity and Intersectionality

As the foregoing discussion makes clear, granularity has a lot to do with intersectionality. Intersectionality can be understood as a 'framework checker' (Garry 2011): rather than supplying an account of social kinds, social identities, oppression, and so on, it sets a standard that accounts of these phenomena should meet. I explained how I am understanding the different components that make up this standard in §2.4. I'll now outline how the CEF accords with each of these components of intersectionality.[21]

The first component of intersectionality is the thought that oppression is *non-additive*, which is to say that we cannot gain adequate insight about Black women's oppression, for example, simply by adding together some general claims about race-based oppression and some general claims about gender-based oppression. This is not to say that oppression can *never* function in additive ways, just that it often does not, and therefore we cannot count on it doing so. Second, there is the closely related thought that oppression is *non-separable*: the oppression experienced by a Black woman cannot be separated into oppression experienced "on the basis of race" and oppression experienced "on the basis of gender". Again, this does not rule out the possibility of cases where oppressions *can* be separated out but is rather a caution against assuming that such separation is always possible. The third thought, which is a rather stronger claim than the first two, is that oppressive categories involve *cross-constitution* or mutual construction. It is not just that race and gender interact to underpin forms of oppression that are non-additive and non-separable; rather, race plays a crucial role in constructing the reality of gender, and vice versa. In other words, gender could not be what it is if race did not exist, and race could not be what it is if gender did not exist (Garry 2011; Bernstein 2020). I am committed to all three: *non-additiveness*, *non-separability*, and *cross-constitution*.

The CEF accords with *non-additiveness* because it is not the case that there are constraints and enablements for single-moniker race kinds and single-moniker gender kinds that can be added together to yield the constraints and

---

[21] I am here treating intersectionality as a feature of social kinds. For a contrasting approach that treats intersectionality instead as a feature of social *properties*, see Jorba and Rodó-Zárate 2019. However, note that in my view, social kinds are unified by shared properties, which suggests that there may not be as much distance between treating intersectionality as a feature of kinds and treating it as a feature of properties as Jorba and Rodó-Zárate take there to be.

enablements for intersectional race and gender kinds. Rather, intersectional kinds have their own, *distinctive* constraints and enablements, which contribute to determining the constraints and enablements for single-moniker kinds. This reverses the common, though problematic, understanding of the experiences of Black women, for example, as being determined by the experiences of Black people of all genders and women of all racial groups. Rather, the experiences of Black people of all genders, for example, are understood to be determined partly by the experiences of Black women.

The CEF also accords with *non-separability*, because when we specify the constraints and enablements for single-moniker race kinds and for single-moniker gender kinds, these should be understood as *one description* of the constraints and enablements that is useful for *certain explanatory purposes*; they should not be understood as implying that those constraints can be definitively or perfectly separated into those relating to race and those relating to gender.[22] In other words, the level of description at which all women, for example, are understood to share social constraints and enablements is explicitly positioned as a generalisation or abstraction, one that must serve our explanatory purposes if we are to be justified in using it.

Finally, the CEF accords with *cross-constitution*. As we have seen, the experiences of Black people of all genders is understood to be determined partly by the experiences of Black women; since Black women are a gender group as well as a racial group, we here find gender contributing to making race what it is. More generally, any single-moniker kind is extrapolated from a more complex patterned distribution of constraints and enablement in which 'other' single-moniker kinds are always also at play in shaping those patterns. Thus, race plays a role in constituting the reality of gender, and gender plays a role in constituting the reality of race.

In Chapter 2, I also mentioned a fourth component that is sometimes understood as part of intersectionality, namely, *explanatory priority*. This is the thought that intersectional kinds have greater explanatory power than the single-moniker kinds that are their apparent 'constituents'—for example, that we can get further with our explanations if we use intersectional kinds such as *Black woman* rather than single-moniker kinds such as *Black* and *woman*.

I see no reason to accept *explanatory priority* as a blanket claim.[23] That is to say, I reject the claim that it is always the case that for any intersectional kind K

---

[22] For a similar view, see Gunnarsson 2017, 124–25.
[23] For a view that accords with this, see Crenshaw 2010. For a contrasting view, see Bernstein 2020.

and any set of other kinds (whether single-moniker or simply less complexly intersectional) that feature in K (K1, K2 . . . Kn), K has greater explanatory value than any of K1, K2 . . . Kn. Which level of granularity is most explanatory depends on the kinds in question and on the explanatory purposes; it's not always the case that a more granular kind is always more explanatory than a less granular kind. For example, in a certain context and for certain explanatory purposes, the kind *Asian woman* may be more explanatory than the kind *disabled Asian woman*, and the kind *upper-class White Anglo man* might be more explanatory than *upper-class White gay Anglo man*. I do allow that there may be specific cases in which certain intersectional kinds are consistently more explanatory than the corresponding single-moniker kinds, and I explore this idea more in Chapter 4. In general, however, the level of granularity that is most explanatory depends on the particular kinds in question and on our explanatory purposes; we cannot make a blanket claim about the priority of intersectional kinds over single-moniker kinds. The CEF, appropriately in my view, leaves this open on the level of human social kinds in general, although I will argue in Chapter 4 that we can and should say something more about certain race and gender kinds in particular.

Establishing the level of granularity that is helpful for a particular inquiry is a substantive task, and I take it that one of the lessons of intersectionality theory is that we ought to be very careful not to assume that the most general level of description is usually going to be the most helpful. Granted, this pluralist model is somewhat messier than one on which we *only* acknowledge the existence of the most coarse-grained, single-moniker kinds; but the social world *is* messy, and emancipatory theorists should expect some of this messiness to have to be reflected in our theories of it.

3.7. Advantages of a Pluralist Framework

The pluralist framework I have offered in this chapter, the CEF, gives us a unified overview of how different accounts of specific varieties of social kinds, such as those theorised by Brännmark, Ásta, and Mallon, fit together. This constitutes a novel contribution to our understanding of these social kinds. For example, although both Ásta (2018, 52) and Mallon (2016, 212) state that their accounts can be seen as largely compatible with each other, neither gives much explanation of how exactly we might understand the relationship between the two accounts. Brännmark (2019; 2021) is silent on the question of how institutional kinds relate to other social kinds. Using the framework developed here, we can tell a more detailed story about how the kinds identified by Brännmark, Ásta, and Mallon coexist in the same society.

The kinds theorised by Brännmark are the kinds we arrive at when we take a narrow focus on deontic interpersonal constraints and enablements within a particular context, and they can be specified at different levels of granularity. The kinds identified by Ásta are the kinds we arrive at when we take a slightly wider, but still rather narrow, focus on interpersonal constraints and enablements in general but still within a specific context. As with institutional kinds, these kinds can be specified at different levels of granularity, depending on what features are salient in the relevant social context (Ásta 2018, 124). The kinds identified by Mallon are the kinds at which we arrive if we take a broad focus on constraints and enablements, including the interpersonal, the psychological, and the structural, but adopting the limitation that they must relate to a common-knowledge conception of a social role. This limitation constrains granularity: the resulting kinds can only be as granular as the conceptions of social roles that people in the relevant society hold. For example, if people do not have a conception of the social role *disabled Black lesbian woman*, then we cannot specify a social kind at this level of granularity.[24]

Thus, the CEF offers us the resources to position these other accounts in relation to one another within a pluralist framework. Moreover, I take the CEF to be compatible with all three of these accounts, since it treats them as identifying different varieties of social kinds that are useful for different explanatory purposes, all of which are constituted by social constraints and enablements. The only way in which the CEF could be seen as contradicting these other accounts would be if we were to interpret those accounts as encouraging us to draw sharp boundaries around different sorts of constraints and enablements and *always* to theorise kinds based on these constraints and enablements separately, or if we were to read them as encouraging us to think that kinds based on one sort of constraints and enablements have *unique and overriding* explanatory power. I do not interpret any of the accounts as involving either sort of claim.

The CEF has advantages that go beyond Ritchie's structural account of feature social groups as nodes in social structures, which we encountered

---

[24] We can also arrive at kinds by taking a similarly broad focus on interrelated constraints and enablements without adopting a common-knowledge constraint; these kinds would be very similar to those identified by Mallon.

in §3.3.1. Ritchie takes her account to be compatible with various different specific accounts of the nature of particular social kinds (Ritchie 2020, 416). For example, she takes it to be compatible with Ásta's conferralist account of gender as well as with other non-conferralist accounts (2020, 416–17). However, Ritchie's account does not include apparatus for understanding how different accounts relate *to each other*. Whilst Ritchie compellingly makes the case that her structuralist framework is compatible with different accounts of the nature of specific kinds such as gender kinds, the account does not purport to help us figure out whether or not we must choose between these accounts, nor to give us resources for positioning them in relation to one another if they are deemed to be compatible. Thus, the CEF is a helpful supplement here as well.

3.8. Conclusion

In this chapter, I have introduced and motivated the constraints and enablements framework (CEF) for theorising constitutively constructed human social kinds. The CEF holds that a given human social kind is an explanatory kind that is unified by a particular bundle of social constraints and enablements. An individual is a member of a human social kind in virtue of falling under that bundle of constraints and enablements. What determines the bundle of constraints and enablements that unify a particular kind is the mechanisms that enable them to support explanation in the context of a particular explanatory project. A bundle of constraints and enablements is individuated by having a certain scope, breadth, and granularity:

1. **Scope:** The *context* in which the kind is explanatory.
2. **Breadth:** The *varieties* of constraints and enablements that are included in the bundle.
3. **Granularity:** The level of *generality* at which the constraints and enablements are specified.

This gives a framework for comparing different human social kinds and understanding how they relate to one another, because we can ask how they differ in terms of scope, breadth, and granularity and thereby map the relationships among them.

4

Hegemonic Race and Gender Kinds and Ontic Oppression

4.1. Introduction

In this chapter and the next two, I use the CEF to identify several different varieties of race and gender kinds that should be of particular interest to emancipatory theorists, and I assess, in each case, whether the kinds are ontically oppressive.[1] I will argue that whilst some varieties of race and gender kinds can straightforwardly be understood to be ontically oppressive, others cannot, and some even include kinds that play an important emancipatory role. A brief reminder of the definition of ontic oppression from Chapter 2:

> **Ontic oppression:** An individual suffers ontic oppression if and only if they are socially constructed as a member of a certain social kind where that construction consists, at least in part, of their being subjected to a set of social constraints and enablements that are systematically interrelated and that steer them towards social positions characterised by suffering at least one of the following: exploitation, marginalisation, powerlessness, cultural imperialism, violence, and communicative curtailment.

I will begin, in this chapter, by considering a variety of race and gender kinds that I term 'hegemonic kinds'. I first introduce these kinds and show how they are explanatorily important from an emancipatory perspective. I then discuss some details of how the kinds fit into the CEF and some different varieties of hegemonic kinds. Finally, I argue that many hegemonic kinds are ontically oppressive.

---

[1] My focus is on the ontology of gender (and race) kinds; note that a related but orthogonal debate concerns the ontology of gendered individuals (Witt 2011).

Ontology and Oppression. Katharine Jenkins, Oxford University Press. © Katharine Jenkins 2023.
DOI: 10.1093/oso/9780197666777.003.0005

Before I begin, I need to make an important point about how I will use language in talking about race and gender kinds. In this chapter and the next two, I aim to discuss some kinds in the world that I think have at least a prima facie claim to be understood as race and gender kinds. I am not giving an account of the meaning of race and gender terms, such as 'race', 'gender', 'Black', 'woman', 'White man', and so on. I follow Elizabeth Barnes in thinking that '[t]he project of developing a philosophical theory of gender can and should come apart from the project of giving definitions or truth conditions for sentences involving our gender terms' (Barnes 2020, 704), and I take this also to apply to race terms.

In Barnes's view, and mine, it is one thing to try to describe the social reality that explains gender (and race) and another thing to try to identify either the meaning of our gender (and race) terms or the precise people to whom they apply. Here I'm only engaging in the first of these tasks. In doing so, I use terms like 'race and gender kinds' to refer to kinds that are intuitively 'in the vicinity of' our race and gender talk, in the sense that if someone claimed that one of these kinds was the referent of our race and/or gender talk, we might agree or disagree, but we would not think that the person was deeply confused or that there had been a fundamental error of communication. To borrow Rowan Bell's evocative phrase, I am concerned with kinds that have '*travelled under the banner of* gender' (or, in this case, race) (Bell 2022, 9, emphasis in original). I am aiming to give an account of these kinds, understood as explanatory kinds. I intend my usage of terms such as 'race and gender kinds' to keep open the possibility that only some of these kinds, or indeed none of them, may turn out to be the referents either of our current everyday race and gender talk or of the race and gender talk we should be aiming to cultivate.

It is worth noting here that the CEF is a framework for theorising human *social* kinds. Using it to theorise race and gender kinds thus does not preclude us from acknowledging the existence of related non-social kinds. For example, some scholars of race have argued that races are biological kinds, which is to say that they are groupings of people that are unified by an explanatorily significant biological property or a cluster of biological properties. Nuanced forms of biological realism about race, framed as compatible with anti-racist commitments, have been defended by Robin Andreasen (2004; 2005), Philip Kitcher (2007), and Quayshawn Spencer (2014; 2018; 2019; Glasgow et al. 2019, pp. 73–110, 203–244; see also Jenkins 2019). Others claim that race kinds are 'thin kinds', in my terminology, that are unified by physical properties (Glasgow and Woodward 2015; see also Glasgow et al. 2019, 111–49 and 245–73). The members of a thin kind (also sometimes termed a 'basic kind') share a mind-independent property, but this property need not have any particular explanatory significance. In each case, these claims about non-social kinds can sit alongside the CEF, provided we interpret them in a pluralist spirit (i.e., as not denying that there may be other sorts of race kinds, in the sense of 'race kinds' just outlined). The same goes for gender/sex kinds.

4.2. Introducing Hegemonic Race and Gender Kinds

One way of conceiving of race and gender kinds that has been much discussed in the literature is to focus on large-scale patterns of constraints and enablements within a wide context, such as a country, a larger region, or even the whole world. Accounts of race and gender kinds of this sort have been developed by philosophers including Monique Wittig (1996) and Catharine MacKinnon (1989), with respect to gender; Charles W. Mills (1999), with respect to race; and Sally Haslanger (2012a), with respect to both race and gender. These accounts converge in identifying two important features of the large-scale patterns of constraints and enablements that constitute gender kinds. First, these constraints and enablements align with people who are taken to have certain bodily features, and, second, they exhibit a systematic pattern of subordination and domination.

In what follows, I will focus mainly on Haslanger's account, which is particularly useful for my purposes because it spans both gender and race kinds.[2] For Haslanger, being gendered as a man or a woman consists of occupying a certain hierarchical social role on the basis of having observed or imagined bodily features that are taken to indicate the role one can play in biological reproduction. To be a woman, for example, is to be regularly and for the most part subordinated on the basis of observed or imagined bodily features presumed to be evidence of a female's biological role in reproduction (Haslanger 2012a, 235). To be a man is to be regularly and for the most part privileged on the basis of observed or imagined bodily features

---

[2] Haslanger first proposed this account as an account of gender concepts ([2000] 2012a), specifically an ameliorative or prescriptive account, which is to say, an account of the concept as we ought to come to use it. However, in subsequent work (2005), she has suggested that the account might also capture gender kinds, and I am here considering the account as an account of gender kinds.

presumed to be evidence of a male's biological role in reproduction. With race, Haslanger focuses on relations of subordination and privilege based on social perceptions of the geographically marked body. So to be Black, for example, is to be regularly and for the most part subordinated on the basis of observed or imagined bodily features presumed to be evidence of ancestral links to Africa (237). To be White is to be privileged on the basis of observed or imagined bodily features presumed to be evidence of ancestral links to Europe.[3]

The basic thought here with respect to gender is that when we look at all the constraints and enablements that are at play across all different contexts in a given society—all the various schools, workplaces, homes, streets, and so on—the pattern that emerges is one in which those whose bodies are perceived as female are pushed towards subordinating social positions, and those whose bodies are perceived as male are pushed towards privileged social positions. The same goes for race with respect to ancestral links to geographic regions. It's important to note that the picture with race is more complicated than for gender, because ideologies of race vary more strongly between different societies.[4] For example, being Roma may be a possible way of being racialised in one country and not in another (for discussion, see Mallon 2004). Perhaps the most that can be said on a general level, following Mills (1999), is that in most societies, those whose bodies are perceived as indicating ancestral links solely to Europe are by and large directed towards privileged social positions, and those whose bodies are perceived as indicating ancestral links to other continents are pushed towards various different subordinated social positions.

How can we situate this account of race and gender kinds within the CEF? Recall that the CEF identifies three variables that can be used to individuate social kinds: scope (the context in which constraints and enablements are investigated), breadth (which varieties of constraints and enablements are taken into consideration), and granularity (the level of detail at which the

---

[3] Haslanger's account of gender resembles that of Wittig, and her account of race resembles that of Mills. MacKinnon's account of gender is slightly different in that she focuses specifically on *sexualised* (in the sense of 'eroticised') subordination and dominance; although MacKinnon's account is an important one, and although it shares many features with the account of structural gender kinds I will advocate, I do not find it plausible that *sexualised* hierarchy fully captures the relevant constraints and enablements. Accordingly, I follow Haslanger (and Wittig) in adopting a wider focus on various different aspects of subordination and privilege.

[4] This is not to say that ideologies of gender are completely without variation; see the discussion of colonialism and gender in §4.3. But ideologies of race exhibit more variation.

constraints and enablements are specified). Let us consider each of these three variables in turn.

In terms of scope, Haslanger's account and others like it adopt a very wide scope: something like the whole world over a time period of at least a few hundred years. In terms of breadth, the account seems to be picking up on the whole range of different varieties of constraints and enablements discussed in Chapter 3: interpersonal, psychological, bodily, and environmental.[5] Finally, in terms of granularity, the account is operating at a maximally course-grained level that yields single-moniker kinds such as *woman*, rather than intersectional kinds such as *Black woman*. Interpreted in this way, the key claim of the account is that when we adopt this focus in terms of scope, breadth, and granularity, the gender and race kinds we will identify are unified by a bundle of constraints and enablements that are subordinating or privileging (as the case may be for the kind in question), which tracks the fact of being perceived in a certain way with regard to one's reproductively or geographically marked body. I find this claim plausible.

I will term these kinds, as theorised within the CEF, 'hegemonic kinds', because looking at kinds in this broad-brushstroke way brings into focus only the most dominant social dynamics.[6] We can think of this similarly to zooming out on a picture: what stays visible when we lose the fine-grained detail is the largest and most strongly marked lines, the most sharply differentiated areas of colour, and so on. For now, I will define hegemonic kinds as having a very wide scope, having maximally expansive breadth, and being at least fairly coarse-grained; I will discuss the parameters for scope and granularity in more detail in §4.3.

Hegemonic kinds capture the high-level patterns and regularities produced by interlocking constraints and enablements affecting individuals who stand in social relations to one another and to other phenomena such as material resources. Since, as I explained in Chapter 2, oppression also relates to the complex interlocking of constraints and enablements in people's lives as a whole, hegemonic kinds have significant explanatory value for emancipatory theorists. As Lola Olufemi says, 'While it is important to start locally and build movements in our communities, the most radical work is work

[5] Mills's discussion highlights especially clearly the psychological and environmental constraints and enablements involved in the construction of hegemonic race kinds (1999, 41–89).

[6] The term 'hegemonic kinds' may bring to mind the concept of 'hegemonic masculinity' (Connell 1987; for discussion, see Connell and Messerschmidt 2005). While there is certainly a general connection here, I am not intending to use the term 'hegemonic' in precisely the way is it used in the literature on 'hegemonic masculinity', nor do I take my discussion here to rely on that literature.

that looks beyond borders and nations, and finds subversive ways to link the work of oppressed people across the world' (2020, 17). Hegemonic race and gender kinds link the social situations of people across the world who are oppressed in relation to these dimensions of experience.

To be clear, this account of hegemonic race and gender kinds is completely compatible with there being *specific social contexts* in which other characteristics of people serve as prompts for differential forms of treatment—for example, social spaces in which gender self-ascription is what prompts people to respond differently to individuals they meet, rather than perception of bodily features linked to reproduction (I return to this point in Chapter 5). The claim is simply that if we look at the *overall patterns* of what people are and are not able to do across society as a whole, what we will see is a tendency for those with differently marked bodies to be subject to different sets of constraints and enablements, some more subordinating and others more privileging. The types of marked bodies that are significant *here*—that is, which best serve to predict these broad patterns—are reproductively marked bodies, in the case of gender, and geographically marked bodies, in the case of race.

One might wonder why the focus for gender is on the reproductively *marked* body, rather than simply the reproductive body *as such*. The claim I am making—following Haslanger and others—is not that reproductive capabilities in themselves do not matter. Clearly, experiences such as pregnancy and childbirth, for example, are of huge personal and social significance in and of themselves and also play a role in maintaining social structures. Rather, the claim is that the patterns of subordination that surround reproductive differences are also related to those differences via social perceptions. For example, a woman who is not, in fact, capable of becoming pregnant but who is *perceived* as capable of becoming pregnant may nevertheless be discriminated against in a hiring process in this regard. So it is social perceptions that serve as the best predictor for people becoming caught up in social structures of subordination and privilege. This is partly because social perceptions of these features do often match up with actual capabilities. Accordingly, taking this view is compatible with thinking that bodily differences that are not socially produced play a role in constituting hegemonic gender kinds also, for example by being part of a homeostatic property cluster.[7]

---

[7] For further discussion, see §3.5.4.

4.3. Hegemonic Race and Gender Kinds, Scope, and Granularity

I have said that I take hegemonic kinds to have a *very* wide scope, to have a *maximally* expansive breadth, and to be at least *fairly* coarse-grained. The maximally expansive breadth is clear-cut, but I want to return to consider scope and granularity in more detail. I have described the variables of scope, breadth, and granularity as being like sliders on a sound-mixing board. To extend this metaphor, although these sliders can be adjusted separately, some combinations of settings will give a muddy, tinny, or otherwise unpleasing sound, while other combinations of settings will exhibit synergy. It is the same with the variables of the CEF: some combinations of settings for scope, breadth, and granularity will have a kind of synergy in virtue of which they will tend to have high explanatory value, while others will have a kind of anti-synergy that makes them likely to have little explanatory value, if any.

For example, with hegemonic kinds, there is a weak sort of synergy between the wide scope and the expansive breadth. To see how this works, we could look at a high-breadth kind within a certain specific social space—a public library, for example—and there would be some patterns of interaction between interpersonal, psychological, and environmental constraints and enablements in this context; but we will get much richer patterns of interaction if we increase our scope to the town or city as a whole and still more so if we broaden it further to the country as a whole. This is both because the constraints and enablements continue to interact and produce patterns as individuals move between more particular social spaces and because the constraints and enablements play out over the course of people's lives. However, there are some limitations to this: as we widen our scope more and more, we may end up trying to describe constraints and enablements that are so varied that the description of them that we can offer becomes more and more minimal, until it ceases to be informative.

Many discussions of (what I am calling) hegemonic kinds imply a very wide scope but do not precisely specify *how* wide. My suspicion is that the scope that gives us the most illuminating results will often stop short of being the whole world, because the variations between the dynamics of race and gender oppression vary significantly in different geographical regions. I suspect that we will be well advised to begin by trying to specify hegemonic kinds on something like the level of particular countries or regions and adjust up and down to suit our particular explanatory purposes. This is what I mean by saying that hegemonic kinds have a very wide scope.

Turning now to granularity, it is significant that the structural accounts of race and gender proposed by Haslanger, Mills, and Wittig all adopt a maximally coarse-grained approach, dealing with what I term single-moniker categories such as *woman* and *White*.[8] However, there is reason to think that a slightly more granular approach, dealing in race–gender intersectional kinds such as *White woman*, will often be more useful to emancipatory theorists. This is why I did not want to *define* hegemonic kinds as being maximally coarse-grained. Thinking about the granularity of hegemonic kinds is important in relation to intersectionality.

In Chapter 2, I argued that intersectionality, understood as a 'framework checker' (Garry 2011), requires us to recognise that race and gender, for example, are non-additive, are non-separable, and involve cross-constitution. Accordingly, if we want to understand the hegemonic kind *Black woman*, for instance, we cannot merely take what we know about those who are subordinated on the basis of being perceived to be female and those who are subordinated on the basis of being perceived to have ancestral links to Africa and assume that Black women experience 'both' forms of subordination. Rather, we need to look specifically at the way those who are perceived as *both* female *and* ancestrally linked to Africa are constrained and enabled, treating this as a distinctive form of subordination.

When introducing intersectionality in Chapter 2, I also mentioned what is sometimes understood to be a fourth component of intersectionality that I do not in general accept: *explanatory priority*. This is the idea that intersectional categories have greater explanatory power than the single-moniker kinds that are their apparent 'constituents'—that as a rule, we can get further with our explanations if we use intersectional kinds such as *Black woman* rather than single-moniker kinds such as *Black* and *woman*. As I explained in Chapter 3, I see no reason to accept *explanatory priority* as a blanket claim about kinds in general. Rather, I hold that the level of granularity that will be most explanatory depends on the particular kinds in question and the explanatory interests with which they are approached. However, it is nevertheless the case, in my view, that intersectional race and gender kinds *specifically* do very often have greater explanatory value than race or gender single-moniker kinds for the purposes of the emancipatory theorist. This is

---

[8] Jones 2014 critically discusses this feature of Haslanger's account.

due to the deep intertwinement of these kinds in processes of colonisation and exploitation.

Maria Lugones's (2007) account of the relationship between race and gender shows how these kinds as we know them have been, and still are, produced, reproduced, and enforced in conjunction with one another, as well as with categories of class and sexuality. This happens through the workings of capitalist colonialism and results in a situation in which racialised and gendered embodiment cannot be sharply separated. Lugones draws on the insights of Third World and women of colour feminists and of theorists of coloniality to describe this 'colonial/modern gender system':

> Colonialism did not impose precolonial, European gender arrangements on the colonized. It imposed a new gender system that created very different arrangements for colonized males and females than for white bourgeois colonizers. Thus, it introduced many genders and gender itself is a colonial concept and mode of organization of relations of production, property relations, of cosmologies and ways of knowing. (2007, 186)

An example of this process, which Lugones discusses, is the imposition of gender roles on Yoruba society, as theorised by Oyèrónkẹ́ Oyěwùmí (1997). Prior to colonisation, Yoruba concepts existed that correspond roughly to 'anatomical male' (okunrin) and 'anatomical female' (obinrin), which are often translated as 'men' and 'women'. However, these categories are importantly different from European categories of 'men' and 'women' in that they are not binary opposites, nor are they hierarchically related. The imposition of European gender categories on Yoruba people through processes of colonisation resulted in the exclusion of women from leadership roles and state structures, in contrast to social practices prior to colonisation. Thus, colonialism created not only a subordinated class of racialised colonial subjects in contrast to European colonisers but *also* a subordinated class of *colonised women* through the introduction of hierarchical gender as an organising social principle.

Another example, which Lugones does not use but which in my view fits with her analysis, is the de-gendering effects of the processes to which enslaved Black people were subjected in North American chattel slavery. As Hortense Spillers (1987) has argued, the conceptualisation and social positioning of Black people as property often overrode the social marking of individuals as male and female. For example, captive Africans were often treated as cargo to be packed as densely as possible into the holds of ships without differentiation between male and female individuals. To the extent that socially marking gender often involves differentiating between those understood as male and those understood as female, especially in the context of organising intimate spaces, this undifferentiated treatment can be understood as *de-gendering* in the sense that considerations of profit displaced rules of gendered behaviour as an organising social principle (Spillers 1987, 72). 'Under these conditions', Spillers writes, 'we lose at least *gender* difference *in the outcome*, and the female body and the male body become a territory of cultural and political manoeuvre not at all gender-related, gender-specific' (67, emphasis in original).

Building on Spillers's analysis, Christina Sharpe also analyses how similar processes continue to occur in the 'spaces of terror' of contemporary racist societies. For example, she describes a group of Black women being stopped and searched by male police officers ostensibly looking for a male rapist. Sharpe argues that in this situation, the logic of "protecting women" from the terror of male violence does not extend to the Black women who are terrorised by the police search itself. 'Once again', Sharpe writes, echoing Spillers, 'in these spaces of terror, heteronormative Euro-gender relations disappear in the outcome' (Sharpe 2016, 85). Heteronormative Euro-gender relations would prohibit the male police officers' search of the women, classifying it as a violation of their gendered modesty, dignity, or privacy (for related discussion, see Bettcher 2017). However, the women's status as Black makes them targets for just such an intrusion, and, ironically, this intrusion can even be presented as a way of 'protecting women'. Evidently, the women who are presumed to merit protection are not *these* women, and the threats from which they are deemed to need protection are not conceived of as including the male police officers who stop and search them. This shows us that being racialised as Black can still place someone outside the purview of at least certain conceptualisations of gender in at least some contexts.

Overall, then, there is a stark contrast between gender arrangements for people racialised other than as White and for people racialised as White. To overlook these different constructions of gender is to lay a shaky foundation for feminist action, as Lugones (2007) and others (hooks 2000; Spelman 1990) point out, and the parallel point can be made about opposition to racial oppression that fails to account for gender difference (Lugones 2007; Crenshaw 1991). This motivates Lugones's claim that these important differences find expression in the ontology of gender and race, such that women racialised as White and women racialised other than as White, for example, do not occupy the same gender category (Lugones 2007; see also Curry 2017 for a related point concerning masculinity).

It is worth noting here that Lugones's analysis changes in some important ways between the 2007 paper on which I am focusing here and her later work (Lugones 2010), in which a similar evidence base is used to argue that gender is seen as a social status reserved for colonisers, with the dehumanisation of colonised people resulting in their exclusion from gender categories altogether. I have focused on her earlier work because it fits my analysis in this chapter better, but it would be interesting to explore this contrast in more detail. However, engaging with this issue is unfortunately beyond the scope of this chapter. The key point for my purposes here is that the specific histories of colonialism and slavery, and their implications for gender as well as more obviously for race, mean that emancipatory theorists have good reason to engage with hegemonic kinds that are defined at a more granular level that engages the intersection of race and gender.

It is a virtue of the CEF that, as a pluralist framework, it can allow for the existence of *both* maximally coarse-grained single-moniker hegemonic race and gender kinds of the sort characterised by Haslanger *and* more fine-grained intersectional hegemonic race–gender kinds of the sort characterised by Lugones. To the extent that each has some explanatory value for specific purposes, each exists according to the framework, and I think they are similar enough to both be included under the label 'hegemonic kinds'. My contention here, though, is that the intersectional race–gender kinds are very often the ones that we need in order to do explanatory work in the service of emancipatory theory, given the dangers inherent in overlooking racialised difference when theorising gender, for example.

To be clear, I am not claiming that the hegemonic single-moniker race and gender kinds picked out by Haslanger's definitions, for instance, are such that they *in themselves* inappropriately erase the intersectional nature of these kinds or that their use should be avoided *in all cases*. I am merely suggesting that we should be careful to select the level of granularity that best serves our explanatory purposes and that we will very often—though not always—make more headway, as emancipatory theorists, by thinking in terms of hegemonic intersectional race–gender kinds rather than in terms of hegemonic gender kinds that are undifferentiated by race and hegemonic race kinds that are undifferentiated by gender.[9] This is not because of any blanket tendency for more fine-grained kinds to be more explanatory but because of the specific ways in which race and gender categories have been co-constructed through social structures and ideologies that are at once capitalist, colonialist, patriarchal, and heterosexist.

If it is helpful to approach hegemonic social kinds as fine-grained to this extent, we might wonder whether it would be even more helpful to define them in even more fine-grained ways. I think this is worth exploring, although I cannot do so here for reasons of space. However, I think there is a limit to how fine-grained we can go whilst keeping such a wide scope. This is because there is a kind of anti-synergy between looking at kinds across a very expansive range of social settings and looking at highly complex intersectional kinds. The level of detail we would gain by going more fine-grained is cancelled out by the fact that the only generalisations we can make need to range across a broad context. As we reach a certain level of detail, we will no longer be able to say anything general enough to apply across the context in question. This is not to say that we should not consider significantly more fine-grained kinds, but when we do so, we should probably not think of ourselves as exploring hegemonic kinds but rather be willing to adjust the scope slider to focus on a narrower context and treat this as a different variety of kind.

4.4. Hegemonic Gender Kinds and Gender Modality

Alongside attending closely to hegemonic intersectional race–gender kinds for the reasons just outlined, emancipatory theorists need to pay close attention to more fine-grained hegemonic gender kinds in order to capture the social situation of trans people. The account of hegemonic gender kinds I have been working with so far has two features that call for further discussion in this regard: it emphasises the reproductively marked body, and it is binary. It is important to clarify how trans people are positioned in relation to hegemonic gender kinds, so understood.

Let me emphasise here two points. First, hegemonic gender kinds are just one variety of gender kinds among several that I shall discuss in this chapter and the next two. In describing hegemonic gender kinds, I do not take myself

---

[9] I take my position here to be in agreement with that of Crenshaw 2010.

to be describing everything that gender is. Second, the account of hegemonic gender kinds that I am proposing here aims to capture the actual patterns of different constraints and enablements that exist in society. It is not intended to provide a recommendation for how gender kinds *should* exist or (as I said in the introduction to this chapter) for how we should use gender terms. Furthermore, it is not intended to function as a normative basis for feminist action (on the latter point, see Mikkola 2016). In this sense, the account is descriptive rather than prescriptive.

On a descriptive level, it is undeniable that Western society is extremely cissexist and that gendered social practices, background ideologies, and so on, are heavily shaped by a binary and biological notion of sex difference: being perceived as having female or male bodily features does usually function as a cue for differential (and hierarchical) social treatment, where this treatment has cumulative psychological, bodily, and environmental implications. These social practices and ideologies are extremely harmful, including to trans people. At the most coarse-grained or broad-brushstroke level—generalising across many different social contexts—a pattern emerges from these practices and ideologies in which those perceived as female are subordinated and those perceived as male are privileged. To say that this is the case is not to endorse those social practices and ideologies, nor is it to deny that these dynamics manifest in distinctive ways for those who are trans, as Talia Mae Bettcher, among others, has shown (2007).

A trans person's membership in structural gender kinds at this maximally coarse-grained level is based on how they are perceived and accordingly socially positioned, rather than how they identify. Accordingly, some trans women are members of the hegemonic gender kind *woman*, whilst others are members of the hegemonic gender kind *man*, and vice versa for trans men. In most Western societies, it's not yet possible to be regularly and for the most part perceived as non-binary; many non-binary people are regularly and for the most part perceived as cis men or as cis women, and this determines their membership in a hegemonic gender kind. (There are some exceptions to this, however, to which I shall return.)

Of course, though, there are also differences in the constraints and enablements facing trans and cis women, just as there are differences in the constraints and enablements facing straight and queer women, for example. And the same applies for trans and cis men. These differences don't render maximally coarse-grained hegemonic kinds useless, but they do mean that we *also* need more fine-grained hegemonic gender kinds, kinds such as *trans woman* and *cis woman*, as well as more complexly intersectional kinds that include race, such as *Black trans woman* and *Asian cis woman*.

I am inclined to think that at least within the contemporary United Kingdom, and perhaps many other places, the trans/cis contrast shares with race and gender a hierarchical nature: on the whole, trans people are systematically subordinated, and cis people are systematically privileged. As Riki Wilchins puts it, describing the United States, 'Being transsexual is like a tax: you pay it to get a job, rent an apartment, find a lover, just exist' (2017, 160; see also Bailey, Ellis, and McNeil 2014; Pearce 2018). In a phrasing that echoes that of Wilchins, Eva Hayward frames this subordination in terms of a social imperative directed at trans people in general and at trans women of colour in particular: 'Don't exist' (Hayward 2017, 191).

However, when it comes to the feature that predicts the constraints and enablements, I don't think it makes most sense to think about being trans in terms of marked bodies, as with gender and race. Being trans as such is usually defined in terms of having a gender identity that is different from the gender identity one was assigned at birth. In this sense, being trans is not just a matter of how people perceive one's body but rather a matter of the relationship between one's identity and the social position towards which one was initially directed in virtue of the social meaning of one's body at birth.[10] It is *this* property, which Florence Ashley (2022) has aptly termed 'gender modality', that is most strongly linked to a differentiated pattern of constraints and enablements.

Accordingly, I propose to understand the hegemonic kind *trans* as constituted by constraints and enablements that are subordinating and that align with experiencing a contrast between one's gender identity and one's gender assigned at birth. Conversely, I will understand the hegemonic kind *cis* as constituted by constraints and enablements that are privileging and that align with experiencing a correspondence between one's gender identity and one's gender assigned at birth.

Furthermore, I'd like to tentatively suggest that even on the most coarse-grained level, the hegemonic gender kinds of *men* and *women* are not exhaustive. Although there is a very strong tendency for people to interpret the bodily features of others so as to categorise them as male or female, even if this means selectively attending to some features and not others, this

---

[10] I discuss gender identity in much more detail in Chapter 6. For now, I invite readers to work with an everyday sense of gender identity as the way one experiences and/or conceives of one's gender.

tendency does not always yield a binary outcome. In cases where it does not, the individual in question is often perceived, in very negative terms, as a gender anomaly (see Barnes 2020, 716). Wilchins (2017) coins the phrase 'gendertrash', meaning *that which is rejected and thoroughly devalued by the gender system*, to capture those placed in this situation. Conceptions of monstrousness may even enter the picture (see, e.g., Stryker 1994). There are some people who are consistently interpreted as gender anomalies in this way and as a result directed strongly towards severely subordinated social positions.

This suggests that there may be a third hegemonic gender kind: those whose reproductively marked bodies register regularly and for the most part as *anomalous* and who are severely subordinated as a result. Some trans people—including, although not only, some non-binary people—are members of this hegemonic gender kind, though many are not, and some cis people may also be members of this hegemonic gender kind (see, e.g., the experiences described in Watson 2016). Again, here I want to be cautious regarding scope; this analysis seems to me to accurately capture the social situation at present in the United Kingdom, the United States, and probably some other parts of the world, but it should not be assumed to apply in all social locations, given the various different cultural practices that exist concerning genders other than *man* and *woman*.

C. Riley Snorton (2017) has argued that the intimate co-production of race and gender described in the previous section has particular implications for the relationship of gender modality to race (see also Bey 2017; Gill-Peterson 2018). For example, Snorton argues that the un-gendering of enslaved persons identified by Spillers, and described earlier, was at play when fugitive slaves used 'cross-dressing' to avoid recapture, giving rise to 'an understanding of gender as mutable and as an amendable form of being' (2017, 57) that paved the way for contemporary conceptualisations of trans identities. Snorton's nuanced investigation proceeds primarily via a selection of complex case studies, but insofar as an overall analysis can be briefly summarised, I take this to be that we should understand the often-violent social processes that give rise to race and gender categories—categories that superficially and misleadingly appear to be stable and fixed—as inextricably intertwined in a way that closely links Black experience with trans experience. Or, as Jules Gill-Peterson puts it, 'Blackness problematises the category trans—and vice versa' (2018, 25).

On this analysis, as Snorton puts it, 'to feel black in the diaspora ... may be a trans experience' (2017, 8), insofar as to be socially positioned as Black is already to stand in a precarious relationship to dominant social practices of gender categorisation. Moreover, 'sex and gender [are] racial arrangements' (Snorton 2017, 11), in that racist violence—for example, the torture of enslaved Black women in the name of gynaecological research—has played a central role in producing and stabilising social conceptions of sex and gender difference. To link this back to my discussion in §4.3, Snorton's analysis highlights once again the need for emancipatory theorists to pay close attention to hegemonic intersectional race–gender kinds, where this intersection includes gender modality.

4.5. Hegemonic Race and Gender Kinds and Ontic Oppression

Those hegemonic race and gender kinds (including gender modality kinds and various intersectional kinds) that are characterised by subordination rather than privilege—being a woman or a gender anomaly, being trans, the various ways of being racialised other than as White, and the intersections thereof—are all ontically oppressive. This follows quite naturally from the accounts of these hegemonic kinds that have been given. The kinds are constituted by interlocking constraints and enablements that have an overall tendency, where that tendency is a subordinating one. This neatly fits the definition of ontic oppression—indeed, I take it that to describe hegemonic race and gender kinds as ontically oppressive is mostly to draw out and to formalise a thought that is implicitly present in many accounts of these kinds.

On these accounts, what it is to be a member of a particular race and gender kind *is*, at least in part, to be constrained and enabled in certain systematic ways. It's not only that, for example, a Black person is more likely to be stopped, assaulted, or murdered by the police; it's that *being* more likely to be stopped, assaulted, or murdered by the police *is part of what constitutes the person's being Black*. The further step I want to take—which I take to be a modest one—is to say that every Black person, including the person who is *never* stopped, assaulted, or murdered by the police, has been wronged by this state of affairs. The concept of ontic oppression serves to bring this wrong involved in hegemonic race and gender kinds characterised by subordination into sharper focus.

Recognising these hegemonic race and gender kinds as ontically oppressive fits particularly closely with analyses of the continuities that persist through the shift from more formalised or de jure forms of racial and gender oppression to more informal or de facto forms. For example, Sharpe argues, with regard to the US context, that 'the means and modes of Black subjection may have changed, but the fact and structure of that subjection remain' (2016, 12), and she goes on to describe this subjection as an 'ontological negation' (14).

An example that fits this analysis is the continuity between killings of Black people in law-enforcement contexts and historic forms of officially or informally sanctioned violence against Black people, notably lynching and fugitive slave laws. For instance, Stephen C. Ferguson II and John H. McClendon III (2013), Timothy Joseph Golden (2013), and Vanessa Wills (2013) all discuss the killing of Trayvon Martin, a seventeen-year-old young Black man, who was shot and killed by George Zimmerman, a neighbourhood watch member, in Florida in February 2012. Zimmerman had followed Martin as he walked home from a shop, and he claimed to have been acting in self-defence under Florida's notorious 'Stand Your Ground' law. He was charged with murder and acquitted.

Ferguson and McClendon describe the presumption that Martin was obliged to prove to Zimmerman's satisfaction that he was entitled to be in the gated community as being '[a]kin to a runaway slave or the pass laws of former Apartheid South Africa' (2013, 50). In a similar spirit, Golden compares Martin's death to an incident from the autobiography of Frederick Douglass in which Demby, a slave, runs into a creek to escape a flogging from the overseer. The overseer orders him to come out and shoots him dead when he refuses. Golden observes:

> Demby had neither the protection of the positive law nor the social and cultural practices of his day. And although the positive law has changed, Trayvon Martin is in a situation that is worse than Demby's: the positive law affirms his humanity, but the social and cultural context does not. (2013, 79)

I agree with Golden that the continuity between the two cases is striking, and although I am not sure to what extent it is possible to determine whether or not Martin's situation is straightforwardly 'worse' than Demby's, there is certainly something particularly perverse about the mismatch between formal laws about the right to life of Black people and the frequency and impunity with which they are killed. Wills highlights the fact that the lack of formal laws supporting this frequency and impunity does not prevent us from accurately understanding the racial basis on which differential vulnerabilities are structured. When Wills asked her students to consider a situation analogous to Martin's death involving a White seventeen-year-old being pursued by a Black adult man, '[t]he classroom rippled with nervous laughter. . . . The students recognized [the scenario] as totally impossible—and indeed, it might as well be a piece of science fiction' (2013, 230).

These discussions of the killing of Martin highlight the continuing 'fact and structure' of Black subjection to which Sharpe refers. On my view, this social structure gives rise to a kind—the hegemonic race kind *Black*—that is ontically oppressive, where that ontic oppression carries through from times of explicit enslavement of Black people to the current situation of more informally maintained racial oppression. The wrongful constraints and enablements that constitute the hegemonic kind *Black* are very similar, despite being maintained by different 'means and modes'.[11] As Saidiya Hartman puts it:

> black lives are still imperilled and devalued by a racial calculus and a political arithmetic that were entrenched centuries ago. This is the afterlife of slavery—skewed life chances, limited access to health and education, premature death, incarceration, and impoverishment. (2007, 6)

This 'afterlife of slavery' amounts, on my account, to a continued ontic oppression enacted through the hegemonic kind *Black*. The wrong of this ontic oppression is ultimately a moral injury (a form of *devaluation*, to echo Hartman) that affects everyone who is constructed as a member of that kind.

A similar continuity of ontic oppression can be seen with regards to other hegemonic kinds, such as gender. For example, the marital rape exemption discussed in Chapter 1—the law that prevented non-consensual sex within marriage from being considered a crime—was formally ended in England and Wales in 1991 (and in Scotland two years previously). Yet the 'afterlife' of this law can be detected in the high number of women experiencing severe sexual violence, where more than half of those cases involve a perpetrator who is the victim's current partner.[12] The chances of a given instance of

---

[11] Another example of similar constraints and enablements being enacted by different means is the ways in which racist regimes of criminalisation and incarceration play a similar role to that played in the past by laws upholding forced labour, disenfranchisement, and segregation (Alexander 2012).

[12] One in five women in England and Wales reports experiencing some form of sexual offence at least once since the age of sixteen, and one in twenty reports experiencing rape, attempted rape, sexual assault, or attempted sexual assault. The Ministry of Justice estimates that about 85,000 women

severe sexual violence resulting in a legal conviction are vanishingly small.[13] This picture suggests that the legacy of sexist laws such as the marital rape exemption still shapes the social and cultural context severely constraining women's ability to uphold their sexual autonomy (for discussion, see, e.g., Card 1991; Brison 2003). This constraint is part of the ontic oppression suffered by members of the hegemonic kind *women*.

Let me here make an important aside: although I am pointing to low conviction rates for rape—and indeed in relation to the killing of Black people—as evidence for the presence of ontic oppression, I do not intend thereby to endorse criminal and carceral systems as appropriate responses to harm. Rather, my claim is that *whilst* such systems *are* the socially sanctioned response to serious harm, the fact that they systematically overlook certain forms of harm creates effective impunities that are morally and politically significant. When rape, especially by a current partner, is so underreported and underprosecuted as to be effectively legal, and when someone can shoot and kill an unarmed Black teenager who is walking in his own neighbourhood without being convicted of murder, those targeted by these harms are devalued and wronged. One can (and I do) think this whilst *also* thinking that a truly just response to harm would require a radical and fundamental social shift away from our present criminal and carceral systems, institutions, and logics.

The constraints and enablements that I have discussed so far are all obviously such as to be oppressive to any human individual who falls under them. Accordingly, the type of ontic oppression I have identified is one that is suffered by *all* human individuals who are socially constructed as members of the relevant hegemonic race and gender kinds. I think there is a further type of ontic oppression that is suffered only by *some* members of these kinds and that is also suffered by *some* members of other hegemonic kinds that are associated with privilege. However, in order to explain this second form of ontic oppression affecting structural race and gender kinds, I need to have

per year suffer one of these crimes in England and Wales, compared with 12,000 men, and of these women, 56 percent were raped or assaulted by their current partner (Ministry of Justice 2013).

[13] In England and Wales, only 15 percent of women who experience rape and other forms of sexual assault report the incident to the police, and only 7 percent of reported rapes result in a conviction. The possibility of multiple offences being committed by the same person or perpetrated against the same person makes it difficult to estimate the proportion of actual rapes that result in a rape conviction. However, combining the 7 percent conviction rate for reported rapes with the 15 percent reporting rate for rape and other sexual assaults would suggest that the percentage of actual rapes that result in a rape conviction is around 1 percent (Ministry of Justice 2013).

some further varieties of race and gender kinds, notably *identity* kinds, on the table. Accordingly, I will reserve discussion of this type of ontic oppression for Chapter 6, when I will have introduced those kinds.

4.6. Conclusion

I have introduced hegemonic race and gender kinds, which capture the high-level patterns and regularities produced by interlocking constraints and enablements affecting individuals who are subordinated or privileged based on their reproductively and/or geographically marked body. In terms of the three variables of the CEF, hegemonic kinds have a very wide scope, have a maximally expansive breadth, and are at least *fairly* coarse-grained. With regard to the last, I argued that whilst existing accounts of hegemonic race and gender kinds tend to focus on single-moniker kinds, hegemonic intersectional race–genderkinds very often have greater explanatory value than hegemonic single-moniker race or gender kinds for the purposes of the emancipatory theorist, due to the ways in which race and gender have been co-constructed through social structures and ideologies that are at once capitalist, colonialist, patriarchal, and heterosexist.

Furthermore, I suggested that our understanding of hegemonic kinds should include the gender modality kinds *trans* and *cis* and a gender kind something like *gender anomaly* that sits alongside the gender kinds *man* and *woman*. I also highlighted the importance of attending to the intersections not only of gender modality kinds and gender kinds (e.g., *trans woman*) but also to the intersection of both of these with race kinds (e.g., *Black trans woman*). Finally, I argued that all hegemonic race and gender kinds (including gender modality kinds) that are characterised by subordination rather than privilege—being a woman or a gender anomaly, being trans, the various ways of being racialised other than as White, and the intersections thereof—are ontically oppressive. Recognising them as such brings into focus the wrong suffered by all members of those kinds, as well as helping to highlight the continuity across the shift from more overt to more covert forms of racial and gendered oppression.

5

Interpersonal Race and Gender Kinds and Ontic Oppression

5.1. Introduction

In Chapter 4, when I introduced hegemonic race and gender kinds, I acknowledged that these kinds may not capture what it means to be gendered or racialised in a certain way in a specific context. Fortunately, there is a second variety of race and gender kinds that philosophers have identified that can help us here: kinds grounded by *interpersonal* constraints and enablements only, in a given, narrowly defined context. These are the sorts of kinds picked out by Ásta's conferralist account of social categories (2018), which I discussed in Chapter 1 and in Chapter 3. As I explained there, Ásta holds that constraints and enablements, amounting to a social status, are conferred upon an agent A in a social context by the actions and attitudes of other agents in the context, which are typically a response to some perceived feature or features of A (the 'base property') to produce what she terms 'social categories'. I take these to be explanatory kinds in the sense discussed in Chapter 3, and I will term them 'interpersonal kinds' because they are grounded by interpersonal constraints and enablements and not by other varieties of constraints and enablements.

In this chapter, I first introduce interpersonal race and gender kinds, drawing on Ásta's account of social categories. I then show how they fit into the CEF and argue for a particular understanding of the role that deontic normativity plays in constructing interpersonal kinds, which is a point of departure from Ásta's account. Finally, I argue that some interpersonal race and gender kinds are ontically oppressive, but others are not, and some even have an emancipatory function.

Ontology and Oppression. Katharine Jenkins, Oxford University Press. © Katharine Jenkins 2023.
DOI: 10.1093/oso/9780197666777.003.0006

5.2. Introducing Interpersonal Race and Gender Kinds

5.2.1. Ásta on Conferred Properties

A prominent account of what I am here calling 'interpersonal kinds' is Ásta's account of social categories.[1] This account is especially useful for my purposes because it is a general account of social categories that is specifically applied to both race kinds and gender kinds. Accordingly, I adopt it as a starting point for theorising interpersonal race and gender kinds.

Ásta holds that social categories depend on conferred properties: constraints and enablements, amounting to a social status, are conferred upon an agent A in a social context by the actions and attitudes of other agents in the context, which are typically a response to some perceived feature or features of A. To be a member of a social category is to have the relevant social status. Ásta offers a schema to show how conferrals work, which consists of five aspects that matter in a conferral.

Conferred property: what property is conferred...

Who: who the [conferring] subjects are....

What: what attitude, state, or action of the subjects matters....

When: under what conditions the conferral takes place....

Base property: what the subjects are attempting to track (consciously or not), if anything.... (2018, 8)

I want to expand on this conferral schema by adding a further component, which I will term the 'indictor property'. This is because I think it will be helpful for the schema to reflect the fact that sometimes the way the subjects attempt to track the base property runs via another property. That is, it may be that subjects respond differently to different people based on an immediate cue, but the reason they respond to this cue is that they think it is evidence of some other property, which is what really matters to them.

An example of this is military uniforms and military rank. Military uniforms function to communicate information about the wearer's rank. When a member of the military responds to other members of the military whom they

---

[1] Ásta's account is informed by, and has features in common with, Butler's performative account of gender (Ásta 2018, 54–69; see Butler 1990; 1993).

do not know personally, uniform functions as an immediate indicator of rank which guides responses. But of course, what the person is really trying to track (i.e., the base property) is the official record of the other people's rank; wearing a certain uniform only guides their responses because it is a reliable indicator for this official record of rank. If a member of the military found out that another member was wearing a uniform that did not tally with the official record of their rank, it is that record that would guide responses going forward, not the uniform. Call a property that functions in this way an 'indicator property'.

> Indicator property: what the subjects are using as a proxy for, or evidence of, the base property (consciously or not), if anything.

In general, identifying indicator properties is important because indicator properties are frequently strongly policed, with penalties being applied to those who are perceived as displaying a misleading indicator property. Moreover, they are often policed *precisely because* of their role in organising conferrals. The case of military uniforms is a good example of this: there tend to be severe penalties for wearing a uniform to which one's rank does not entitle one. Indicator properties will therefore often be relevant to how systems of social kinds are maintained. Of course, not every social status property will include an indicator property, because in many cases, the subjects are able to access the base property directly. I'll argue shortly that including a space for 'indicator property' in the conferral schema helps us when it comes to understanding race and gender interpersonal kinds.

I propose to understand interpersonal kinds roughly in line with Ásta's account of social categories. Within the CEF, interpersonal kinds can be understood as narrow in scope (focusing on a tightly defined context) and restricted in breadth (focusing only on interpersonal constraints and enablements). As with hegemonic kinds, interpersonal kinds have usually been discussed at a very coarse-grained level, but I will show in §5.3 that they can be defined at various different levels of granularity, including finer levels than are possible with hegemonic kinds.

5.2.2. Institutional Kinds and Communal Kinds

Ásta's account of (what I am calling) interpersonal kinds distinguishes between two sorts of kinds: institutional kinds and communal kinds. What she terms 'institutional properties' are conferred by those in positions of formal authority (which is to say, a collectively recognised status that entitles them to make decisive pronouncements on the relevant matters) and involve explicitly deontic constraints and enablements, such as rights and duties. By contrast, 'communal properties' are conferred by those with informal social standing (which is to say, the practical ability to get others to go along with them), and they involve non-deontic constraints and enablements, roughly, what people can or cannot manage to do. An example of an institutional property is 'being the president' (in a particular state); an example of a communal property is 'being cool' (in a particular school).

The institutional/communal contrast is intuitive in many ways—and as we shall see, it plays an important role in Ásta's accounts of race and gender kinds—but I have a reservation about the use of the deontic/non-deontic contrast to demarcate the two sorts of interpersonal kinds. I take it that Ásta is operating with a narrow conception of deontic power according to which right, duties, and so on, must be fairly explicit and formal in order for them to count as deontic. By contrast, following Brännmark, I am operating with a more expansive conception of deontic normativity according to which it can be subtle and implicit (see §3.5.1). On this more expansive conception, deontic constraints and enablements are characterised by the presence or absence of tendencies for normatively laden corrective responses, rather than by people explicitly thinking of others as having rights, duties, and so on. On this more expansive conception of deontic normativity, the properties that Ásta considers to be paradigmatically communal seem also to involve deontic constraints and enablements.

To see how this is so, consider Ásta's paradigmatic example of a communal property: being cool. As she says, 'the cool kids are able to say or do things that others can't', such as to set fashions (2018, 20). On the broader understanding of deontic constraints and enablements that I favour, this plausibly amounts to a deontic power. For example, suppose that I, a decidedly un-cool person, were to attempt to set a new trend by saying the following: 'On Wednesdays, we wear pink!' Now, it may well be that other people will have a corrective response along the lines of 'Oh yeah, says who?' In other words, who do I think I am to attempt to set such a trend? Not only will I not manage to get everyone else to join me in wearing pink on Wednesdays, but I will be treated as having overstepped the mark in even suggesting it. One difference between myself and a cool person is that the cool person would be able to get such a trend off the ground whilst I would not; but a further difference is that I would be treated as having overstepped the mark in attempting to set a trend, and they would not. Thus, coolness seems at least in part to be a matter of deontic properties, once we adopt a broader conception of deontic normativity.

This may sound like a merely verbal disagreement, and an uninteresting one at that: Ásta is using the term 'deontic' more narrowly, and I am using it more broadly. However, I think that we have a good reason to use this term more broadly, which is that the narrow usage risks obscuring social dynamics that are ubiquitous and that play an important role in maintaining race and gender oppression. I'll argue for this claim in §5.4. But first, I need to outline Ásta's account of race and gender properties specifically.

5.2.3. Race and Gender Interpersonal Kinds

In her accounts of gender and of race, Ásta distinguishes in each case between institutional properties (in the case of gender, this is termed 'sex'; in the case of race, 'institutional race') and communal properties ('gender' and 'communal race', respectively). Let's start with race.

Ásta argues that there are both institutional and communal race properties in the United States (the main context on which she focuses) at present (2018, 94) and also in other places such as the United Kingdom (2018, 104–5) Institutional race properties are created wherever formal institutions, such as governmental and non-governmental agencies, schools, colleges, and so on, authoritatively categorise people by 'race' and use these categories in ways that make a difference to people's lives. For example, a person's institutional racial categorisation may determine whether they are eligible for a certain kind of scholarship, or it may influence (together with the categorisations of other individuals in the same area) the allocation of resources, such as public transport and road maintenance, that the local government makes to the neighbourhood the person lives in. By contrast, communal race properties are created whenever people are informally categorised by 'race' in a way that affects what they are able to do. For example, if a person is perceived by his friends as White, and this leads them to censure him for wearing dreadlocks, this would be an example of a communal race property.

It is worth noting, again in connection with race, that conferrals of social status need not be conscious, explicit, or overt in either communal or institutional cases. Conferring institutions—whether government bodies such as the US Office of Management and Budget (OMB) or more local institutions such as a specific college or university—may take their practices of categorisation to be merely describing a pre-existing feature of the world; nevertheless, when the categorisation is used as a basis for differential social treatment, however slight, this creates conferred properties.

Here is the schema Ásta gives for institutional race properties:

Property: being of the institutional race R, for example, Black or African American, White or Caucasian, Asian, Native Hawaiian or Other Pacific Islander, American Indian or Native Alaskan

Who: legal and political authorities, drawing on self-identification in official documents

What: the recording of a race identification in official files and documents

When: in each context where the official document plays a role in decision-making

Base property: supposed actual geographic ancestry, but the evidence for it is self-identification (2018, 99)

I find the way that Ásta specifies the base property in this schema a little unclear. She refers to 'supposed actual geographic ancestry'; however, it's not clear why she needs to include the caveat 'supposed', since the idea of a base property has already been defined as 'what the subjects are *attempting* to track' (2018, 8, emphasis added). Presumably, institutions are attempting to track *actual* geographic ancestry, not *supposed* actual geographic ancestry (indeed, it's not obvious what *attempting* to track *supposed* ancestry would involve). If we split up the base property into a base property and an indicator property that are treated separately, as I have suggested, we get a more straightforward picture. The base property is what the subjects are attempting to track, which in this case is 'actual geographic ancestry'. The fact that the OMB tends to rely on self-reporting, at least in most cases, comes into the picture as the indicator property, which is 'self-identification'. So we get:

Indicator property: self-identification.

Base property: actual geographic ancestry.

Some readers may think that this suggestion gets things the wrong way around and that the base property should, in fact, be simply 'self-identification' (in this case, my suggestion to add an indicator property would be redundant). After all, in many cases, people declare their race, and that declaration is entered into the institutional system without any evidence of their ancestry being consulted. Doesn't this mean that what is being tracked—the base property—is really self-identification?

Ásta argues, compellingly in my view, that this is not correct, because self-identification is not really being treated as decisive (2018, 95–98). As she sees it, the institution uses its authority to set up racial categories based on ancestry and decides to treat the self-identification of individuals as evidence of their having the relevant ancestry plus, in some cases, other properties (e.g., affiliation with a tribe in the case of being classified as 'American Indian' by the OMB). The individual's self-identification is not the real base property; rather, it is merely treated as an indicator of the base property, which is (for the most part) the individual's actual geographic ancestry. If the institution chose to do so, it could challenge someone's racial self-identification, asking for further evidence of their geographic ancestry. More radically, an institution could introduce a requirement to supply additional evidence of geographic ancestry along with or in place of self-identification. That these possibilities are so readily to hand suggests that Ásta is right to claim that self-identification is not being treated as decisive and therefore is not the base property but rather—in my terms—the indicator property.

When it comes to communal race kinds, Ásta emphasises how context-specific conferrals of race properties are. In the context of a discussion between two people in the United States about how to avoid racist police violence, having the status of Black might require having grown up being perceived as Black *in the United States* (and therefore having a store of specific cultural knowledge). In the context of a police arrest, by contrast, having the status of Black might simply require having a certain appearance, regardless of where a person is from (Ásta 2018, 103). The different racial categories that are available, the constraints and enablements associated with each category, and the base property that guides category allocation all vary very significantly from context to context.

With regard to gender kinds, as I previously mentioned, Ásta operates with a distinction between sex and gender that maps onto the institutional/communal distinction. Sex, according to Ásta, is 'a conferred legal status' (2018, 73) or institutional property. Here is how Ásta gives the schema:

Property: being female, male

Who: legal authorities, drawing on the expert opinions of doctors, other medical personnel, and parents

What: the recording of a sex in official documents

When: at birth (in the case of newborns); after surgery and hormonal treatment (in the case of older individuals)

Base property: the aim is to track as many sex-stereotypical characteristics as possible, and doctors perform surgery in cases where that might help bring the physical characteristics more in line with the stereotype of male and female (2018, 72)

Again, I would split up the base property into an indicator property and a base property proper:

Indicator property: the testimony of parents, doctors, and others as to what sex role would be most fitting, given the biological characteristics present

Base property: Actual preponderance of sex-stereotypical characteristics

This account of sex establishes a close link to bodily features such as chromosomes and genitals; these are the base property, which conferrals of sex are intended to track. However, sex remains a social kind, not a biological kind, because 'the determination of which physical properties are important for sex assignment, and, in particular, the assignment of people into one of two sexes, is shaped by societal values and interests' (Ásta 2018, 73).

As with communal race properties, Ásta takes gender—the communal counterpart to institutional sex—to be 'radically context dependent' (2018, 73). The vignette she uses to make this point is evocative:

Consider this scenario: you work as a coder in San Francisco. You go into your office where you are one of the guys. After work, you tag along with some friends at work to a bar. It is a very heteronormative space, and you are neither a guy nor a gal. You are an other. You walk up the street to another bar where you are a butch and expected to buy drinks for the femmes. Then you head home to your grandmother's eightieth birthday party, where you help out in the kitchen with the other women while the men smoke cigars. (2018, 73)

As this example highlights, communal gender kinds vary radically between different social contexts in many respects, including the categories that are available ('gal', 'butch', 'woman'), the base property that conferrals are supposed to track (social role, sexual role, body type, self-identification), and the constraints and enablements that constitute the status. The example also highlights the possibility of a person being made into a gender 'other' when they don't fit into any of the gender categories that are available to the conferrers in that context.

As with race and sex, Ásta's account of gender is augmented by adding in the category of indicator property as something distinct from the base property, because in many contexts, the property that people rely on in gendering others is different from the property that would ultimately determine what conferral they would make if they had complete knowledge. To use a benign example, I have often been in contexts where people have conferred gender status in a way that ultimately aims to track gender self-identification but relies on preferred pronouns as a proxy and where information about preferred pronouns is circulated fairly explicitly, perhaps by nametags or by being mentioned in verbal introductions.[2] In such a context, perceiving that someone's nametag says 'she/her' typically leads people to make a conferral of a gender status 'woman', and so on, but the ultimate aim is to track the way a person self-identifies their own gender. This distinction between pronouns and self-ascription comes to the fore in some cases. For example, one might meet a person whose preferred pronouns are 'they/them' and mentally place them as 'non-binary', only then to learn that the person identifies as a woman but uses gender-neutral pronouns because they want to facilitate a social switch to the blanket use of gender-neutral pronouns for everyone. This new information would reliably lead people in these contexts to revise their gender conferral for that person to 'woman'.

A much more unpleasant example can be found in Talia Mae Bettcher's work on transphobic oppression (2007). Drawing on research in sociology and ethnomethodology, Bettcher argues that in many contexts, genital status is understood as the "concealed truth" of sex. Thus, if a person has a penis, for example, they are seen as "really a man", regardless of their gender

---

[2] As Ásta notes (2018, 104), there is an important difference between gender and communal race in this regard: one rarely encounters contexts in which the base property for race conferrals is self-ascription, such that it would not be conceptually possible to inquire whether a person's self-ascription is appropriate. Granted, there are contexts in which self-ascription functions as an *indicator* property, and there are even contexts in which it's not considered good etiquette to *question* someone's self-ascription, but that does not suffice to make self-ascription the *base* property.

presentation and gender identity. Furthermore, as Bettcher puts it, '[g]ender presentation is generally taken as a *sign* of sexed body [i.e., genital status], taken to *mean* sexed body, taken to *communicate* sexed body' (2007, 52). This sets up an appearance/reality contrast between gender presentation and genital status which is mobilised to enact harm, including violent assault and even murder, against trans people who are perceived as "misaligning" their gender presentation and genital status and therefore understood as engaging in a form of "deception". In such contexts, genital status is the base property, as this is what is understood ultimately to determine whether someone is "really a man" or "really a woman", whilst gender presentation is the indicator property. The forms of social punishment that are imposed on those who are perceived as displaying the "wrong" gender presentation for their genital status function as a form of policing aimed at ensuring continued correlation between the indicator property and the base property.

5.2.4. The Explanatory Value of Interpersonal Kinds

Attending to race and gender interpersonal kinds is worthwhile, from an emancipatory perspective, for four main reasons. The first reason is that people who are positioned in a complex way relative to a hegemonic gender kind are often going to have strongly varied experiences in different contexts when it comes to how they are treated by others. For example, Adrian Piper, a Black woman, describes how, based on her appearance, she is regularly assumed to be White by people who do not know her actual family history and life experience (Piper 1992). Piper also describes how people's responses towards her shift when they become aware of her ancestry and of how she racially identifies. Operating at the level of 'regularly and for the most part', as with hegemonic gender kinds, obscures the detail of these experiences. We also need to look at the shifting detail of the way people are constrained and enabled in different contexts in order to understand how oppression operates in practice. Otherwise, we will risk marginalising the complex experiences of those individuals who are most unstably situated relative to dominant frameworks of meaning. Interpersonal kinds bring these more complex experiences into focus, by allowing us to say that Piper, for example, is made into a member of different race kinds in different contexts, due to the interaction between people's beliefs about her and the schemas that govern the conferral of race properties in those contexts.

Second, and related to this, interpersonal kinds are explanatorily useful from an emancipatory perspective because they allow us to capture the regional differences in how race and gender classifications are enacted and understood. In the literature on the metaphysics of race, this point has been an important focus of discussion, where it has been formulated as the claim that race 'does not travel': someone who is a member of one race at one spatio-temporal location may be a member of a different race at a different spatio-temporal location. As Michael Root puts it:

> Race does not travel. Some men who are black in New Orleans now would have been octoroons there some years ago or would be white in Brazil today. Socrates had no race in ancient Athens, though he would be a white man in Minnesota. (2000, S631–32)

This is to say more than just that someone's race might be *perceived* differently in different contexts; rather, it is to make the claim that their race might actually *be* different, in the sense that they are a member of one race kind in one location and another race kind in another location. Of course, the idea is not that race *never* travels but only that it *need* not—that is, that a person's race is dependent on the culture in which they live in such a way that there are at least some cases where context makes a difference to someone's race. The idea that race does not travel has been treated as a constraint on an adequate account of the metaphysics of race (Mallon 2004; see also Glasgow 2007). Although hegemonic race kinds have some limitations to their context, they do not capture the thought behind this constraint, because they allow for extensive travelling. By contrast, interpersonal kinds are well able to capture the sense in which race does not travel: when someone leaves one context and enters another, they may well cease to be a member of one interpersonal race kind and become a member of another.

The third reason interpersonal kinds are explanatorily useful from an emancipatory perspective is that, as I argued in §3.4, social change requires, among other things, that people come to understand the texture of their own lives in different ways, leading to affective shifts as well as changes in beliefs. What is more, we don't typically relate to the social world 'all at once', as it were; rather, we tend to experience it piecemeal, as specific situations in which we find ourselves. These context-specific experiences are therefore important for emancipatory theory, as can be seen in feminist understandings of consciousness raising (MacKinnon 1989, 83–105). Through considering forms of treatment and responses directed at people who are perceived as female in a certain context, for example, an individual may come to realise that treatment she thought was specifically targeted at her as an individual, perhaps due to her own actions or inactions, is, in fact, part of a pattern of treatment systematically directed at those perceived to be female in that context. This in turn may direct her towards other constraints and enablements in other contexts, enabling her to build up a picture of gender-based oppression as a structural phenomenon based on an initial understanding that is quite context-specific. In order to facilitate this kind of building of resistant consciousness, emancipatory theorists therefore need to attend to more narrowly contextual race and gender kinds, such as interpersonal race and gender kinds, as well as to the kinds based on wider contexts, such as hegemonic kinds.[3]

Finally, interpersonal race and gender kinds are important for emancipatory theorists because they are important sites of adjustment when it comes to making emancipatory social change. Those of us working to end oppression cannot change hegemonic kinds all at once, because they depend on a complex pattern of interaction of different factors. However, it may at times be within our power to create social spaces in which the interpersonal constraints and enablements that are imposed are ones that we can wholeheartedly endorse. We may even, sometimes, be able to bring the kinds created in these resistant spaces into dominant contexts (for a suggestion to this effect regarding gender, see Dembroff 2018, 36–38). In other words, interpersonal kinds offer distinctive opportunities for fostering emancipatory social change.

5.3. Interpersonal Race and Gender Kinds, Granularity, and Intersectionality

The discussion so far should have made clear the scope (narrow) and breadth (restricted to interpersonal constraints and enablements) that characterise interpersonal kinds, but what about granularity? Although Ásta's account of (what I am calling) interpersonal race and gender kinds is specified primarily in terms of single-moniker race and gender properties, she allows that

---

[3] For further discussion of resistant consciousness, especially resistant imagination, see Medina 2013.

these constraints and enablements can combine in potentially non-additive ways and clearly intends for her account to be sensitive to intersectionality (2018, 6, 81, 125). In regard to the intersectional nature of social properties, she writes:

> The general story is that we have features, and some of those features have social significance in a context, and the status we enjoy in a particular context is *the result of the constraints and enablements that the presence of each and every one of our socially significant features brings*, where the presence of some features can trump others. (2018, 125, emphasis added)

The acknowledgement that 'the presence of some features can trump others' conforms with the idea that oppression is non-additive, which is the first component of intersectionality. I take it that the thought here is that although a person's overall social status is the result of all the different constraints and enablements that they are under as a result of each of their various socially significant features, this result is not a straightforward matter of adding up all the different constraints and enablements but something much more complicated, in which different features can interact.

The way Ásta talks about overall, intersectional status as the 'result of the constraints and enablements that each and every one of our socially significant features brings' (2018, 125) seems to imply that there is *a set* of constraints and enablements that any given feature brings. This impression is strengthened by the fact that Ásta gives separate conferral schemas for race and gender properties. That is, she gives conferral schemas for properties such as *being a woman* (2018, 74–75) and *being Black* (2018, 99), and these conferral schemas do not make reference to one another. I have previously (Jenkins 2020a) articulated a reservation about this approach, which is that emphasising separate conferral schemas for single-moniker properties—even ones that are described as interacting non-additively— seems not to go far enough in acknowledging the non-separable and cross-constituting nature of race and gender kinds. This is because it seems to place single-moniker race and gender categories prior to intersectional race-gender categories in some (possibly ontological) sense and to suggest that they can be separated from one another more neatly than I think is the case.

In response, Ásta clarifies her view:

[T]he intersectional status is the status you get by being taken to have base features B1 and B2 and B3, but the constraints and enablements need not be the product of the constraints and enablements that come with being taken to have B1 plus the constraints and enablements that come with being taken to have B2 plus the constraints and enablements that come with being taken to have B3. (2019, 282)

She adds that she takes this approach to meet all three of *non-additivity*, *non-separability*, and *cross-constitution*. This strikes me as a step in the right direction. However, there still seems to be a gap in the account when it comes to explaining where the constraints and enablements for single-moniker kinds come from. Given the complexity of each person's deeply intersectional experience of being constrained and enabled in a context, we need to explain how it is that we can arrive at a specification, or conferral schema, for a single-moniker property such as *being a woman*.

Situating interpersonal kinds within the CEF enables us to draw on my account of granularity (given in §3.6) to fill this gap. On this view, specifications of the constraints and enablements for single-moniker race and gender interpersonal kinds are only approximate descriptions of the complex patterns made up of each individual's experiences. Accordingly, there is no sense in which our different features bring different constraints and enablements that then combine to produce an overall status in a context. Rather, the richly intersectional overall statuses of all the people in the context can be theoretically and imperfectly disaggregated to yield conferral schemas for single-moniker race and gender properties. As with hegemonic race and gender kinds (§4.3), and for the same reasons (which I shall not rehearse again), I take it that although sometimes single-moniker race and gender interpersonal kinds will be explanatorily useful, often emancipatory theorists will do better to work with interpersonal intersectional race-gender kinds.

5.4. Interpersonal Race and Gender Kinds and Deontic Constraints and Enablements

I have said that I would argue that we should prefer a broader understanding of deontic power over the narrow understanding on which Ásta relies, for example in demarcating institutional and communal properties. Here I will make good on this promise. Ásta herself sees communal race and gender kinds as involving a kind of after-the-fact normativity: there are normative expectations placed on members of communal race and gender kinds, but this normativity is not part of what constitutes the kind. By contrast, I see normative expectations as part of the constraints and enablements that actually constitute kind membership, in the form of deontic interpersonal constraints and enablements. This is because I think this treatment of normativity better illuminates some important social dynamics.

The dynamics that interest me concern the informal policing of racialised and gendered modes of behaviour. These constraints and enablements are deontic in the broader sense of the word (which, following Brännmark 2019 and 2021, I prefer) but are not deontic in the narrower sense that I understand Ásta to be using. For instance, someone whose racialised or gendered mode of presentation does not match the interpersonal kind that they are made a member of in that context will often be treated as overstepping social boundaries—as doing what they are not *entitled* to do—and 'corrective' responses ranging from chilly body language to explicit verbal censure to outright violence may follow.

These kinds of norm-laden responses can be the case even where there are no explicit beliefs about what's appropriate or inappropriate for differently racialised and gendered people in the picture. For example, if a Black woman and a White man speak an equal amount in a meeting, she may be perceived as pushy and arrogant whilst he is perceived as confident and helpful. This, too, can be understood as a deontic constraint if we adopt a broader understanding, because it involves race- and gender-patterned perceptions of what is and is not socially appropriate. It is important to acknowledge, though, that some of the interpersonal constraints that constitute race and gender social status kinds are not deontic in character even in this broader sense. If a Black woman's idea is simply less likely to be taken up in a meeting than a White man's but she is not viewed negatively for attempting to put ideas forward, this is not a deontic constraint, merely an interpersonal one.

The reason I think we should prefer the broader understanding of deontic power over the narrower is that the narrower understanding risks making it seem as though there are only two sorts of interpersonal constraints and enablements: those that are explicitly deontic and those that are not deontic at all. In other words, it places the category of constraints and enablements that are deontic in the broader sense but not in the narrower sense at risk of merging into the background of constraints and enablements that are not deontic in any sense—those constraints and enablements that merely concern what is more or less likely to happen but are not maintained by way of any perceptions of social boundaries or any tendency towards corrective responses. What is more, this intermediate category of constraints and enablements looms large in people's experiences of race and gender.

Consider how comedian Nish Kumar, who is British Asian, describes the racism he encounters when he articulates left-wing opinions:

> There's a narrow band of opinions you are expected to have, if you are born in this country and your parents are of ethnic minorities. If you are a person of colour and you don't just tell everybody how wonderful Britain is, how it's not racist, there is a sense of your ingratitude. There is a sense that you were given plenty, so how dare you? People like me, who come from an ethnic minority, who are born in this country, if we do anything that even vaguely tries to interrogate Britishness or British history, *there is a sense that we should just be quiet and be grateful*. (quoted in Lamont 2021, emphasis added)

The 'should' here is best understood, in my view, as expressing a *deontic* constraint imposed by those who respond to Kumar with racist attitudes. This interpretation tallies with Kumar's use of the phrase 'how dare you?' to evoke the attitudes he has in mind. Those responding to Kumar don't just *expect* or *predict* that he will be quiet and grateful, but rather they take him to be under an *obligation* to be so—and they respond with hostility when he does not live up to this perceived obligation.

A more violent example comes from another comedian, Hannah Gadsby. In her stand-up show *Nanette*, Gadsby describes being accosted by a man who was angry that she was talking to his girlfriend. The man then said that he had thought that Gadsby was 'a faggot', which is to say, a gay man. When he realised she was a woman, he backed off, saying that he did not hit women. (As Gadsby comments: what a charmer!) He then returned, however, saying, 'Oh no, I get it, you're a *lady faggot*, I'm *allowed* to beat the shit out of *you*'. Gadsby continues: 'And he did. He beat the shit out of me, and nobody stopped him' (Gadsby, Olb, and Parry 2018). The 'allowed' here again seems to me deontic in character. It is not just that this man thought (correctly) that he could in practice *get away with* assaulting Gadsby, given that she is a lesbian (an interpersonal intersectional gender-sexuality kind); he also seems to have felt that he was *socially entitled* to do so—a perception that the inaction of the bystanders who witnessed the attack without intervening can only have served to confirm.

We can also see deontic normativity at play when people try to resist oppressive constraints and enablements. Here is Piper's description of how people tend to respond to her when she asserts herself:

> To those who in fact believe (even though they would never voice this belief to themselves) that black people are not entitled to this degree of respect, attention, and liberty, the sight of a black person behaving as though she were can, indeed, look very much like arrogance. It may not occur to them that she simply does not realize that her blackness should make any difference. (1992, 22)

Here people form a negative appraisal of Piper's behaviour, conceptualising it as 'arrogance', since, as Piper says, they take her to be demanding things (respect, attention, liberty) to which, in their view, she is not entitled. Again, these responses seem to me to be deontic in character and to condition what is socially possible for Piper—in other words, to constrain and enable her. Thus, it makes sense to treat them as part of what constitutes the interpersonal kind *Black* in the social contexts in question.[4]

These cases support my claim that deontic normativity forms an important, if often subtle, aspect of race and gender kinds. Being expected not to criticise Britain, being seen as a legitimate target of violence, and being seen as not entitled to respect, attention, or liberty are all part of what it is to have the social status *Asian*, *lesbian*, or *Black*, respectively, in the relevant contexts. The broader understanding of deontic constraints and enablements brings this form of normativity and its role in constructing social kinds into focus. If we were to see communal interpersonal kinds only in terms of the power to effect certain outcomes, we would miss out on these important dynamics of race and gender oppression and of people's resistance to it. To avoid this, I think we should adopt the broader understanding of deontic power (as something that comes in both explicit and implicit forms) rather than the narrower one (as always and only explicit).

Switching to a broader understanding of deontic constraints and enablements has implications for the institutional-versus-communal distinction that Ásta draws, which exclusively associates deontic constraints and enablements (narrowly understood) with the institutional side of

---

[4] For more on what determines which constraints and enablements constitute the social kind and which are incidental, see §7.4.

the distinction, because the kinds I have shown to involve subtly deontic constraints and enablements—*Asian, lesbian, Black*—seem intuitively like communal kinds. Certainly, they are not formalised, or conferred by those with particular authority, like the paradigmatic cases of institutional kinds. I find the idea of an institutional/communal contrast intuitive, however, and we saw in the previous subsection that it does helpful work in Ásta's accounts of race and gender/sex.

I therefore want to propose an alternative account of the contrast between institutional and communal interpersonal properties that does not rely on the role of deontic normativity. I suggest that we can understand it (1) as a matter of degree and (2) as involving several different aspects. An interpersonal kind is institutional, on this view, to the extent that the relevant social status is formally or explicitly conferred and is backed by an organisational structure. Correspondingly, an interpersonal kind is communal to the extent that the relevant social status is informally or tacitly conferred and is not backed by an organisational structure. Although deontic normativity does not here play a role in defining this contrast, we can say as a general rule that institutional kinds are more likely to involve explicitly deontic constraints and enablements, though communal kinds may involve explicitly deontic constraints and enablements and will often involve implicitly deontic constraints and enablements. On this view, the institutional/communal distinction is a matter of degree, with plenty of borderline cases, rather than a perfectly clear-cut distinction. I believe, however, that the reworked distinction is quite sufficient to allow us to retain the insights Ásta offers about institutional and communal race and gender/sex kinds.

5.5. Interpersonal Race and Gender Kinds and Ontic Oppression

Due to the sheer quantity of race and gender interpersonal kinds that exist and their pronounced heterogeneity, it is far from straightforward to assess which interpersonal race and gender kinds are ontically oppressive. Often, the interpersonal constraints and enablements that constitute non-dominant social status race and gender kinds will be oppressive. Piper, for example, describes various ways in which 'whites have tried to put [her] in [her] place upon discovering [her] racial identity', including:

the grammar school teacher who called my parents to inquire whether I was aware that I was black, and made a special effort to put me in my place by restricting me from participating in certain class activities and assigning me to remedial classes in anticipation of low achievement; and the graduate school classmate who complimented me on my English; and the potential employer who, having offered me a tenure-track job in an outstanding graduate department (which I declined) when he thought I was white, called me back much later after I'd received tenure and he'd found out I was black, to offer me a two-year visiting position teaching undergraduates only, explaining to a colleague of mine that he was being pressured by his university administration to integrate his department. (1992, 20)

These are all interpersonal constraints and enablements and would partially constitute the kind *Black woman* in the contexts (a school, a university department, etc.) in which Piper was situated. Since these constraints and enablements are plainly oppressive to the person who falls under them, the interpersonal race–gender kind *Black woman* in this context is ontically oppressive.

However, it is far from being the case that the relevant interpersonal constraints and enablements are always oppressive towards members of non-dominant race and gender kinds. In a significant subset of contexts, being a member of a non-dominant race or gender kind brings a net-positive set of constraints and enablements. An example of this can be found in Ta-Nehisi Coates's description of his experience as a Black student at Howard University, a historically Black university in the United States. Describing this growing awareness of the complexity of racial identity and experience, he writes:

And still and all I knew that *we were* something, that we were a tribe—on one hand, invented, and on the other, no less real. The reality was out there on the Yard, on the first warm day of spring when it seemed that every sector, borough, affiliation, country, and corner of the broad diaspora had sent a delegate to the great world party. I remember those days like an OutKast song, painted in lust and joy. . . . A dude in a TribeVibe T-shirt walks up, gives a pound, and we talk about the black bacchanals of the season—Freaknik, Daytona, Virginia Beach—and we wonder if this is the year we make the trip. It isn't. Because we have all we need out on the Yard. We are dazed here because we still remember the hot cities in which we were born, where the first days of spring were laced with fear. And now, here at The Mecca, we are without fear, we are the dark spectrum on parade. (2015, 56–67)

Coates's experience suggests that in the context of Howard University at that time, the interpersonal contextual kind *Black* is constituted by a set of constraints and enablements that is very positive, even empowering. Being perceived as Black in this context enables social interactions and shared experiences that would not be possible in the same way for someone perceived as White in that context. These shared experiences, and by extension the enablements to participate in them, are evidently extremely valuable. Other examples of similarly valuable sorts of interpersonal contextual kinds may include being a woman at a feminist gathering or being a trans person in a trans-centred social space (for discussion of the latter, see Bettcher 2013).

Clearly, then, even non-dominant race and gender kinds can be constituted by very positive sets of interpersonal constraints and enablements in particular contexts. These interpersonal race and gender kinds are *not* ontically oppressive. The fact that some interpersonal race and gender kinds are ontically oppressive whilst others are not enables us to see how individuals can experience their race or gender kind membership as positive even when the relevant category is bound up with oppression and to see that such experiences often do not rest on any kind of mistake or oversight.

In some cases, as with the experience Coates describes at Howard, these positive interpersonal race and gender kinds are an active part of liberatory or resistant social currents. However, this need not always be the case. In other instances, the positive interpersonal kinds may be more tied up with ideologies that support oppressive social structures. For example, in certain contexts to do with childcare—a nursery school, perhaps—women might be treated as more authoritative than men; for instance, their assertions about their children's needs may be taken more seriously. Although this might be experienced positively by some women, it is directly linked to a broader ideology that positions women as primarily suited to, and solely responsible for, caring work—an ideology that has many other negative implications. Even so, a tight contextual focus on the nursery school might identify an interpersonal gender kind *woman* that is constituted by a broadly positive set of constraints and enablements that cannot be described as oppressive. In both the emancipatory case and the case tied to problematic ideologies, it is coherent for people to value membership in the interpersonal contextual race and gender kinds. The former case is perhaps more straightforwardly valuable, but even the latter can also reasonably be valued, although it is counterproductive from an emancipatory perspective if such kinds are valued to a degree that blocks the ideology in question from criticism.

It is important to remember, though, that individuals who are members of empowering interpersonal contextual race and gender kinds are still also, at the same time, members of other interpersonal race and gender kinds in different contexts, as well as members of hegemonic race and gender kinds, and may suffer ontic oppression in virtue of those other kind memberships. When it comes to non-dominant race and gender kinds, the empowering nature of a particular interpersonal contextual race or gender kind cannot outweigh or cancel the subordinating nature of other interpersonal and hegemonic kinds. This again is brought home powerfully by Coates, as he reflects on the killing by a police officer of one of his friends from Howard at the age of twenty-five:

> I thought of all the beautiful black people I'd seen at The Mecca, all their variation, all their hair, all their language, all their stories and geography, all their stunning humanity, and none of it could save them from the mark of plunder and the gravity of our particular world. (2015, 81)

Since ontically oppressive interpersonal race and gender kinds are often enforced by powerful social agents, whereas emancipatory interpersonal race and gender kinds are often created at sites of resistance, it will often be the case that the latter cannot 'save' people, as Coates puts it, from the former.

Consider, for example, a queer and trans activist group whose members go together to a protest march. Within the group, conferrals of communal gender properties might be entirely based on self-identification. However, if the members of the group are arrested on the march, their treatment within the criminal system will likely be determined by their institutional sex, as signified by markers on official documentation, or perhaps by their communal gender in contexts such as the police station. Both the genders that members of the group confer on each other and the sexes and genders that the state and the police confer on them are interpersonal kinds, but these different interpersonal kinds exist within complex nested structures of power. The conferrals of the state, enforced by the police, can override the conferrals of the group members amongst themselves, but not vice versa. These nested structures of power are important for establishing what we might think of as the *reach* of ontically oppressive interpersonal kinds, which is to say, the contexts into which their imposition can intrude, by force if necessary.

5.6. Conclusion

In this chapter, I have introduced interpersonal race and gender kinds and argued that they, like hegemonic race and gender kinds, are useful to emancipatory theorists. I have also assessed whether interpersonal race and gender kinds are ontically oppressive and have argued that the picture here is complex in virtue of the many different interpersonal kinds that exist in different contexts. Some of these kinds are ontically oppressive, but others are not, and some even serve an important emancipatory function.

Considering this conclusion alongside my conclusion in Chapter 4—that non-dominant hegemonic race and gender kinds *are* ontically oppressive— shows us that it would be a mistake to make broad claims, such as 'the kind *woman* is ontically oppressive', or more colloquial versions of this, such as 'to be a woman is to be oppressed'. Rather, we need to make narrower claims about different specific varieties of race and gender kinds. In Chapter 6, I'll add a final element to this picture by considering a third variety of race and gender kinds and showing how attending to these kinds brings into focus a distinctive form of ontic oppression.

6

Race and Gender Identity Kinds and Ontic Oppression

6.1. Introduction

In this chapter, I consider a third type of race and gender social kind, which I term 'identity kinds'. These kinds relate to a person's experienced relationship to a social category. After introducing race and gender identity kinds and assessing their explanatory value from the perspective of emancipatory theory, I show how these kinds fit within the CEF. I then argue that, similarly to interpersonal kinds, some race and gender identity kinds are ontically oppressive, while others are not, and some are even conducive to emancipation.

Finally, I show that attending to identity kinds brings into focus a distinction between two types of ontic oppression. The first type affects *any* human being who is constructed as a kind member, because it is oppressive in virtue of being at odds with moral entitlements that all human beings share. The second type affects only *some* individuals, because it is oppressive in virtue of moral entitlements that those individuals have in virtue of some more specific feature, such as their identity. Having this distinction in place enables me to look back at hegemonic and interpersonal race and gender kinds and identify a further instance of ontic oppression that has not yet been discussed: ontic oppression that affects some (but not all) members of the hegemonic or interpersonal kind in virtue of the relation between their race and/or gender identity and the constraints and enablements that constitute kind membership.

6.2. Introducing Identity Kinds

6.2.1. Two Senses of 'Identity'

The term 'identity' is used in many different ways, both in general and specifically with regard to race and gender. Sometimes it is used in a way that

Ontology and Oppression. Katharine Jenkins, Oxford University Press. © Katharine Jenkins 2023.
DOI: 10.1093/oso/9780197666777.003.0007

is equivalent to 'category'—one's racial or gender identity is simply the race or gender category that one belongs to. This sense of identity does not lend itself to being contrasted with the hegemonic or interpersonal kinds described in the Chapter 5. Accordingly, it is not what I shall focus on. Rather, I am interested in another sense of identity, which concerns (to put it very broadly) an *experienced relationship* to a category. Identity in this sense *can* come apart from hegemonic or interpersonal kind membership, because a person can experience their relationship to a category in a way that is different from the way they are positioned within dominant social structures (the hegemonic kind of which they are a member) and from the ways in which other people are perceiving and responding to them in a particular context (the interpersonal kind of which they are a member in that context).[1] This second sense of identity is what I want to capture under the label of 'identity kinds'.[2]

In talking of identity in this sense, I have in mind a family of accounts, rather than one specific account. Within this family of accounts, there are two broad clusters.

The accounts within the first cluster focus quite narrowly on a felt relationship to race and gender norms (on gender, see Jenkins 2016a; Ásta 2018, 114–26; on race, see Cross 1991; Haslanger 2012e; see also Tanesini and Lance 2000 on sexual orientation for a structurally similar account). This relationship can stop short of endorsing the norms, committing to following the norms, or actually following the norms. Rather, it is a matter of having the norms function as a reference point for one's own experience of one's behaviour: the norms shape and structure one's embodied social experiences. Norms can play this role for one even if one adopts a critical stance towards them.

---

[1] These two ways of talking about identity are not always sharply differentiated. For example, I take Linda Martín Alcoff's (2006) work on 'visible identities' to span both of them. For Alcoff, 'social identities' such as races and genders 'are not simply social locations or positions, but also hermeneutic horizons comprised of experiences, basic beliefs, and communal values, all of which influence our orientation toward and responses to future experiences' (2006, 287). The first part of the quote speaks to the first way of talking about identity that I describe here, and the second part speaks to the second way. Although Alcoff's analysis is rich and fruitful, and although I am broadly sympathetic to her account of race and gender, especially her claim that race and gender identities 'are not per se oppressive' (2006, 287), the differences in how we use the term 'identity' mean that a full comparison of my position with hers is outside the scope of this chapter.

[2] A third, less often discussed sense of identity concerns a projected or communicated invitation for people to categorise and treat us in certain ways rather than others. See Dembroff and Saint-Croix 2019 for an account of this sense of identity, which they term 'agential identity'.

For instance, gender identity, on this type of account, is a matter of a person's felt relationship to norms of gender (Jenkins 2016a; 2018a). Imagine a woman who does not remove her underarm hair, who wears clothing that reveals that hair, and who feels subtly as if she is doing something transgressive when she does so. This woman is experiencing a feminine norm ("women should not have underarm hair") as relevant to her, even though she does not comply with it. She may still have this experience of feeling as though what she is doing is transgressive even if she consciously believes that people of different genders should not face different expectations about their body hair or even that all gender norms are entirely pernicious and ought to be rejected altogether. This kind of felt relationship need not involve an active exercise of agency but can simply be a feature of someone's experience; one can experience certain norms as relevant in this sense without ever making any kind of decision about which norms those will be.

By contrast, accounts within the second cluster conceive of identity as something much more active and agential (Appiah 1996; Bettcher 2009). Kwame Anthony Appiah, for example, holds that an individual must engage in an active process of 'identification' in order to have a certain identity, where identification involves using a category or label to shape one's intentional acts. For instance, consider someone who uses the label *Black* in developing their conception of what is valuable and in planning their life. They may choose to live in a neighbourhood they conceive of as a Black neighbourhood, attend a church they conceive of as a Black church, volunteer with and donate to charities they conceive of as Black charities, and so on. Such a person is engaging in identification with the category or label *Black*. Appiah notes that this use of a label or category to shape one's projects need not be experienced as *voluntary*, in the sense that it does not need to be the case that one feels one could just as easily have chosen to take up a different label instead; however, it does need to be *active*, in the sense that one exercised one's agency in choosing to shape one's values and projects with reference to the label rather than without it (1996, 69–71).

In a similar spirit, Talia Mae Bettcher discusses gender identity in relation to the experiences of trans people and argues that identity in this sense (which she terms 'existential self-identity') centrally concerns the ways in which 'people are partially guided by what is important to them' (2009, 111). Identity in this sense is not about an explicit self-conception, Bettcher tells us. Rather, it is to be understood as an answer to the question 'Who am I, really?', where this question is understood as meaning 'What am I about? What moves me? What do I stand for? What do I care about the most?' (Bettcher 2009, 110). Thus, there is slightly less emphasis on *labels* in Bettcher's account than there is in Appiah's. However, both accounts are about how we actively make sense of ourselves and our actions, and for this reason, I see them as sharing an important feature that sets them apart from the first type of account of identity that I considered.

I'll refer to the first type of account of identity as an account of 'identity as norm-relevancy' and the second as an account of 'identity as identification'. Although these two types of accounts of identity pick out slightly different phenomena, they are not incompatible. We are the sort of beings who implicitly experience ourselves in light of the norms that are operative in our social context, and we are also the sort of beings who can actively fashion our life, our projects, and our sense of self using the categories and labels that are available to us. However, it's important to note that these two senses of identity can come apart from each other. Someone might, for example, navigate the social world in a way that takes the norms for women's behaviour as a reference point but never consciously take up the label of *woman* or use it to shape their plans for their life. Such a person has a female gender identity in the sense of identity as norm-relevancy but not in the sense of identity as identification.

We have seen how these two senses of identity can come apart from each other. They can, of course, come apart from interpersonal and hegemonic kinds as well. For example, someone might have a strong identity in both senses as Asian, and they might normally spend most of their time in contexts in which their geographically marked body prompts this categorisation. They might then temporarily inhabit a social context in which they are considered by others around them *not* to be Asian, perhaps due to a lack of cultural connection which is considered particularly important in that context, and they may be treated accordingly. In that context, their racial identity (in both senses) has come apart from the interpersonal race kind of which they are a member at that time and place. The same can happen with hegemonic gender kinds. Someone may have an agender gender identity (in both senses) and be perceived and treated as agender in some social contexts but as a man in many others. Due to their spending most of their time in contexts where their agender identity is *not* recognised, their life may be woven into larger patterns in a way that makes them a member of the hegemonic gender kind *man* even though this is not their gender identity. In other words, they experience constraints and enablements that are, at a broad-brushstrokes level, characteristic of those whose bodies are socially marked as male, even though they differ from many of the people with whom they share those constraints and enablements in that they have an agender gender identity rather than a male gender identity.

6.2.2. The Explanatory Value of Identity as Norm-Relevancy

Each of these senses of identity does important explanatory work from the perspective of emancipatory theory. Identity as norm-relevancy is useful for capturing experiences that some trans people have. For example, consider Julia Serano's description of her experience as a child who had been assigned male at birth (Serano is a trans woman):

> I had an unexplainable feeling that I was doing something wrong every time I walked into the boys' restroom at school; and whenever our class split into groups of boys and girls, I always had a sneaking suspicion that at any moment someone might tap me on the shoulder and say, 'Hey, what are you doing here? You're not a boy'. (Serano 2016, 78)[3]

It's clear from Serano's broader description of her experiences around this time that on a conscious level, she was fully aware that other people, in fact, expected her to follow the norms associated with boys, so her experience can't be explained by thinking about the interpersonal gender kind of which she was a member in the relevant context. What is more, Serano did not consciously identify with any category other than "boy" at the time of the incident she describes, meaning that identity as identification does not help us to capture the experience, either. Identity as norm-relevancy is what we need here, because identity in this sense can come apart from interpersonal gender kind membership whilst also not needing to be accompanied by an explicit self-association with the relevant gender category.

---

[3] Serano herself would not describe this sense as gender identity, because she reserves the term for 'the way [one] consciously relate[s] to [one's] own gender'—what I term identity as identification. Instead, she describes it as one consequence of what she terms 'subconscious sex', which centrally concerns one's feelings about one's sexed body (2016, 81–83).

Identity as norm-relevancy can also help to bring into focus some of the wrongs that can be involved in misgendering someone, which is to say, treating them in ways that do not accord with their gender identity.[4] Stephanie Kapusta argues, and I agree, that misgendering causes psychological harms such as anxiety, stress, fear, and depression; moral harms, such as the undermining of self-respect; and political harms, such as unjust additional burdens and discrimination, which amount to oppression and domination (2016, 504–5). As I have previously argued (Jenkins 2018a), identity as norm-relevancy draws our attention to one particular way in which misgendering enacts such harms, which is by its impact on people's agency. This impact can be identified by considering what Alissa Bierria has termed 'the social dialectic of agency' (2014, 131). Bierria observes that although it seems natural to many to locate agency solely within the agent who acts, in fact, our understanding of agency in a social context should extend to the reception of the action by observers. In general, an agent not only acts intentionally but also acts on the presumption that her act will communicate to observers at least roughly what she meant it to, including at least a partially accurate sense of her intentions in so acting. In this sense, the acts we end up performing are co-constructed by ourselves and by others around us who perceive those acts. As Bierria puts it, 'even if an agent develops her intentions and acts accordingly, others who observe the agent's action also construct narratives of meaning about her actions, empowering them as social authors of her autonomous action' (2014, 131).

According to the norm-relevancy sense of identity, to have a certain gender identity ('woman', for example) is to experience one's actions as norm-compliant or norm-violating with respect to the norms for that gender, rather than the norms for any other gender. For example, a person with a female gender identity in a Western society would tend to experience wearing a dress as norm-compliant behaviour, rather than as norm-violating behaviour. Now, suppose that such a person is perceived by others as a man and that she wears a smart dress to a relatively formal occasion, such as a university graduation. Her intention, let us suppose, is to dress in an aesthetically pleasing but not particularly remarkable way that is sensitive to

---

[4] In previous work (Jenkins 2018a), I suggested that gender identity as norm-relevancy could also individuate gender identities in a way that facilitates trans liberatory politics. However, I no longer think this. For persuasive arguments criticising my previous suggestion that gender identity as norm-relevancy can do this work, see Dembroff 2020b.

the formality of the occasion. Those observing her, however, interpret her as dressing in an extremely conspicuous and deliberately challenging way that undermines the formality of the occasion. This is because whilst wearing a smart dress to an occasion of this sort is norm-compliant relative to the norms of femininity, it is highly transgressive relative to the norms of masculinity. Thus, there is a marked disconnect between the intended meaning and the perceived meaning of this agent's action.

Continuously experiencing this sort of disconnect amounts to a serious form of social disempowerment. To employ terminology that Bierria borrows from María Lugones (2003), it constitutes 'disenfranchisement', a deprivation of the authority to prompt social recognition of one's intentions (Bierria 2014, 132). Accordingly, identity as norm-relevancy is important because sustained disrespect for a person's gender identity in this sense leads to disenfranchisement of the kind identified by Lugones and Bierria. This kind of disenfranchisement is experienced by people whose gender identity is routinely ignored, denied, or invalidated. This makes identity as norm-relevancy significant for emancipatory theorists, especially (though not only) in relation to the goal of securing trans liberation.

6.2.3. The Explanatory Value of Identity as Identification

The second sense of identity, identity as identification, is also important for emancipatory theorists. Since people can and do make active decisions about how to shape their projects in response to labels, and these decisions can have oppressive and emancipatory tendencies, it is useful to distinguish this from the less active sense of social location that most people tend to have by default. This enables us to draw attention to the domain in which we do have a choice and where this choice may present an opportunity to resist oppression. In this vein, Robin Zheng (2018) has argued that we should seek to do our part in combating structural forms of injustice through the ways in which we occupy social roles.

According to Zheng, social roles are sets of predictive and normative expectations that apply to individuals in virtue of the relationships in which they stand to others, which are maintained by people in that social context by means of social sanctions (2018, 873). For example, the social role of "teacher" consists of expectations for how teachers should behave in relation to students, to parents, to other teachers, and so on, and a teacher who departs from these expectation risks negative responses (for a similar account of gender roles, see Witt 2011). Zheng argues that people's identification with social roles, which I understand along the lines of identity as identification in the sense discussed earlier, is 'part of what enables roles to preserve social structure' (2018, 875). This is because identification in this sense tends to incentivise people to act in accordance with at least some of the expectations that make up the relevant social roles. If the expectations that make up social roles are such that they tend to maintain unjust social structures, then we can expect to see people acting in ways that tend to maintain unjust social structures. Thus, social roles are a key interface between individual agency and social structures.

This perspective, Zheng argues, enables us to hold each other accountable for resisting structural injustice; by occupying our social roles in ways that are innovative and oriented towards resistance, we can engage in boundary-pushing actions that shift the expectations that constitute the role and therefore change the role itself so that it no longer facilitates structural injustice. This is something that cannot be done by trying to step *outside* the relevant social role. One can contribute to shifting the norms around the social role of being an "academic", for example, by acting *as* an academic in ways that are different from current expectations—a course of action that is incompatible with disavowing the role of "academic" altogether. Thus, Zheng concludes, 'we are responsible [for structural injustice] *through* and *in virtue of* our social roles' (2018, 884).

Unlike Zheng, I am not here directly concerned with the question of *responsibility for* structural injustice. I do, however, agree with Zheng's account of *how it is possible* for individuals to contribute to resisting structural injustice through occupying social roles in resistant ways. At minimum, I think Zheng shows that acting as an occupant of a race and/or gender social role—which is to say, having a race and/or gender identity in the identification sense—is one potentially fruitful way in which to resist structural injustice. This makes identity as identification relevant to emancipatory aims.

6.3. Race and Gender Identity Kinds in the Constraints and Enablements Framework

Given the interest that both identity as norm-relevancy and identity as identification hold for emancipatory theorists and given that, as we have seen, having a certain race and/or gender identity can come apart from being a member of the associated hegemonic or interpersonal kinds, I want to include race and gender identity kinds, in both of these senses, within the pluralist account I am developing. In order to fit within the CEF, membership in race and gender identity kinds will have to be shown to be unified by constraints and enablements, in the sense discussed in Chapter 3. I think that this is possible although not entirely straightforward. I'll consider each sense of identity in turn.

In the norm-relevancy sense, having a certain race and/or gender identity is a matter of falling under certain constraints and enablements that concern the ways in which we are able to interpret our actions and experiences. Someone with a female gender identity in this sense can choose whether or not to remove her underarm hair, but she may well not be able to choose whether or not to experience it as transgressive if she keeps it and shows it in public. It is important to note that the constraints and enablements that ground identity as norm-relevancy do *not* concern what actions we are actually able or unable to perform. A person with a female gender identity may be just as able to keep and show her underarm hair as someone with a male gender identity is to keep and show his. The constraint she may be under merely concerns whether she has the ability to experience this action as socially norm-compliant.[5] Accordingly, identity as norm-relevancy kinds have quite limited explanatory power because the constraints are very minimal— they are about whether one can do X *and experience it as transgressive or compliant*, not about whether one can do X or not, full stop. This is important and interesting for understanding people's experiences, but it does not by itself allow us to predict very much about how someone's life will go.

Turning now to identity as identification, the constraints and enablements that ground these race and gender identity kinds are the ones we have *chosen* to hold ourselves to. If someone takes up a race or gender label in a way that then shapes what they feel able or not able to do—for example, someone cannot bring themself to join the women's caucus of their trade union because they do not feel that they are a woman—then this is also a psychological constraint (or enablement, as the case may be). A complication with incorporating this sense of identity into the CEF is that one might think that identity as identification is not properly conceived of as involving constraints

---

[5] I say she *may* be under this constraint because having a female gender identity in the norm-relevancy sense does not require someone to be attuned to *all* of the norms associated with femininity in that context, merely some of them (for further discussion, see Jenkins 2018a).

and enablements at all, because we can always choose to rethink our relation to the label, which would open up different avenues of action to us.

However, I contend that identities in the identification sense *do* involve constraints and enablements *at a given point in time*, because if one's identification is genuine, then it may well be that one cannot rethink one's relation to the relevant label on the spot, so to speak. Although identities in the identification sense are the product of our agency, once we have created them, they structure what is psychologically possible for us until and unless we put in the work of changing them. If this seems doubtful, consider a comparable case involving a physical constraint. If I have built a fence in a square around myself, then it constrains my movement until and unless I dismantle it. For the span of time for which the fence exists, I am no less constrained by it than if it had been built by someone else. The same is true of enablements. If I have built a bridge over a river, I am at that time enabled to cross the river without getting my feet wet, even though I myself built the bridge at an earlier time. Accordingly, we *can* say that identity as identification gives rise to kinds that are constituted by constraints and enablements. In contrast to the kinds that arise from people's experiences of identity as norm-relevancy, these constraints and enablement do concern what people are actually able to do or not do.

Having established that identity kinds in both senses can be thought of as being unified by constraints and enablements, situating accounts of race and gender identity within the CEF requires us to specify the scope, breadth, and granularity of the relevant bundles of constraints and enablements. Here the two accounts of identity point towards slightly different specifications, resulting in two different sets of kinds, but there are some key similarities that justify terming all of the resultant kinds 'identity kinds'.

In terms of scope, accounts of both senses of race and gender identity do not usually focus on very specific social contexts, such that someone would be understood to have a different race or gender identity as they move through different social spaces during the course of a single day. On the other hand, both race and gender norms and the scripts attached to race and gender labels vary significantly across different times and places, such that it would not make much sense to talk about a race or gender identity without specifying *some* time and place (e.g., the twentieth-first-century United Kingdom) that one has in mind. This suggests a medium scope: less context-specific than interpersonal kinds but more context-specific than hegemonic kinds.

In terms of breadth, accounts of both senses of identity suggest that we should restrict our focus primarily to psychological constraints and enablements. This is because, as we have seen, an individual's identity (in both senses) can come apart from the ways in which other people respond to that individual and from the ways in which an individual is situated within social arrangements such as built environments. However, I think the ways in which identities are experienced as embodied mean that it is helpful to also include bodily constraints and enablements. As we saw in §3.5.3, there is a close connection between psychological and bodily constraints and enablements. Recall, for example, Young's (1980) description of the ways in which women can experience feelings of being inhibited from involving all of the body in a movement and from adopting an open stance, which in turn can make it more difficult to perform certain physical actions, such as throwing a ball hard and far. These types of constraints operate through embodied psychological experiences of felt limitation and inhibition. My account classifies this kind of constraint as a bodily constraint. Accordingly, I think we should specify the breadth of identity kinds as including psychological and bodily constraints, rather than being restricted to psychological constraints only. Again, this breadth places race and gender identity kinds between interpersonal kinds (which include only one type of constraint and enablement) and hegemonic kinds (which include all four types of constraint and enablement).

Finally, both accounts of identity have tended to be articulated with regard to single-moniker race and gender kinds, but I think we would do well to also attend to more fine-grained kinds. This is because we can expect that intersectional race–gender identity kinds will often have greater explanatory value than single-moniker race or gender identity kinds, for the same reasons as those considered in relation to hegemonic kinds and interpersonal kinds (see §4.3), namely, the historic co-production of race and gender through social processes that are at once patriarchal, heterosexist, colonialist, and capitalist. These fine-grained identity kinds include kinds such as *working-class White straight woman*, for example.

Another important similarity between the two varieties of identity kinds is that in both cases, the best evidence of someone's kind membership is their own testimony (see Bettcher 2009; Jenkins 2018a). Whether we are trying to establish someone's race and/or gender identity in the norm-relevancy sense or the identification sense, we can do no better than to ask them how they identify and accept their answer as authoritative. I do not mean to say that their answer will necessarily always be correct, even when it is sincere, because facts about identity kind membership are constituted by the actual constraints and enablements the person falls under, and these might be obscured from someone's introspection for various reasons. However, there is not, it seems to me, any *better* way to find out about the psychological constraints and enablements someone experiences than listening to what they have to say about their experiences.

Thus, there are some significant similarities between identity as norm-relevancy and identity as identification. The main *difference* between these two senses of identity is that they focus on slightly different subsets of psychological constraints and enablements, with the former prioritising those that are implicit and experienced as given, and the latter prioritising those that are actively taken up in an exercise of agency. However, I think the two varieties of race and gender kinds that result are similar enough to justify my treating them together as 'identity kinds' for the purposes of contrasting them with hegemonic and interpersonal kinds. Where necessary, I will disambiguate them as 'identity (as norm-relevancy) kinds' and 'identity (as identification) kinds'.

6.4. Race and Gender Identity Kinds and Ontic Oppression

In this section, I consider whether race and gender identity kinds are ontically oppressive. I will suggest that race and gender identity (as norm-relevancy) kinds cannot themselves be ontically oppressive, but that race and gender identity (as identification) kinds can, and some are.

Let us begin by considering whether race and gender identity (as norm-relevancy) kinds can be ontically oppressive. The constraints and enablements that ground these kinds concern how someone is able to make sense of their actions—which is to say, whether they experience one set of norms or another as providing a benchmark in relation to which their actions feel compliant or transgressive. However, the simple fact of whether one experiences a norm as a reference point for one's actions in this way is not the sort of thing that can itself be oppressive. This is because the experience of transgressing norms is not always negative; one might joyfully revel in transgressing the norm, which could be an experience that tends towards emancipation. Thus, even if a certain *norm* is oppressive, the fact that *someone experiences that norm as relevant to them* is not necessarily oppressive. To put the point another way, identity (as norm-relevancy) kinds are grounded by constraints and enablements that are too distant from the facts about the kinds of actions we can and cannot perform to directly contribute to someone's being oppressed.

Now let us consider race and gender identity (as identification) kinds. These kinds are grounded by psychological and bodily constraints that *do* relate to what actions we can or cannot perform. We come to fall under these constraints and enablements in virtue of the ways in which we have chosen to shape our lives in response to the labels that are available in our social context. These labels offer default 'scripts', or ways of using the label to shape one's life plans. So these identity kinds do involve constraints and enablements that may be oppressive. What is more, many of these scripts reflect hierarchical social structures. For example, imagine someone who takes up the label of *middle-class White heterosexual woman* in such a way that she shapes her life plans so as to prioritise meeting conventional beauty standards and having an immaculate home over things that she would, in fact, have found more fulfilling, such as pursuing creative hobbies and fostering meaningful connections in her community. It's tempting to say that this person is oppressively constrained and enabled by her gender identity.

I think this is broadly right, but remember that identity as identification kinds are very fine-grained. Saying that the woman we just considered is oppressively constrained and enabled *by her particular gender identity* is different from saying that she is oppressively constrained and enabled *by simply having a 'female gender identity'*. Other people who also have a female gender identity (in the identification sense) are not similarly constrained and enabled, because they are responding to different social scripts. This includes people who share the particular intersectional identity *middle-class White heterosexual woman*. We can say that some gender identity kinds are oppressive, but these will not be kinds like *woman*. Rather, they will be much more fine-grained kinds relating to particular intersectional identities that involve specific hegemonic scripts.

So race and gender identity (as identification) kinds can be sites of ontic oppression, but the kinds in question will be very fine-grained. They will relate not to identities such as *woman* but rather to particular hegemonic conceptions of femininity to which race, class, sexuality, and other dimensions of social experience are relevant. Of course, as well as scripts that reflect hierarchical structures, there are plenty of resistant scripts, too, and people often take these up when they identify with labels. For example, Appiah talks about people who take up the label *Black* and shape their lives so as to prioritise joining together with others to resist racism (1996, 71). Thus, some race and gender identity (as identification) kinds can serve a positive emancipatory function.

It might be objected that the psychological and bodily constraints and enablements that unify race and gender identity (as identification) kinds cannot be oppressive (and so such kinds cannot be ontically oppressive) because those constraints and enablements are *chosen*. However, the fact that this is so does not preclude the possibility that identity (as identification) kinds might be ontically oppressive. Oppression very often includes constraints and enablements that are in some sense chosen by those who fall under them, and theorists of oppression tend to draw attention to the circumstances under which those choices were made, rather than treating the presence of choice as automatically legitimating unequal outcomes. Ann Cudd (1994), for example, argues that oppressive societies often feature vicious cycles in which a social group comes to suffer serious harm in part through the individually rational decisions of the group members. Where these choices are made in the context of an unjust framework, one that unfairly distributes options and power unevenly, the mere presence of choice does not block the conclusion that the group suffers oppression (Cudd 1994, 40–41). Accordingly, the fact that race and gender identity (as identification) kinds involve choice does not mean that they cannot be oppressive, at least on most accounts of oppression.

Overall, then, race and gender identity (as identification) kinds are quite similar to interpersonal race and gender kinds in terms of their relation to ontic oppression: some race and gender identity (as identification) kinds are ontically oppressive, but others are not, and some even serve an emancipatory function. Thus, we cannot make blanket claims to the effect that race and gender identity (as identification) kinds associated with oppressed groups are ontically oppressive.

6.5. Two Types of Ontic Oppression

I will now move beyond the question of whether race and gender identity kinds are themselves ontically oppressive to show how considering race and gender identity kinds enables us to identify a distinction between two different ways in which hegemonic race and gender kinds and interpersonal race and gender kinds can be ontically oppressive. In the Chapters 4 and 5, I considered forms of ontic oppression relating to race and gender kinds that applied to everyone who was constructed as a member of the kind in question. In other words, the constraints and enablements that grounded these kinds were such that they would be oppressive *for any human individual*. However, I think it is also possible for constraints and enablements to be such that they are oppressive *for some human individuals* but not for others. When this happens, it is because the constraints and enablements function to funnel some people towards subordinated social positions (characterised by exploitation, marginalisation, powerlessness, cultural imperialism, violence, and communicative curtailment) but do not function to similarly funnel others, due to differences between the individuals in question. The most obvious form of difference that is relevant here relates to the needs of individuals.

For example, in our own society, a constraint that prevented people from using glasses or contact lenses would be liable to result in marginalisation for individuals who need to use glasses or contact lenses in order to read text or navigate social spaces, but it would not result in marginalisation for those who do not need to use glasses or contact lenses. I will call ontic oppression that impacts all human individuals who are constructed as members of the kind in question 'generalised ontic oppression', and I will call ontic oppression that impacts only some human individuals based on the interaction of the constraints and enablements with their particular needs 'selective ontic oppression'.

One situation in which selective ontic oppression can occur is through the way that someone is constructed being at odds with their identity. For example, if a person, Dara, is constructed as a member of the interpersonal kind *man* in most contexts but has a female gender identity, then she is subject to constraints that are liable to result in her experiencing various aspects of subordination such as marginalisation. If Dara needs to use a public facility such as a toilet or a changing room, for instance, she may be constrained from using women's facilities, leaving her with no appropriate alternative and perhaps even curtailing her ability to leave her house (Jones and Slater 2020; for further discussion, see §8.4.2). Dara may be required to present herself as male as a condition (either official or unofficial) of employment, and she may not be able to bring herself to do so (for a case of this kind, see Williams 2020; on the wrongs of misgendering in general, see Kapusta 2016). Being

prevented from traversing public space and being unable to secure employment are both paradigmatic instances of marginalisation, one of the aspects
of subordinated social positions according to my account (see Chapter 2). It
seems clear that Dara is oppressed in virtue of falling under these constraints.

Now imagine a cis man, Ethan; he is constructed as a member of the same
interpersonal kinds *man* as Dara, but he differs from Dara in having a male
gender identity. Like Dara, he is constrained from using women's facilities
and presenting as female, but *unlike* Dara, he does not need to be able to do
these things. Accordingly, being prevented from using women's facilities and
from presenting as female does not result in Ethan being unable to traverse
public space or secure employment. As a result, although Ethan is subjected
to the same constraints as Dara, he, in contrast to her, does not experience
marginalisation or other aspects of subordination. Dara is oppressed in
virtue of falling under the constraints and enablements, but Ethan is not.

Thus, Dara suffers a selective ontic oppression in virtue of being socially
constructed as a member of the interpersonal kind *man*, while Ethan does
not, even though Ethan and Dara are both socially constructed as members
of the same interpersonal kind. This example highlights that one and the
same kind—an interpersonal kind *man*, in this case—can be selectively
ontically oppressive to some of those who are constructed as kind members,
even if it is not generally ontically oppressive, in the sense that not all human
individuals who are constructed as kind members are thereby oppressed.

We need to be careful here. I don't want to say that *anytime* someone is
socially constructed as a member of a kind that is at odds with their identity,
they suffer ontic oppression. That would, I think, be too broad. Rather, the
claim is that having a certain identity *can* give rise to genuine needs that are
such that if a person cannot meet those needs, they are oppressed. When a
person is socially constructed as a member of a kind that is constituted by
constraints and enablements that are at odds *with those needs* but not at odds
with the needs of all human individuals, and where the mis-match between
needs and constraints/enablements gives rise to oppression, then this is an
instance of selective ontic oppression. I take the needs of trans people to be
able to navigate society in accordance with their gender identity to be a paradigm instance of this phenomenon.

I suspect that disentangling selective and general ontic oppression on
an individual level may prove difficult. It may in practice be hard to distinguish between constraints and enablements that are subordinating for any
human individual, on the one hand, and constraints and enablements that

are only subordinating for some human individuals based on their particular needs, on the other. In some cases, one and the same constraint or enablement might be both implicated in the oppression of human individuals in general *and* particularly disadvantageous for some human individuals based on their particular needs, albeit in different ways. Nevertheless, on a macro level—which is to say, when we are talking about ways in which race and gender hegemonic and interpersonal kinds are ontically oppressive, rather than the ways in which a given individual suffers ontic oppression—it makes sense to distinguish these two ways in which kinds can be ontically oppressive. Kinds can be ontically oppressive for all human individuals, and kinds can be ontically oppressive for certain human individuals in virtue of their particular needs, which can include identity-based needs; some kinds are both. So far, I have mostly discussed general ontic oppression, but attending to race and gender identity kinds brings selective ontic oppression into focus because it directs our attention to the needs that can arise from having a certain race or gender identity.

6.6. Conclusion

In this chapter, I have introduced race and gender identity kinds, distinguishing between identity as norm-relevancy and identity as identification and showing that both types of identity kind can be incorporated into the CEF. I have argued that race and gender identity (as norm-relevancy) kinds cannot be ontically oppressive, because they do not involve the right sort of constraints and enablements, but that race and gender identity (as identification kinds) can. However, as with race and gender interpersonal kinds, I argued that race and gender identity (as identification) kinds are not always ontically oppressive and can sometimes even serve an emancipatory function. Finally, I have shown how attending to identity kinds and the needs to which they can give rise draws our attention to the possibility of selective ontic oppression, as contrasted with general ontic oppression, and I have illustrated how someone can suffer selective ontic oppression in virtue of needs arising from their race and/or gender identity.

7

The Constraints and Enablements
Framework Revisited

7.1. Introduction

In the last three chapters, my main claim has been that we cannot make the blanket statement that race and gender kinds are ontically oppressive. We need to attend to different varieties of kinds, including hegemonic race and gender kinds, interpersonal race and gender kinds, and race and gender identity kinds. Some of these kinds are ontically oppressive, some are not, and some even serve an emancipatory function. We also need to be alert for different sorts of ontic oppression, including both general and selective forms of ontic oppression.

Having this detailed picture is useful because, as emancipatory theorists, we need to focus our efforts on eliminating or radically changing oppressive kinds and on fostering and bolstering emancipatory kinds. Exactly *how* we should do that is an even more complicated question, one that I think cannot be addressed at the level of generality at which I have been operating. Rather than setting out to develop a plan for countering ontic oppression specifically, my suggestion is that we need to approach particular emancipatory struggles with an awareness that ontic oppression is one form of oppression that we may encounter.

This picture also serves to further illustrate the CEF. In this chapter, I revisit the CEF now that the accounts of the three different varieties of race and gender kinds that I am drawing attention to—hegemonic kinds, interpersonal kinds, and identity kinds—are on the table. I first outline some benefits of integrating these three different varieties of race and gender kinds into a unifying framework. Then I consider four objections to the pluralist account of race and gender kinds within the CEF that I have offered. These are the strongest objections that I have encountered so far, and, moreover,

Ontology and Oppression. Katharine Jenkins, Oxford University Press. © Katharine Jenkins 2023.
DOI: 10.1093/oso/9780197666777.003.0008

responding to each of them enables me to highlight something important about the pluralist account I have offered.

7.2. The Benefits of Integration

In this chapter and Chapter 6, I have integrated hegemonic race and gender kinds, interpersonal race and gender kinds, and race and gender identity kinds into the CEF. A major benefit of integrating these different accounts of race and gender kinds into the CEF is that it enables us to understand the relationships between these different kinds within a systematic framework. As explained in §3.7, even among philosophers who appear friendly to pluralist accounts of the metaphysics of social kinds (such as gender), the way the different sorts of kinds fit together has seldom been discussed in detail. The CEF fills this gap.

According to the CEF, when A and B advance different conceptions of race and/or gender kinds, they are not, or at least they need not be, engaging in fundamentally different types of analysis or working with radically different sorts of ontologies that are mutually unintelligible. Rather, each of them can be understood as identifying an explanatory kind where an individual is a member of the kind in virtue of falling under certain constraints and enablements. To understand the ontology of these kinds, we need to understand the scope, breadth, and granularity of the constraints and enablements that an individual must fall under in order to be a member of the kind. It follows that we can think of A and B as using the same tools to pick out different kinds according to their different purposes, and we can inquire further into the scope, breadth, and granularity of the different constraints and enablements that A and B are each picking up on to understand this contrast in more detail. Thus, the CEF offers a systematic framework for understanding how different kinds relate to one another.

Without this sort of systematic framework, we may face difficulties when it comes to identifying and resolving disagreements. Davina Cooper puts it well when she states that (those whom I would call) emancipatory theorists need to find

> ways of sustaining incommensurate progressive conceptions [e.g., of gender], attuned to different tasks. This, however, begs a difficult question: can clashing conceptions be sustained *in fruitful relation to each other.*

This is an important question for a range of left projects, where the conceptual terms that support critique may not be the ones that support experimentation or hopeful notions of progress. (2019, 26)

Without an account of how different kinds relate to one another, it is very hard to adjudicate a disagreement between those who advocate different accounts of what appears to be the same kind. A lurking worry here is that without a framework, we will be confronted with a sort of ontological free-for-all, a mish-mash of different accounts of race and gender in which anything goes and it is impossible to understand and assess disagreements in any kind of systematic way. A further benefit of integrating race and gender kinds into the CEF is that it helps to avoid such a situation by facilitating and structuring productive discussion in cases where there seems to be disagreement about the nature of these kinds. It does this by offering resources for distinguishing different types of disagreement, as I shall now show.

Using the CEF, we can identify a number of different things that might be going on when person A and person B appear to disagree about the nature of gender kinds. First, it may turn out that there is no genuine disagreement after all. Since, as we have seen, the CEF holds that human social kinds are explanatory kinds and that kinds have explanatory value only in relation to explanatory purposes, it follows that A and B might simply have different explanatory purposes from each other. In this case, each kind might be most useful for the relevant set of purposes, and each purpose might be a genuinely valuable one, meaning that there is no real conflict—merely a need to be careful with language to avoid misunderstandings. For example, if I am trying to investigate a certain economic disparity, and you are trying to figure out who should be able to participate in a certain activist space, then we are just trying to do different things, and it will be no problem if we settle on different accounts of gender kinds. We can think of this as a *mere divergence*.

However, it does not follow that all apparent disagreements that stem from different purposes are mere divergences, and not genuine disagreements, because we can have genuine disagreements *about the normative appropriateness of explanatory purposes*. For example, suppose someone's explanatory purposes are geared solely around understanding how wealthy White women are oppressed, with a view to emancipating solely this limited group of women, and those purposes lead them to pick out a certain social kind as explanatorily useful. Those explanatory purposes can legitimately be criticised on a political and ethical basis: adopting these purposes is contrary to the goal of genuine, collective emancipation because it is liable to further obscure and entrench the oppression of less privileged women (hooks 1984, 1–15; Lugones 2007).

Of course, it's also possible that interlocutors who disagree about a social kind *do* share the same explanatory purposes, such that the disagreement between them must be located elsewhere. Here, again, the CEF helps to structure these disagreements. Such disagreements can involve either disagreement about the empirical facts, for example, about what kinds of constraints and enablements exist, or disagreement about what explanatory role different kinds play, for example, about which predictions and explanations are more informative. Suppose that we are trying to explain and counteract pregnancy-related discrimination in the workplace. An example of the former type of disagreement—call it *empirical disagreement*—would be if we were to disagree about the frequency with which pregnancy-related discrimination occurs in workplaces, based on a shared understanding of what constitutes such discrimination. An example of the latter—call it *interpretative disagreement*—would be a disagreement about how we should understand the precondition for someone experiencing pregnancy-related discrimination (and accordingly which incidents we should be capturing in our data); options here might include (1) actually being pregnant, (2) being capable of becoming pregnant, (3) being perceived as being capable of becoming pregnant, or (4) being perceived more generally as a woman. If we want to gather statistics that will help us tackle pregnancy-related discrimination, which of these kinds of people would it be most helpful to focus on? These two different forms of disagreement require different investigations to resolve them. Empirical disagreement requires further investigation of empirical states of affairs, whereas interpretative disagreement requires comparative assessment of different theories and explanatory models.

To sum up, when faced with an apparent disagreement about social kinds, the CEF directs us to ask the following questions:

1. Do the parties share the same explanatory purposes?
2. If not, does each party accept the others' explanatory purposes as legitimate?
3. Do the parties agree about the empirical facts?
4. Do the parties agree about the best theoretical interpretation of the empirical facts?

(See Figure 7.1 for a visual representation.)

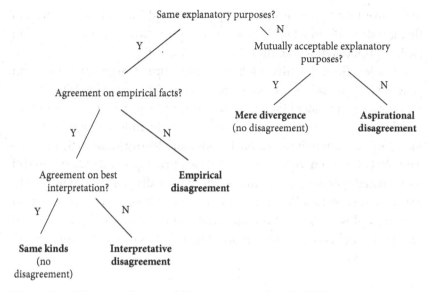

Figure 7.1. Diagram of types of disagreement within the CEF

In this chapter and Chapter 6, I have set out a selection of race and gender kinds that I claim can indeed, as Cooper puts it, 'be sustained in fruitful relation to one another'. However, as I have shown, the CEF goes beyond this particular suggestion in offering resources to distinguish different types of disagreement in a way that points towards the best avenue for further investigation to resolve the disagreement. This capacity is a significant benefit of the account.

Finally, a third benefit of integrating the three different accounts of race and gender kinds that I have considered here into a pluralist framework is that some objections that have been raised against one or another account can be mitigated or avoided when it is considered as one part of a larger pluralist picture. For example, several worries often raised against accounts of (what I have called) hegemonic race and gender kinds are assuaged by adopting a pluralist picture that situates these kinds as one among several varieties each of which plays important explanatory role. Mikkola (2009) has argued that it is a problematic result that some very privileged people who seem to be women do not count as members of the kind *woman* as Haslanger defines it. Mikkola (2016, 104–42) and Alison Stone (2007, 160) have both argued that it is unhelpful to think that there is no way to preserve a category of women whilst ending subordination. In a similar vein, Chike Jeffers has argued that hegemonic accounts of race overlook important cultural aspects of people's experiences of race and that it is desirable to allow that race in a cultural sense could outlast racism (Jeffers 2013; Glasgow et al. 2019, 38–72 and 176–202).

However, these putative problems only arise if hegemonic race and gender kinds are taken to be all there is to race and to gender. When hegemonic race and gender kinds are seen as one variety among several, each of which can do some explanatory work, these objections lose much of their force; we can turn to interpersonal kinds and identity kinds to do the relevant work. For example, we can say that very privileged individuals can still have a female gender identity and be interpersonally gendered as women in many contexts even if they are not members of the hegemonic gender kind *woman*, and we can say that both racial identity kinds and interpersonal race kinds could outlast racial oppression, which is to say, the end of hegemonic race kinds.[1]

7.3. The Proliferation of Kinds

7.3.1. Mason's Challenge

In the remainder of this chapter, I will consider and respond to four objections to the CEF and the pluralist picture of race and gender kinds that I have used it to articulate. The first of these has been advanced in print: in a response to the material presented in this book as Chapter 1, Rebecca Mason (2020) has argued that my claim that social kinds are at least partly constituted by social constraints and enablements, which I take to capture a view shared by many social ontologists, should be rejected.[2] The paper to which Mason

---

[1] We would, of course, then owe a story about exactly how this could be, which is to say, about how the social structures that underpin interpersonal and identity kinds could persist through the kinds of social changes that would bring about the end of hegemonic kinds. I say a little more about this shortly, but the important point at this juncture is that pluralism creates space in which such a story can be offered.

[2] A slight complicating factor in considering Mason's criticism is that she targets the claim that 'social kinds are constituted by social constraints and enablements' (Mason 2020, 1), which is more general than the claim I have, in fact, made (either in the paper to which Mason is responding or in this book), namely, that social kinds are *at least partly* constituted by social constraints and enablements. In order to avoid attributing a misreading of my work to Mason, I will interpret her talk of constitution as allowing for partial constitution, such that the claim 'social kinds are constituted by social constraints and enablements' is compatible with the claim 'social kinds are partly constituted by social constraints and enablements and partly constituted by something else'. Here I will continue to stress the possibility of partial constitution, including in reporting Mason's argument, since it is important.

is responding (Jenkins (2020b) did not include a full account of the CEF but merely the claim that many social ontologists agree that social constraints and enablements at least partly constitute social kinds. However, she interprets my brief remarks in accordance with the direction in which I in fact develop them in constructing the CEF, namely, as positing a form of constitutive social construction in the sense discussed in Chapter 3. In this sense, I take Mason's criticism of my briefer treatment of social kinds as partly constituted by constraints and enablements to pose a challenge that the CEF, as a fuller development of the view she criticises, should be expected to meet.

Mason argues that viewing social kinds as at least partly constitutively constructed by social constraints and enablements 'leads to a proliferation of social kinds that significantly undermines our ability to make empirical generalizations and engage in inductive reasoning about kinds and their members' (2020, 3). This is because, for example, the constraints and enablements that people we intuitively think of as women fall under seem to vary across different times, places, and social contexts. It therefore seems as though we will end up with a large number of different kinds on our hands, rather than one kind *woman*. For example, Mason lists 'Women in the United States prior to 1919 [when American women gained the formal right to vote]' and 'Women in the United States after 1919' as distinct kinds in virtue of the fact that membership of the first kind is partly constituted by falling under the constraint 'cannot vote', but membership of the second kind is not (5).

Mason argues that this is a problem:

> Individuating social kinds in such a fine-grained way undermines our ability to make empirical generalizations and engage in inductive reasoning about social kinds and their members. If women at different times and in different places belong to numerically distinct social kinds, then we cannot say that, for example, women (all women) are more likely to experience sexual assault than men. Given the proliferation of constraints and enablements, and the corresponding proliferation of social kinds, there is no single social kind available to support generalizations about women simpliciter. Yet many empirical generalizations about women simpliciter are well founded. (2020, 6)

I agree with Mason that feminists need to be able to make generalisations about women simpliciter and that many such generalisations are well founded. However, I explicitly welcome the proliferation of numerically distinct social kinds that serve different explanatory purposes. The fine-grained kinds she lists, such as 'Women in the United States prior to 1919', are examples of interpersonal kinds that I am more than willing to include within my pluralist account. The CEF provides resources for systematising the relationship between these different kinds, as I have explained. It is important, though, that the CEF also provides resources for identifying other sorts of social kinds.

In particular, the variable of granularity enables us to specify some kinds in very coarse-grained ways by offering coarse-grained descriptions of the relevant constraints and enablements. For example, here is a constraint:

(a) 'not being legally permitted to stand for political office'.

Here is a similar but much more coarse-grained constraint:

(b) 'being less able to hold political office'.

Some women at certain times and places have fallen under (a). Those women *and also many more women at other times and places* have fallen under (b). This is because there are lots of factors besides legal restrictions that can make women less able to hold political office than men. Here are just two examples from among many such factors: candidates being subject to sexist stereotypes that make it less likely they will get elected, and political office being difficult to combine with family and caring responsibilities due to policies such as office holders not being entitled to maternity leave.[3] More coarse-grained gender kinds are individuated by constraints such as (b) rather than by constraints such as (a). These more coarse-grained kinds, grounded by more coarse-grained constraints and enablements, can support generalisations about women at different times and places.

I submit, then, that the proliferation of fine-grained kinds per se is not a problem from the point of view of the kinds of explanatory purposes Mason has in mind. A problem would indeed arise if we *lacked* other, coarse-grained

---

[3] I am working here with single-moniker gender kinds in order to align with Mason's treatment of the examples; however, I think this is a good example of an instance in which race–gender intersectional kinds are more explanatorily useful than single-moniker kinds. For example, it seems to me unhelpful to think about the restrictions faced by women running for political office without thinking about how these restrictions are different for women who are differently racialised, and it likewise seems unhelpful to contrast the situation of women in this respect with that of men without considering the restrictions faced by men of colour.

kinds that could do that explanatory work, but I have argued that the CEF can also include such kinds. Thus, pace Mason, it is not the case that '[i]f women at different times and in different places belong to numerically distinct social kinds, then we cannot say that, for example, women (all women) are more likely to experience sexual assault than men' (Mason 2020, 6), because the antecedent of this conditional is compatible with it being the case that women at different times and in different places *also* belong to one and the same (more coarse-grained) social kind, which *can* support the relevant generalisation.[4] Since I think this is, in fact, the case, I can admit many fine-grained gender kinds into my pluralist ontology without losing the ability to do the sort of explanatory work Mason has in mind, and which I agree is important for feminist purposes.

Thus, I think that the CEF does have the resources needed to respond to the objection Mason levelled against my earlier, more minimal claim that social kinds are at least partly constituted by social constraints and enablements.

7.3.2. The Unification Question

Although I think that Mason's challenge can be met, it brings into focus a question that the CEF as I have stated it so far does not yet include the resources to answer. This is the question of what ties together the different kinds I have been calling 'gender kinds' and 'race kinds' such that they are all properly conceived of as *gender* kinds or as *race* kinds. Call this the 'unification question'. The unification question arises from considering the proliferation of kinds because this proliferation might seem worrying if we have no way of knowing which kinds are race and/or gender kinds and which are not.

At this juncture, it is helpful to bring in a fruitful distinction developed by Brian Epstein (2015). Epstein offers a framework for social ontology that centres on a distinction between two different metaphysical relationships, 'grounding' and 'anchoring'. This distinction rests on the claim that '[a]ny given social fact has building blocks, and also metaphysical reasons why that fact's building blocks are what they are' (2015, 74). Epstein terms the former the 'grounds' of a social fact and the latter, its 'anchors'. Let's see how

---

[4] One might worry that the coarse-grained kinds cannot support the generalisations Mason wants them to explain because these generalisations are too close to the (coarse-grained) constraints and enablements that constitute the relevant kinds; but this is now in my view a different worry about the direction of explanation, to which I will respond in §7.5.

this distinction works in relation to a specific social fact: the fact that a small, metal, painted figurine F is a holy statue of a certain religion.

According to Epstein, the grounds of this social fact (that F is a holy statue) are the facts in virtue of which F counts as a holy statue, say, the fact that F has a certain appearance A in virtue of which it depicts a recognisable deity and that it has been made in accordance with ritual R. Anchors are the facts in virtue of which *these are the things* that make it the case that F is a holy statue. As Epstein puts it, anchors are the facts that 'set up or put in place the grounding conditions for social facts' (2015, 84) such as *F is a holy statue*. In this case, then, the anchors might include the fact that the religious texts describe the appearance of the relevant deity as A and state that R is the appropriate ritual to employ in making a holy statue, the fact that the religious authorities of the day agree that this is so, and the fact that day-to-day judgements of which objects are holy statues are based on the perception of which objects meet these criteria. Epstein describes criteria such as these as 'frame principles'; social facts are *grounded*, whereas frame principles are *anchored*. One of the main implications of this distinction is that the question of how social facts are grounded should be separated from the question of how frame principles are anchored, with social ontologists pursuing a 'grounding inquiry' and an 'anchoring inquiry' as separate projects (2015, 86).

A number of critics responding to Epstein's framework have challenged his claim that grounding and anchoring are distinct metaphysical relationships (Hawley 2019; Mikkola 2019). Epstein terms the position these critics adopt—that anchoring is a subspecies of grounding—'conjunctivism'. Note, though, that even if we were to adopt a conjunctivist position, the distinction between *what Epstein terms* 'grounding' and *what Epstein terms* 'anchoring' remains on the table. That distinction is not what is at issue in the conjunctivism debate. All parties seem to grant that there are two relations that are worth differentiating, one concerning social facts about kind membership such as *F is a holy statue* and the other concerning social facts in the form of frame principles such as *if some object has appearance A and has been made in accordance with ritual R, that object is a holy statue*. Whether it's worth drawing *some sort of distinction* between these types of relations is not what is at issue. Rather, the disagreement concerns the nature of that distinction: are grounding and anchoring best thought of as two distinct sorts of metaphysical relations, or are they better conceived of as one sort of metaphysical relation (grounding, perhaps) that takes different forms, one in relation to facts about the kind memberships of individuals and one in relation to frame principles? Given that the disagreement between Epstein and those he calls 'conjunctivists' is so restricted, we can use the grounding/anchoring distinction, and hence Epstein's framework, to help us understand social kinds *without* taking a stance on the deeper metaphysical questions that are at stake in the conjunctivism debate.

The grounding–anchoring framework is compatible with the CEF and indeed complements it in a useful way. The claim that social kinds are explanatory kinds, which is an important part of the CEF, can be understood as the claim that social kinds are *anchored* by whatever features of the situation underpin the patterns and regularities that make the kind suitable for playing an explanatory role. Against this backdrop, we can explain the role of constraints and enablements even more precisely: constraints and enablements *ground* social facts about the kind membership of individuals.

To break this down, let's consider a fact about a human social kind: the fact that someone, call them 'Zadie', is a priest. According to the CEF, the social fact *Zadie is a priest* is grounded by facts about the ways in which Zadie is constrained and enabled—for example, the fact that Zadie is entitled to perform certain religious ceremonies and is obliged to visit the sick and dying. But what makes *these* constraints and enablements the decisive factor in determining whether or not Zadie is a priest? This is the anchoring question, and the answer the CEF gives is that the social practices that exist in Zadie's context give rise to regularities centred on these constraints and enablements that make the kind *individuals so constrained and enabled* suitable for use in explanation in the context of a broadly sociological inquiry. Thus, the social practices anchor a frame principle according to which individuals constrained and enabled in specific ways are members of the kind *priest*, and then the fact that Zadie is so constrained and enabled grounds the fact *Zadie is a priest*.[5] We can see, then, that the CEF is an answer to what Epstein terms 'the grounding inquiry' and therefore that it sits comfortably within the grounding–anchoring framework.[6]

---

[5] Here I'm treating the explanatory purposes in relation to which the kind has explanatory value as separate from its anchors. On this view, for a given explanatory kind, there are grounds that make things into members of the kind, anchors that give rise to patterns and regularities that make the kind suitable for use in explanations of some sort or another, and explanatory purposes according to which kind has actual explanatory value. Alternatively, one might view explanatory purposes as *also* falling into the category of anchors. This is an intriguing thought but one that I cannot pursue here, since my main concern is with the grounding inquiry. Thanks to Esa Diaz-Leon for helpful discussion on this point.

[6] Recall that making use of the grounding–anchoring framework in this kind of way does not require us to endorse Epstein's claim that grounding and anchoring are distinct metaphysical relationships.

I propose to think of the 'unification question' as sitting alongside the 'grounding question' and the 'anchoring question' that Epstein helpfully demarcates. The latter two questions are about a given social kind, specifically about what makes an individual a member of the kind (the grounding question) and what makes the kind have the membership conditions that it has (the anchoring question). The unification question, on the other hand, is about the relationship between distinct social kinds that are nevertheless intuitively related, perhaps in the sense of all being plausible candidate meanings for certain terms or perhaps in the sense of doing related sorts of explanatory work. Stated in general terms, the unification question is: what makes it the case that the kind belongs to a certain category of social kind, for example, the category 'gender kinds'?

The unification question only arises for pluralists about social kinds. One approach to answering it is suggested by the work of Elizabeth Barnes (2020), whose pluralist account of gender kinds attributes a special explanatory role to the sorts of social structures that anchor (what I have called) hegemonic gender kinds. Gender is many things, according to Barnes, but all of these things 'can ultimately be explained in terms of the basic binary social structure that attributes social significance to perceived biological sex, and which privileges some and disadvantages others based on assumptions about what ought to follow from being perceived as male or female' (2020, 715). As Barnes points out, understanding gender social structures as organised along binary lines is compatible with positing many gender kinds, including some that fall outside the man/woman binary, because there are more than two ways in which a kind can relate to a binary structure (e.g., it might confound the binary).

I think one available reading of this claim is to view Barnes as suggesting an answer to the unification question. Understood in this way, Barnes's claim is that 'the basic binary social structure that attributes social significance to perceived biological sex, and which privileges some and disadvantages others based on assumptions about what ought to follow from being perceived as male or female', is what ultimately explains why a given social kind is (or is not) a gender kind. And the parallel claim about race would be that the basic social structure that attributes social significance to perceived biological ancestral links to different geographic regions, and privileges some and disadvantages others based on assumptions about what ought to follow from being perceived to have such links, is what ultimately explains why a given social kind is (or is not) a race kind. I think both of these claims are plausible and serve as the basis for good answers to the unification question.

At this point, the question arises of what *sort* of relation must hold between a kind K and the relevant social structures picked out by Barnes in order for us to say that K is a race and/or gender kind. I'm wary of requiring too direct a relationship here, because I want to allow that a kind could, in principle, be a race or gender kind even *after* the oppressive social structures of race and gender have ceased to exist (see Jeffers 2013 for an example of this view regarding race; see Haslanger 2017b for an example of this view regarding gender). Whether we should *aim* for there to still be such kinds is a different question (on this point, see Cull 2019), but it's a question that I think we should be able to treat as a live and substantive one, rather than one to which we are forced to return a negative answer in virtue of the impossibility of such a continuation on our ontological model.

An obvious way to go here is to require a historical relation (Bach 2012). On this approach, we might say that for K to be a race and/or gender kind is for K to be historically related to the race and/or gender social structures. This allows that there could be race and gender kinds after race and gender social structures have been eradicated, because those kinds might originally have been formed in relation to those structures or be the causal successors of kinds that were so formed. It also allows that interpersonal kinds existing within the context of a resistant community can have a base property that has nothing whatsoever to do with perceived biological sex (self-identification, for instance) and nevertheless be gender kinds. All that is required is for these kinds to have been formed in response—a *resistant* response, perhaps—to the oppressive gender social structure, since in this case they would historically related to that structure.

I am, then, attracted to responses to the unification question regarding race and gender kinds that (1) focus on social structures and (2) require a historical relation to such structures in order for a kind to be a race and/or gender kind. However, these are only some preliminary thoughts. Much more needs to be said about exactly how these structures are to be identified, as well the precise nature of historical relationship that is to be required, but I will not take up that task here. As I have said, considerations about ontic oppression are focused on the grounding question, and the CEF is a response to that question only. Like the anchoring question, the unification question, though ultimately important for a full ontological picture, is secondary for my purposes in this project. Whatever answer to the unification question we ultimately settle on, it will not matter for the claims I have defended here about which race and gender kinds are ontically oppressive.[7]

7.4. The Selection of Constraints and Enablements for the Grounding Role

The second objection I will consider is one that I have encountered in various discussions of this work, and it concerns the question of which constraints and enablements are taken to ground race and gender kinds, whether hegemonic, interpersonal, or identity-based. Which constraints and enablements experienced by women, for example, are part of what makes someone a woman, and which are merely something that happens to be experienced by women? To bring this question into focus, consider a coffee shop in which women are entitled to claim a free coffee on International Women's Day.[8] Is this enablement part of what makes someone a woman in that coffee shop? The answer to this question is that this constraint is part of what grounds the interpersonal kind *woman* in the specific context of that coffee shop, because that kind is unified by all the ways in which being taken to have the relevant base property (probably, in this case, self-identification as a woman) makes a patterned difference to how people treat someone. However, the free-coffee enablement is not part of what unifies the hegemonic kind *woman*, because it does not play a significant enough role in maintaining patterns that support structural explanations.

This highlights an important feature of the way in which I am approaching the role of constraints and enablements in unifying race and gender kinds: what matters is *the actual difference that a certain constraint or enablement makes* to the relevant regularities and patterns, not whether it is *considered* to be definitive or constitutive (as opposed to incidental) by the people in the context in question. Interpersonal kinds, with their very tightly specified contexts, require merely that the constraint/enablement makes some systematic difference in that context; hegemonic kinds, with their much more expansive contexts, require that the constraint/enablement

---

[7] Recall that I am using the phrase 'race and gender kinds' in a specific sense; see §4.1.

[8] I am indebted to Elizabeth Barnes for suggesting this example. My thanks to her and to Rae Langton for pressing me to consider this point.

makes enough of a difference to impact on broader patterns in the wider context; and identity kinds of either variety require that the constraint/enablement manifests on a psychological level for the individuals in question in a way that makes a significant difference to either their experience of relevant norms (identity as norm-relevancy) or their self-conception (identity as identification).

I think this approach to the question of which constraints and enablements contribute to unifying a kind is important, because perceptions of which constraints and enablements are relevant in this respect are not reliable. To illustrate this, consider a striking example of racialised vulnerability to violence: the fire at Grenfell Tower, a residential tower block in London, on the 14 June 2017, in which at least seventy-two people were killed and at least seventy were injured. Flammable cladding panels, which did not comply with regulations, had been installed on the exterior of the building to improve its appearance, and these contributed to the rapid and deadly spread of the fire caused by a faulty refrigerator. Residents of Grenfell Tower, and hence victims of the fire, were predominantly racialised other than as White, many were Muslims, and many had either a personal or a family history of migration. The demographics of nearby neighbourhoods, views from which were supposedly improved by the cladding, were much more White and much more affluent. Residents had raised serious concerns about fire safety for many years before the fire took place (El-Enany 2019).

Nadine El-Enany (2019) forcefully argues that the structural causes of the atrocity include Britain's history of colonialism and imperialism, a history that includes the systematic creation of pressures on colonised people to seek to move to Britain, together with negative portrayals of, and punitive responses to, such movement by the British state (see also El-Enany 2020). This history, she argues, offers a structural explanation for why '[t]he marginalised poor housed in Grenfell Tower could not escape their heightened vulnerability to harm and premature death, a condition intensified as a result of rapid gentrification in the area, and the council's prioritisation of the needs of new, predominantly wealthy white residents' (2019, 57). One way in which this structural vulnerability manifested was in hostile and dismissive responses from authorities to whom residents raised safety issues in advance of the fire. As El-Enany notes, 'Some Grenfell survivors reported that "they felt the implicit message from everyone they contacted before the fire for help with the building was 'you are a guest in this borough, and a guest in this country, you have no right to complain' " ' (El-Enany 2019, 58, citing Foster 2017).[9]

Being less able to get the borough council's office to take one's safety concerns seriously may not seem obviously like part of what makes someone a person of colour, but El-Enany shows that it is part of the difference that perceived ancestral links to colonised geographic regions make in contemporary Britain. Therefore, on my account, it is part of what grounds interpersonal race kinds in some of the spaces traversed by Grenfell Tower residents. Moreover, unlike the example of free coffee on International Women's Day, this interpersonal constraint *does* contribute to a broader structural pattern of vulnerability to harm and to premature death, and therefore it *does* make it into the grounds of hegemonic race kinds in the UK context. I contend that this is a helpful approach because it avoids having us ask whether people are "thinking about" or "acting because of" race and/or gender when they interact with others—something that is often very difficult to establish. Rather, we look for patterns in what people can and cannot do, and we consider the implications of these patterns—which can be deadly, as they were in the case of Grenfell Tower.

7.5. The Direction of Explanation

The third concern regarding the CEF that I will consider is also one that I have repeatedly encountered in discussions of this work, and it relates to the direction of explanation between constraints/enablements and kinds.[10] For example, I am presenting hegemonic race and gender kinds, understood to be unified by constraints and enablements, as having explanatory value from an emancipatory perspective, but some readers may wonder how this position squares with the idea that we might reach for race and gender kinds precisely to *explain* why someone is constrained or enabled the way they are. Consider a constraint that seems to be part of what unifies hegemonic kinds, say, the constraint of women not being as easily able to earn certain amounts of money as men (in other words, the gender pay gap). On my view, an individual's being less able to earn money for her labour is part of what

---

[9] Note the resonance here with Nish Kumar's words quoted in §5.4.

[10] My thanks to members of the Cambridge Feminist Philosophy Reading Group and to Alejandro Naranjo Sandoval for encouraging me to address this question and for productive exchanges on the subject.

makes it the case that she is a member of the hegemonic gender kind *woman*. On the other hand, however, it also seems like something that we would want to use the hegemonic gender kind *woman* to explain (Haslanger 2016b). For example, we might want to say that Lisa earns less money than Larry because Lisa is a woman. How do these two things fit together?[11]

This is an important question. My response is that any specific constraint or enablement is only *part* of the story about the nature of the hegemonic kind *woman* and that there are other parts that make it possible to use that kind in giving a substantive explanation of a particular constraint. So imagine that I and a questioner have the following exchange:

Q: Why is Lisa being paid less than her male colleagues for the same job?
A: Because Lisa [is a woman].

What I *don't* want is to be forced to cash the square brackets out as follows:

Q: Why is Lisa being paid less than her male colleagues for the same job?
A: Because Lisa [is being paid less than her colleagues for the same job].

If that's all I could say, I think that the account of hegemonic gender and race kinds within the CEF that I'm advocating here would be in trouble. But on my view, we don't have to say that. For one thing, we can refer to other constraints and enablements that also play a role in unifying the hegemonic kind *woman*, and for another, in the full account, there is a role for the factors that underpin the regularities or patterns in constraints and enablements. As I explained in §7.3, these are what Epstein (2015) calls the 'anchors' of the kind, which are the factors that hold in place the grounding conditions. Anchors, in my view, are things like social practices, which involve shared cultural schemas that shape people's access to material resources (Haslanger 2017a; 2017b).[12] A full explanation of why Lisa is paid less than Larry would also include an explanation of the relevant anchors, although this is beyond the scope of this project.

Instead of being cashed out in the worryingly circular way that we saw earlier, then, the square brackets get cashed out something more like this:

---

[11] Equivalent questions arise for interpersonal kinds and identity kinds, but here I will focus on hegemonic gender kinds; the response I present can straightforwardly be generalised to other sorts of kinds.

[12] For more on this, see §3.3.1.

Q: Why is Lisa being paid less than her male colleagues for the same job?
A: Because Lisa [is subject to a complex interlocking web of social constraints and enablements, one of which is having a harder time getting paid fairly, others of which include things like an expectation to be inter-personally charming and deferential, an expectation to do more than half of the childcare, and so on, and these are held in place by factors like the social practices of Lisa's society.]

On this picture, we can make sense of the (I grant, intuitive) thought that it is genuinely explanatory to say that Lisa is underpaid because she is a woman. Of course, there is also a constitutive relationship going in the other way, where Lisa's being more likely to be underpaid is part of what makes her a woman; but this does not, I contend, render the gender-based explanation of Lisa's being underpaid uninformative once we have the full picture on the table.

7.6. Pluralism about Gender Kinds and Misgendering

The final objection that I will consider is one that has been on my mind throughout the project and that has also been raised on several occasions in discussions of the work.[13] It concerns the implications of gender pluralism for the way people speak to and about trans people. In brief, the worry is that the gender pluralist account I have presented licenses the misgendering of trans people (by 'misgendering', I mean the application of inappropriate gender markers and/or the withholding of appropriate gender markers). As we shall see, though, I think there are actually two different worries in the picture here, which require different responses. I'll respond to the first of them here, while responding to the second will be my task in Chapter 8.

Let's first get clearer on the kind of situation that generates the concern about licensing misgendering. Suppose that Alex is a trans woman working as a programmer in a software company, and she is the only woman pro-grammer who works for that company. Alex is not out to management; the people running the company view her as a man. However, she is out to a few of her co-workers, who fully respect and support her. Two of these co-workers, Brett and Carl, are privately discussing why the company never

---

[13] Thanks to David MacDonald and to Han Edgoose for helpful conversations on this point.

hires programmers who are perceived (by those doing the hiring) to be women, with a view to trying to remedy this state of affairs, which they find deplorable. Consider the following exchange:

BRETT: This company has *never* hired a woman programmer. That's a
·   problem! We need to figure out what's going on with that.
CARL: What about Alex? She's a woman.
BRETT: In the context of what I'm talking about here, Alex is not a woman.

Now, Brett and Carl seem to have purposes (reducing gender discrimination) that are aptly described as emancipatory. Moreover, it seems clear that the gender kind that is relevant for these purposes is an interpersonal kind. The scope of this kind seems to be the company workplace, or perhaps the specific part of the company workplace where hiring happens (the interview room, the boardroom where post-interview discussions take place, and so on). My account suggests that Brett is aiming to talk about these kinds, even though he may lack a detailed philosophical understanding of them. What is more, my account suggests that he is right to do so. Furthermore, it is true that Alex is not a member of the interpersonal gender kind *woman* in the relevant context; the people who hired her thought of her as a man (and still do), and so she is interpersonally constrained and enabled in ways that are characteristic of the interpersonal kind *man* and not the interpersonal kind *woman*.

So Brett has identified a gender kind that is genuinely explanatory relative to his purposes, and those purposes are emancipatory ones. According to my pluralist account, then, everything here has gone as it ought; nevertheless, the worry goes, it is still troubling for Brett to say of Alex that she is not a woman. It seems to constitute misgendering, which is widely understood to always be wrong (Bettcher 2009; Kapusta 2016). Thus, my account faces a problem: it appears to sanction Brett's utterance, where this sanctioning is held to be an unacceptable result. (By 'sanction' here, I mean 'entail that the utterance is an appropriate one to make, all things considered'.) This is the first of the two worries that I think some people may have in connection to this kind of case; I'll respond to it and then turn to the second worry.

I grant that it would be a problem for my account, or at least a significant drawback, if it did sanction Brett's utterance—but I do not think that it does so. This is because there is a large gap between giving an account of the ontology of gender kinds, which is what my account is, and determining which utterances about gender are appropriate. More precisely, there is a *series* of gaps. Recall (from §4.1) that, following Barnes (2020), I take investigating the nature of gender kinds to be a separate philosophical project from that of establishing the meaning of gender terms. I therefore do not take myself to be committed to saying that when Brett says that Alex 'is not a woman', his use of 'woman' refers to the interpersonal gender kind *woman* in the relevant context, such that he says something true. This may be the case, but my account does not establish that it is the case. For that, an account of what the term 'woman' usually means would be needed—in other words, an account of the semantics of 'woman'. I have not offered such an account. So this is the first gap: the gap from ontology to semantics.

However, semantics is not the only thing that is relevant to assessing the appropriateness of utterances. We also need to consider pragmatics: the meaning of particular utterances in particular contexts and the effects of utterances beyond their meaning (for example, what they imply or what speech acts they are used to perform). There are all sorts of ways in which Brett's utterance may be considered problematic on a pragmatic level. Even if what he says is literally true, it might communicate something in this context that is false; for example, it might convey the impression that Alex should not be able to use the women's bathrooms in the workplace (for arguments along these lines, see Dembroff 2018, 44–45; Barnes 2020, 721–22). It might also, or alternatively, be a way of performing a speech act that should not be performed, such as a speech act of subordinating Alex. Either of these possibilities would be enough to make the speech act inappropriate, even if what Brett is directly saying is literally true. So this is the second gap: the gap from semantics to pragmatics.

Suppose, though, that Brett's utterance turns out to be in the clear on a pragmatic as well as a semantic level. There is still a final dimension of analysis that could be used to criticise it, which we can think of as *prescriptive*: How should we be aiming to use words? What collective linguistic practices should we be fostering? One might well think that even if Brett's utterance does not have dubious pragmatics in the context in which it is made (because, for example, Brett and Carl both respect Alex's gender identity, and each knows this about the other), it is the *sort* of utterance that is *liable* to have negative consequences in other contexts (for example, if it was uttered in front of people who do not think that trans women should be able to use women's bathrooms). For this reason, one might think that we should aim to avoid such utterances in order to help contribute to a linguistic shift such that gender terms simpliciter (e.g., 'woman') come to be reserved for gender identity kinds, meaning that they would never be used in a way that is at odds with how someone identifies their own gender. If we adopted this view, we would say that although Brett is trying to express something that is true and important, he should choose different words, given the kind of linguistic practices that it is desirable to foster. So this is the third gap: from pragmatics to prescription.

All that my account entails is that the claim about gender kinds that Brett is trying to convey (i.e., which kinds matter for his purposes and how Alex is situated relative to these kinds) is correct. It does not entail that Brett is right to say, 'Alex is not a woman', for, as we have seen, there might be a problem with this utterance at a semantic level, at a pragmatic level, or in relation to a prescriptive approach that we have good reason to take. This would be so even if there was no other way for Brett to express his point (sometimes saying something true can do more harm than good)—but, in fact, there are plenty of ways for Brett to express that point using alternative language: instead of saying, 'Alex is not a woman', he might say, 'Alex isn't counted as a woman in the context I'm talking about', or, 'the people who matter in the context of what I'm talking about don't perceive Alex as a woman'. Either of these, it seems to me, would avoid misgendering Alex. Given that my account of gender kinds does not entail that Brett's utterance is appropriate, the account does not sanction misgendering.

In my experience of discussing this point, however, I have found that this is not enough for some critics. It seems as though what some people really want here is an account of the *ontology* of gender kinds that makes what Brett says count as false. That is, they want an ontology of gender that *guarantees* that the only correct claim that can be made about Alex's membership in a gender kind is that she is a woman. This is the second version of the misgendering worry: that my account of the ontology of gender kinds does not guarantee that any utterance that misgenders someone will count as false—and that this is a problem.[14] Note that this is a much stronger demand than the first worry: the first worry asked only that my account avoid sanctioning any

---

[14] Notice how the two worries come apart and how the second worry demands something more than is needed to respond to the first worry. An account might avoid *sanctioning misgendering* whilst failing to *guarantee the falsity of misgendering on the basis of ontological considerations*—and, indeed, this is the position my own account actually occupies.

utterances that misgender, whereas this second worry holds that the account must guarantee the falsity of all utterances that misgender.[15]

My account certainly does not offer any such guarantee—but I do not think that this is a problem. Indeed, to aim to offer such a guarantee would be contrary to the ideas about ontic injustice and ontic oppression that are at the core of this project. I believe that the way social kinds exist can be profoundly wrongful and oppressive, and I believe that we need to recognise this fact in order to make progress in emancipatory endeavours. These claims are argued for in Chapter 1 and Chapter 2. What is more, all of the evidence considered in the previous three chapters indicates that gender kinds specifically (along with race kinds) can be ontically oppressive. With regard to trans people in particular, I have argued that most current social structures are cissexist in nature (§4.4) and that trans people often suffer ontic oppression in virtue of being constructed as members of gender kinds that prevent them from meeting the genuine needs that arise from their gender identity (§6.5).

The demand for an account of the ontology of gender kinds that guarantees that kind membership always aligns with gender identity is, quite simply, a demand for the rejection of the analysis of gender kinds that I have offered. What is more, I can only make sense of this demand in the context of a general rejection of the possibility of ontic injustice and ontic oppression. That is to say, I think that those who would criticise my account of the ontology of gender kinds in this way will, in fact, turn out to have a much deeper disagreement with my whole approach to social kinds. Whereas I want to say that the ways in which social kinds exist can be oppressive, this objection is pressing the alternative view: that we should instead say that the only social kinds that exist are ones that are emancipatory. If it would be oppressive for trans people to be members of gender kinds that do not align with their identity and/or to be members of gender kinds that do not align with their gender identity, then this must not be the case. Ontic oppression (along with ontic injustice) is, on the objector's view, an impossibility.

Another way in which this objection to my account might be articulated is to say that I am making a mistake in endorsing pluralism: gender *really is* what I have termed 'gender identity kinds', and the other kinds I have

---

[15] One way of understanding the second worry would be to interpret it as an insistence that my ontology offer a solution to what has sometimes been called 'the inclusion problem', which is the challenge of finding an account of the category of 'woman' that can function as a normative basis for feminist politics in virtue of including everyone who should be included. For a thorough discussion and compelling critique of the inclusion problem and its role in a broader 'gender controversy', see Mikkola 2016, part I. For my discussion of Mikkola's view, see Jenkins 2018b.

identified, while they may exist, are not really *gender kinds*. So gender is, after all, one thing and not (as I have claimed) many things. To this objection, I would respond that it matters a great deal to be clear on what is under dispute. If my interlocutor is merely claiming that the term 'gender' only refers to gender identity kinds (and that gender terms such as 'woman' only refer to the relevant gender identity kind), then we do not have a disagreement: I have here expressed no view on the meaning of such terms. Indeed, this interpretation returns us to the terrain I just covered in response to the first version of the worry. If, on the other hand, my interlocutor is claiming that gender identity kinds have a more ontological sort of primacy, such as being the kinds that are uniquely best suited to doing the explanatory work we have historically asked the notion of gender to do for us, then I disagree, for the reasons already set out in Chapters 4, 5, and 6.

In short, the second version of the objection (the worry that my account of the ontology of gender kinds does not guarantee that any utterance that misgenders someone will count as false) is essentially a wholesale rejection of the arguments made so far in this book. Accordingly, in one sense, I do not have much to say in response to it. The arguments I have already presented are my best attempt to show why I take the approach that I take instead of the approach that I believe underpins this worry, and nothing I could add here would be likely to sway someone who has not been convinced by what I have said so far.

However, in another, sense, I *do* have more to say. This is because I think this second version of the objection partly trades on a concern that I find very compelling. This concern has to do with the *political implications* of putting forward an account of gender kinds that does not ontologically guarantee the falsity of misgendering utterances, *within the current social context*. The concern, as I see it, is that putting forward a view that acknowledges the existence of some gender kinds that do not align with people's gender identities is likely to have effects that run counter to trans liberation in the current social context. I take this concern very seriously. As explained in the Introduction, it is an important part of my emancipatory theory approach to treat the likely effects of presenting my account of ontic oppression and gender kinds in the current social context as relevant to the success of the account as a piece of theorising. Moreover, I can see why someone might think that putting forward a view that acknowledges the existence of some gender kinds that do not align with people's gender identities is likely to have effects that run counter to trans liberation. I believe, however, that I can show that this is not the case and that, on the contrary, the effects of my approach are *conducive* to trans liberation in the current context. This is a significant and complex task, however, and thus calls for a chapter of its own.

7.7. Conclusion

In this chapter, I have clarified the benefits of my pluralist account of race and gender kinds, and I have responded to some objections. I first highlighted three benefits of the pluralist account of race and gender kinds elaborated over this and the previous two chapters. First, the account sheds light on the relations between different accounts of race and gender kinds, which have been underexplored in the literature to date. Second, it offers resources for pursuing productive disagreements about the ontology of race and gender kinds. Third, it protects accounts of particular varieties of race and gender kinds from objections that lose their force when that variety of race and gender kind is not understood as exhausting what race and/or gender is understood to be.

I then considered and responded to four potential objections to my pluralist account. First, I considered Mason's challenge of showing that the account does not lead to a problematic proliferation of social kinds that blocks broad moves of generalisation and induction that are important for emancipatory aims. I argued that although the account does involve some fine-grained kinds that do not support these kinds of moves, it also involves much more coarse-grained kinds that do support generalisation and induction of the kind that Mason highlights as important. Thus, although there is a proliferation of kinds in my account, it is not problematic. The second objection concerned the question of which constraints and enablements are taken to unify race and gender kinds, and I explained how this selection is made on the basis of the actual difference that a certain constraint or enablement makes to the relevant regularities and patterns that make the kind explanatory. The third objection concerned whether the direction of explanation ran the wrong way, from constraints and enablements to kinds, when we might want to use kinds to explain constraints and enablements. I showed that thinking of kinds as unified by constraints and enablements does not prevent their being used in this way and does not give rise to troubling circularity.

Finally, I considered a fourth objection, namely, that the pluralist account of gender kinds that I have presented is morally and politically dubious because it sanctions utterances that misgender trans people. I argued that although it would indeed be a problem if the account sanctioned misgendering, it does not do so. This is due to the fact that it is an account of the *ontology* of gender kinds only; there is a significant step from such an account to a theory of the semantics of gender terms, another step to an account of the pragmatics of particular utterances including such terms, and still another to a prescriptive account of how such terms ought to be used. Utterances that misgender can potentially be criticised on any of these three levels (the semantic, the pragmatic, and the prescriptive), even if the point the person is trying to get across is correct as far as the ontology of kinds is concerned. My account therefore does not entail that utterances that misgender are appropriate all things considered.

However, thinking about misgendering highlighted another possible worry: that the political implications of articulating my pluralist account of gender kinds (and the accompanying claim that some are sites of ontic oppression) in the current social context would be contrary to trans liberation. Addressing this worry will be my task in Chapter 8.

8

Against the Ontology-First Approach
to Gender Recognition

8.1. Introduction

In this chapter, I situate the account of gender kinds and ontic oppression developed in the rest of the book within the present social context, with a view
to establishing its likely effects for trans liberation. I aim to show that the
account is conducive to trans liberation. In doing so, I offer a response to the
concern outlined at the end of Chapter 7, namely, that putting forward a view
that acknowledges the existence of some gender kinds that do not align with
people's gender identities is likely to have political effects that run counter to
trans liberation in the current social context. I will mostly focus on the context in the United Kingdom and, to a lesser extent, the United States, though
some of what I will say applies to other locations as well.

One reason this concern has particular force is that the present political moment in the United Kingdom, and to varying extents in other countries as well, is characterised by severe and worsening transphobia (Pearce,
Erikainen, and Vincent 2020). One major focal point for transphobia has
been public discussions of 'gender recognition',[1] understood as the ways in
which people's genders should be socially recognised, for example, in terms
of how people should be able to navigate gendered social spaces.[2] Although

---

[1] To people in the United Kingdom, 'gender recognition' may call to mind the Gender Recognition
Act 2004, a particular piece of legislation. However, while I will discuss that legislation, I am using
the phrase 'gender recognition' much more broadly, as a loose umbrella term to capture a tangle of
questions about the organisation of social practices on informal as well as official levels. Understood
in this spirit, gender recognition concerns the social conditions of our gendered lives, including, but
not limited to, the legal frameworks that are enforced in our social context. Accordingly, in framing
this chapter around the concept of gender recognition, I do not mean to suggest that legal recognition of trans people's genders by the state is either necessary or sufficient to end the oppression of
trans people or that it should be the primary, much less the sole, focus of emancipatory efforts.

[2] Having focused more or less equally on race and gender in the previous four chapters, in this
chapter, my focus is primarily on gender, though I will briefly discuss race in §8.5.

Ontology and Oppression. Katharine Jenkins, Oxford University Press. © Katharine Jenkins 2023.
DOI: 10.1093/oso/9780197666777.003.0009

decisions about gender recognition affect everyone, insofar as everyone must participate in gendered social practices, these discussions have a particular impact on trans people. This is because the ability of some trans people to navigate gendered social practices as members of the gender with which they identify is placed in jeopardy by many of the proposals for organising gendered social practices that have received attention in these discussions. The same is true for some cis people, but, in addition, public discussions about gender recognition frequently involve problematic scrutiny of trans people's bodies and experiences, often characterised, as we shall see in this chapter, by hostile attitudes ranging from wilful ignorance to outright vilification.

Given this context, I will focus on the interplay between public discussions of gender recognition and the account of gender kinds that I have defended in earlier chapters.[3] I will begin by examining an assumption about the relationship between ontology and social practices that I think is pervasive in public discussions about gender and that I will argue plays a key role in shaping and sustaining them. Roughly, the assumption holds that settling questions about the current ontology of gender kinds will automatically determine what shape our gendered social practices ought to take; I call this assumption the Ontology-First approach. I will show how the Ontology-First approach fuels disagreements about gender recognition and contributes to the perpetuation and amplification of transphobia. The account of ontic injustice presented in Chapter 1 of this book entails the rejection the Ontology-First approach—and given the drawbacks of that approach, I will argue that this is a positive result for my account. I will end by showing how disagreements about gender recognition would appear in a very different light without the distorting effect of the Ontology-First approach, one that is much less likely to perpetuate and increase transphobia. Overall, this suggests that the account of the ontology of gender kinds and of ontic oppression that I have defended is conducive to trans liberation in the current social and political.

---

[3] I take these public discussions to play out primarily through traditional media, social media, political activism, and routine in-person interactions, and accordingly, these will be my focus here. The similarities and differences between academic work engaging with similar topics and the public discussions on which I focus here would need to be assessed before any of my conclusions about the public discussions could be applied to the academic work. Such an assessment is beyond the scope of this chapter. On the topic of philosophy's 'transgender trouble', Dembroff 2020b is illuminating.

8.2. Public Discussions about Gender Recognition

8.2.1. Context of Public Discussions

The public discussions about gender recognition that concern me in this chapter are embedded in a widespread and sustained oppressive social shift characterised by policies, practices, and discourses that are hostile to the overlapping groups of trans people, queer people, women, and people of colour, with particular and heightened implications for those occupying various intersections of these categories. In the United Kingdom, the most recent stage of this social turn dates from around 2017, when plans to reform the Gender Recognition Act were first announced, and involves a 'significant upsurge in public anti-trans sentiment' (Pearce, Erikainen, and Vincent 2020, 680).

The Gender Recognition Act reform consultation and the discussions around it are an important touchstone in my discussion, so some background information will be useful at this point. The Gender Recognition Act 2004 is the legislation that enables some trans people in England and Wales to change their gender for legal purposes.[4] In 2017, the UK government announced that it was considering amending the legislation to a simplified system in which trans people would be able to acquire a Gender Recognition Certificate (effectively changing the gender on their birth certificate) by means of a statutory declaration. This would have been in contrast to the existing process, which involves the submission of 'evidence', including medical records, to a non-accountable panel of assessors and which is expensive, bureaucratic, and inaccessible to many trans people.[5] The proposal was strongly supported by trans rights campaigners and LGBT charities. The practical effect of the change would have been very limited; for example, it would have had no effect on trans people's access to gender-separated services and spaces under equality legislation (which is governed by separate legislation, the Equality Act 2010; Equality and Human Rights Commission 2011). Nor would it have impacted trans people's access to many forms of identity documentation such as passports (for which a Gender Recognition

[4] There was a separate consultation process regarding reform in Scotland, since the relevant legislative powers are devolved to the Scottish Parliament, although the public discussions throughout the United Kingdom were broadly similar in tone.

[5] At the time of the consultation, I argued publicly in support of this reform along with two other philosophers (Finlayson, Jenkins, and Worsdale 2018).

Certificate is not needed). The main effects of the reform would have been to enable trans people to have important life events such as marriages recorded correctly with regard to gender and to avoid the risk of people having their trans status revealed to others against their will due to inappropriate or incongruent gender markers on documentation.

The consultation closed in October 2018, and in September 2020, the government announced that it was not implementing the proposals to move to a system based on statutory declaration but would instead retain the existing system with minimal changes, namely, an online application portal and a reduction in the fee (Truss and Government Equalities Office 2020; for discussion, see Women and Equalities Committee 2021). Although the outcome of the consultation in terms of policy reform was negligible, it served as the focal point for a large amount of public discussion characterised by widespread hostility to trans people, especially trans women. This discussion included a substantial focus on questioning trans women's access to women's spaces and services, such as toilets, changing rooms, and sexual and domestic violence support services—access to all of which, as already noted, would have been unaffected by the proposed changes. Thus, the consultation about the Gender Recognition Act effectively provided cover under which the rollback of trans people's established legal rights could be openly discussed in the mainstream media.

Ruth Pearce, Sonja Erikainen, and Ben Vincent situate this UK-specific 'backlash' within a 'wider trans-exclusionary political climate with international dimensions' (2020, 680). These dimensions include the 'bathroom bills' introduced in some US states, which seek to bar trans people from using toilet facilities consistent with their gender. Discourse around such initiatives typically position "women", assumed to be cis and often implicitly racially coded as White, as uniquely and essentially vulnerable to violence, whilst positioning trans women, typically conceptualised as "men", as inherently dangerous. This discourse presents some bodies as more worthy of protection than others, playing into histories of racist attitudes, and belies the fact that trans women and non-binary people, especially those who are people of colour, are at particular risk of experiencing violence in gendered toilets (Pearce, Erikainen, and Vincent 2020, 680–81; Jones and Slater 2020, 842–43).

This hostility to trans people, and especially trans women, also plays a role in the "culture wars", serving as a rallying point for right-wing and authoritarian regimes. For example, in Hungary in 2020, on the first day that he was granted the power to rule by decree, the dictator Viktor Orbán moved to legally redefine sex, banning trans people from changing the gender they were assigned at birth on official documents (Pearce, Erikainen, and Vincent 2020, 682). Elizabeth Corredor (2019) offers a global analysis of 'antigender campaigns', understood as antagonistic responses to emancipatory claims about sex, gender, and sexuality that are often framed in terms of 'resisting gender ideology', a framing that Corredor terms 'gender ideology propaganda'. She concludes:

> antigender campaigns are flourishing across geopolitical regions, and the deployment of gender ideology propaganda is an effective counterstrategy for mobilizing mass support against feminist and LGBTQ+ politics . . . antigender campaigns are global phenomena that exceed generalized resistance and instead involve coordinated, well-organized, and well-resourced actors whose interests are to preserve traditional values of gender, sex, and sexuality. (2019, 629–30)

My analysis of public discussions about gender recognition takes place in this national and global context. Although I recognise that the discussions are taking place on a global scale, my perspective is inevitably shaped by the fact that I am situated in the United Kingdom. One reason this is significant is that whereas many antigender campaigns globally are explicitly articulated as a defence of religious values and social tradition, the most prominent antigender campaigns in the United Kingdom are superficially presented as a defence of feminist values, aims, and spaces. This surface-level difference should not be overstated. The similarity of the aims (e.g., rolling back access to means of updating gender markers on legal documentation, removing trans people's access to toilets that match their gender identity) and language (e.g., 'gender ideology') between these articulations of gender ideology propaganda is marked. Furthermore, as Katherine O'Donnell has observed, an emphasis on defending a gender taxonomy that is stable, hierarchical, and pure is shared between the purportedly feminist manifestations of antigender campaigns, their overtly religious counterparts, and right-wing and conservative social movements more broadly (2019, 87).[6]

---

[6] O'Donnell also offers an insightful analysis of the historical roots of anti-trans radical feminism in Catholic theology.

8.2.2. "Objective versus Subjective"

What I have said so far serves to pick out the discussions with which I am concerned and to situate them within their political context, but characterising the discussions themselves is rather difficult, for three main reasons. First, discussions about gender recognition, in the sense of the organisation of our gendered social practices, have become discursively linked to a number of other issues that are both practically and conceptually distinct, such as disagreement concerning the safety and appropriateness of transition-related healthcare (especially for trans youth) and meta-disagreement concerning legitimate and illegitimate modes of expression and of protest. Disentangling the disagreements that centrally concern gender recognition from this broader cluster is therefore rather tricky. Second, the discussions typically manifest in the context of particular social practices or proposals for social practices. This makes it difficult to offer a characterisation of them that is sufficiently general to apply across discussions of different specific issues. Finally, these specific discussions often involve different social practices being run together in highly inaccurate ways. For example, as we have seen, disagreements about the Gender Recognition Act in the United Kingdom have featured extensive discussion of the rights of trans women to access women-only spaces and services such as toilets and changing rooms even though the proposed legislative reform would have made absolutely no difference whatsoever to these rights. Given all of this, it is important to note that to describe the public discussions *as they actually manifest*—which is what I aim to do in this section—is not to map conceptual terrain in a logical way but rather to document some of the dysfunctions and distortions of an oppressive discourse.

  With all of these complexities in mind, the first thing that can be said about the disagreements I aim to examine is that on the most general level, they concern the relative importance of what are arguably different aspects of gender in determining the organisation of social practices. Access to gender-separated social spaces looms especially large here, though other aspects of social practices, such as how linguistic terms such as 'woman' should be used, are also implicated. Very often, this question of relative importance is presented as a binary decision between basing gendered social practices on the physical body as sexed by third parties, on the one hand, and basing them on a first-person view of gendered identity, or sense of self, on the other. This characterisation is often framed in terms of "objective" (the material realities of bodies) versus "subjective" (psychological experiences of gender identity). This framing is used to suggest that if the "objectively" sexed body is what matters for gendered social practices, then women's spaces and services should be reserved for cis women, or perhaps for cis women and a certain subset of trans women, namely, those who have received particular kinds of transition-related medical care, such as genital surgery. (Trans men are frequently overlooked in these discussions.) By contrast, it is suggested that if "subjective" gender identity is what matters, then trans women should have blanket access to women's spaces and services. Some alternative framings of what I take to be basically the same contrast are "facts versus feelings", "science versus ideology", and "research versus activism". Charlotte Jones and Jen Slater, for instance, describe a 'construct[ed] . . . battle between "objective and enlightened researchers" and "emotional and volatile activists" ' in relation to questions about trans people's access to public toilets (2020, 840).

As an example of this "objective versus subjective" framing, we can once more consider the case described in the Introduction. On 10 October 2018, shortly before the public consultation about the Gender Recognition Act closed, a full-page advert ran in the *Metro*, London's free commuter newspaper. The advert was run by a group called Fair Play For Women, whose aim, expressed in the advert and in other materials, was to encourage people to respond to the consultation with a negative assessment of the proposals to move to a system based on statutory declaration, on the grounds that the proposed reform would put cis women and girls at risk of harm. The advert posed questions such as 'Do you think fully intact, male-bodied prisoners should be allowed to live with women in prison?' and 'Do you think someone with a penis is a woman?'. Most of the page was taken up with large text reading: 'Think about it. #ChooseReality'.

This advert exemplifies the "objective versus subjective" framing via the appeal to 'reality', which is associated in the text of the advert with trans-exclusionary social practices. Once the issue is set up in this way, the dice are loaded in favour of trans-exclusionary social practices twice over. First, the association of the "objective" side of the "objective versus subjective" contrast with trans-exclusionary social practices is used to make those practices seem more justified than the alternative trans-inclusive social practices, even before any relevant considerations have been assessed. The directive to 'choose reality' carries the connotation that any other choice would be unreasonable. Setting trans-inclusionary social practices up as being in opposition to reality rhetorically frames those practices as difficult to justify.

Second, the "objective versus subjective" framing treats the decision about gender recognition as a binary decision, where one way of organising gendered social practices must be used across all different social contexts and all different types of practices. This sets up a situation where one example of an instance where basing social practices on self-determined gender might conceivably generate some problems is treated as evidence that we should *never* base *any* social practices on self-determined gender. For example, the advert asked, 'Do you think males should be allowed to compete against women in sport, if they feel like women?' However, the proposed reform to the Gender Recognition Act that was the ostensible topic of the advert would have had no impact whatsoever on who is eligible to compete in female categories in sporting competitions. The advert implied that unless we want to base categories in sporting competitions purely on people's statutory declarations of their self-determined gender, we ought not to use such declarations as the basis for being able to obtain a reissued birth certificate with a different gender marker from the original. This is, of course, nonsensical. One can perfectly coherently think that such a declaration is the best basis for obtaining identity documentation whilst thinking that it may not be the best basis for determining categorisation in sporting competitions. By linking the two issues—specific identity documentation (the subject of the proposed reform) and sporting competitions (unaffected by the proposed reform)—the advert created the false impression that if one thinks that using self-declaration as a basis for categorisation within sporting competitions raises some complicated questions that require further consideration, then one has reason to oppose the proposed reform to the Gender Recognition Act.

8.2.3. "Conflict of Interest"

A second way in which these disagreements are often problematically framed is that they purport to identify a "conflict of interest" between cis women, on the one hand, and trans people (with a primary focus on trans women), on the other. One way this is achieved is by associating each of these groups with one of the options in the binary decision just described. The thought is that it is in cis women's interests for gendered social practices to be based on (supposedly "objective") bodily sex and that it is in trans people's interests for gendered social practices to be based on (supposedly "subjective") gender identity. Via a tacit appeal to the background claim that we must choose one and only one of these options to organise all gendered social practices, this licenses the conclusion that there is a "conflict of interest" between cis women and trans people.

As Bettcher points out, this "conflict of interest" framing elides the oppression trans women face and forecloses a much more fruitful approach that would otherwise be open to us:

> Alternatively, we could recognize that what trans women are subject to is a 'double-bind.' We could also remember that, as Marilyn Frye argued, the double-bind is a hallmark of oppression. By recognizing our common interests as feminists, we women could then work together to find the best solution for all. And we would do this, of course, by taking seriously the interests of trans men, genderqueer and other non-binary people. I honestly don't understand an approach that starts off in such an adversarial way, pitting the alleged interests of non-trans women against everybody else. It just doesn't seem very feminist to me. (2018)

Both of these framings of disagreements about gender recognition—as a decision between being "objective" and being "subjective", and as a conflict of interest between trans people and cis women—can be discerned in a statement made by the US-based organisation Women's Liberation Front. The statement was made in the context of a landmark US Supreme Court case that went on to rule that Title VII of the Civil Rights Act of 1964 protects trans people from employment discrimination. Opposing the claim that the Act should be interpreted in this way, Women's Liberation Front told the media:

> Sex is grounded in materiality, whereas 'gender identity' is simply an ideology that has no grounding in science. . . . The redefinition of the word 'sex' to mean 'gender identity' would have myriad harmful effects on women and girls, and women and girls as a distinct category deserve civil rights protections. (quoted in Burns 2019)

The claim that sex is being 'redefin[ed]' away from a meaning that is 'grounded in materiality' exemplifies the first of the two framings, the "objective versus subjective" framing (in its "science versus ideology" formulation). Moreover, the quote shows how easily the move can be made from this framing to the "conflict of interest" framing, via an association between the "objective" side and the interests of cis women and, implicitly, between the "subjective" side and the interests of trans people.

It's worth noting that this talk of 'redefining' the word 'sex' is, in fact, rather peculiar in the context of the remarks by Women's Liberation Front, given that the arguments presented in favour of considering Title VII to protect trans people advocated no such redefinition. Rather, the argument was that discrimination against trans employees necessarily depends on judgements about their sex—judgements with which Women's Liberation Front, as far as one can make out from their comment, would not disagree. As the Supreme Court majority opinion in the case noted:

> An employer who fired an individual for being homosexual or trans-gender fires that person for traits or actions it would not have questioned in members of a different sex. Sex plays a necessary and undisguisable role in the decision, exactly what Title VII forbids. (cited in Williams 2020)

This argument does not appeal to gender identity at all, much less equate it with sex. As with the Fair Play For Women advert, we see here a significant misrepresentation of the legislative issues at stake.

Given the sorts of misrepresentations present in both of these examples, one might take the claims made in support of trans-exclusionary social practices to be deliberately disingenuous: the people making them don't really believe them but are just saying whatever they think will advance anti-trans aims. Alternatively, one might consider these claims to be based on serious factual misunderstandings, perhaps underpinned by prejudice: the people making them have false beliefs about trans people and about the implications of trans-inclusive social practices and perhaps are resistant to counter-evidence due to anti-trans bias. Let me therefore note explicitly that in discussing the claims sketched in this section, I am not assuming that they are usually made in good faith or that they are not usually based on misunderstanding and/or prejudice. Rather, I am interested in the implications of articulating my account of gender kinds in a social and political context in which trans-exclusionary social practices *are* being defended by way of the claims I have described in this section. For this purpose, what matters is not the intentions or other mental states of those who make the claims but simply the fact that the claims are being made and are receiving considerable amplification in the public sphere. Given that this is the case, it is important to

consider what the likely political effects will be of articulating my account of
gender kinds and ontic oppression in this social context.

8.3. Against the Ontology-First Approach

I will argue that the claims described in the previous section implicitly trade
on a way of thinking about gender recognition, the Ontology-First approach,
that is not obviously mistaken or confused and does not depend primarily
on false factual claims. Indeed, I will show that the Ontology-First approach
is also utilised by many people who advocate for trans-inclusive social
practices, such as a self-identification approach to gender recognition. I will
argue, however, that this approach is very unhelpful from the perspective of
trans liberation. Furthermore, I will argue that my account of gender kinds
and ontic oppression helps to displace the Ontology-First approach, thereby
furthering trans liberation.

8.3.1. Characterising the Ontology-First Approach

I will begin by characterising the way of thinking about gender recognition
that I aim to criticise. In order to do this, let us return to the example of the
Fair Play For Women advert and consider the responses that were made to it.
 The intended implication of the slogan 'Choose Reality' in the context of
the other claims made in the advert was that the *reality*—the fact of the matter,
as it were—was that at least those trans women who have not undertaken a
medical transition that includes genital surgery are not women (and, possibly, that no trans women are women) and that for this reason they ought
not to be treated as women socially and politically (and so reform should
be rejected). However, the hashtag was quickly picked up on social media
by people *in favour* of reform who turned it on its head to argue that trans
people were indeed 'choosing reality' by choosing to live in accordance with
their gender identity—something that the proposed legislation would make
much easier. One tweet stated, 'When a person transitions and becomes their
authentic self rather than live a lie that is them deciding to #choosereality.[7]

---

[7] It continued: 'When you fund an [*sic*] run a hate campaign to repress trans* women specifically
you're #choosingtransphobia and #choosingmisogyny' (@mumTdumpty, 5.44 a.m., 10.10.2018).

Another tweet urged people to '#ChooseReality and choose to fight for women's rights, because trans women #really are women and trans women's rights #really are women's rights'.[8] This pushback highlights something very important, which is that arguments against trans people using gender-appropriate facilities deny and obscure many of the realities of trans people's lives. In this sense, it provides an incisive critique of the claims made in the advert.

However, it is noticeable that this way of pushing back at the advert does not challenge an assumption that the slogan 'Choose Reality' implicitly rests upon, which is that the dispute over the legislation *should be settled by establishing what gender kinds are really like.* On this way of thinking, if trans women are "really women", they should be treated as women, and if they are "really men", they should be treated as men. In other words, the responses appear to grant that we should *first* establish the correct account of the ontology of gender kinds such as *woman*—which is to say, how these kinds exist—and *then* treat this as determining what our social practices should be. This is the approach to settling disagreements about gender recognition that I am going to focus on, and I call it the Ontology-First approach.[9]

The Ontology-First approach is a fairly common feature of public discussions of gender recognition. For example, in 2017, the broadcaster Jenni Murray, then presenter of the BBC Radio 4 show *Woman's Hour*, wrote a widely discussed opinion piece that was published in the *Sunday Times*. The piece was headlined 'Be trans, be proud—but don't call yourself a "real woman"', and the subheading read, 'Can someone who has lived as a man, with all the privilege that entails, really lay claim to womanhood? It takes more than a sex change and make-up'.[10] Murray wrote:

[8] It continued: 'It serves none of us to deny anyone their rights because of their biology or because they don't conform to gender norms' (@LauraC_AI, 9:45 a.m., 10.10.2018).

[9] The Ontology-First approach is related to what Dembroff terms the 'Real Gender assumption', which is the assumption that someone should only ever be classified as a member of a certain gender if they are, in fact, a member of that gender. I'll discuss Dembroff's critique of the Real Gender assumption in §8.3.3.

[10] The piece was one of the cruder manifestations of transphobia to appear in the mainstream British press around this time. Its reliance on stereotyping and derogatory tropes (trans people as inauthentic, trans women as superficial, genital surgery as the core component of transition) is apparent from the headline alone and is followed through in the text, which treats remarks by two trans women that Murray finds lacking in feminist insight as evidence about trans women in general. It also extends to the images, which include 'before and after' pictures and a drawn illustration of a stereotypically feminine-looking person casting a masculine-seeming shadow. As noted in §8.2.1, I am not here aiming to document everything that is oppressive about the discussions I am considering, which is why I do not explore this use of transphobic tropes further, despite its undoubted significance for understanding the situation of trans people in the United Kingdom at this time.

my concern, which I know is shared by numerous women who are now to be known as 'cis' (short for 'cisgender'—natural-born women, in the language that's more familiar to most of us), is for the impact this question of what constitutes 'a real woman' will have on sexual politics. And for who has the right to be included in gatherings or organisations that are defined as single sex. (Murray 2017)

Here Murray presents a question—what constitutes "a real woman"?—and the structure of her remarks implies that the way in which this question is settled will have impacts on people's rights concerning the organisation of gendered social spaces ('gatherings and organisations'). Thus, establishing what makes someone "a real woman" is treated as *prior to* and as *determining* questions of gender recognition.

As with the Fair Play For Women advert, some of the most prominent pushback against Murray's piece focused on challenging the claim that trans women are not "real women" whilst appearing to grant that settling this question is important in the ways Murray presents it as being. For example, Rachel Stein, campaigns director of Stonewall, wrote a blog post titled 'Trans Women Are Women' in which she responded to Murray:

Trans women have every right to have their identity and experiences respected, too. They are women—just like you [Murray] and me—and their sense of their gender is as engrained in their identity as yours or mine. (Stein 2017)

Here, again, we see the Ontology-First approach exemplified in the way that Stein bases a claim about trans women's rights on the claim that they 'are women' and specifically that they are women in the same sense that cis women are women.

Overall, I take the Ontology-First approach to be fairly widely adopted by participants in discussions about gender recognition, *including* by those who support trans-inclusive social practices.

8.3.2. The Drawbacks of the Ontology-First Approach

The Ontology-First approach plays a key role in setting up the two framings of questions about gender recognition that were described in the previous section: the framing of trans-exclusionary social practices as the natural outcome of a choice of "objectivity" over "subjectivity", and the framing of this decision as a "conflict of interest" between cis women and trans people. The assumption that social practices should track the reality of gender kinds paves the way for the association of practices that align with existing kinds with "being objective" and practices that depart from existing kinds with "being subjective". And as we have seen, this, in turn, paves the way for associating cis women with the "objective" side of this binary decision and trans people with the "subjective" side, giving the appearance of a stark conflict of interest between these groups.

The Ontology-First approach is not obviously misguided. Indeed, it may even seem like common sense: we want to respond to the way the world is, and so when we are thinking about how we should act, ought we not begin by finding out about the relevant parts of the world—in this case, gender kinds—and take our cue from that? What is more, it might seem that the Ontology-First approach poses no real problem for someone who is committed to trans liberation and who therefore wants to advocate for social practices that include trans people within the gender that aligns with their self-declared gender. We can, we might think, simply argue that the reality of gender kinds is such that it supports trans-inclusive social practices of gender recognition. However, I will argue that this line of reasoning faces some serious problems, such that it is, in fact, very difficult to advocate for trans-inclusive social practices within the Ontology-First approach.

As we have seen, the Ontology-First approach directs us to look for kinds that we can point to and say, 'Look, that's what gender *really is*—so that's what our social practices should track'. For those who want to justify trans-inclusive social practices, a natural choice for which kinds to highlight in this way would be gender identity kinds (see Chapter 6). This is because if we base social practices on gender identity as indicated through self-declaration, then trans people will be able to navigate those practices in accordance with their self-declared gender. Accordingly, the natural strategy for justifying trans-inclusive social practices within the Ontology-First approach is to point to gender identity kinds and say, 'Look, that's what gender really is'.

What this claim really amounts to depends on how you think of social kinds, but one common way of conceiving of social kinds is as groupings of things in the world that can do explanatory work (see Chapter 3). Plenty of philosophers, including myself, think about kinds in this way. Moreover, I think that an imprecise version of this thought is widely held by many

non-philosophers; many people seem to treat the claim that something 'really is gender' as equivalent to the claim that thinking in terms of that thing
helps us to navigate the world. For example, many hostile responses to trans
people's claims about their gender focus on presenting example situations in
which the trans person's self-declared gender allegedly wouldn't be helpful
in navigating or explaining the world.[11] On this quite common view, then,
saying that a certain kind is 'what gender really is' amounts to saying it's
the kind that does the explanatory work that we associate with the idea of
'gender'.

Putting this all together shows that the Ontology-First approach funnels
proponents of trans-inclusive social practices towards making the claim
that *gender identity kinds can do the explanatory work that we've historically
asked the idea of 'gender' to do for us*. This claim, as I have demonstrated in
Chapters 4 and 5, is false. Gender identity is certainly important for many
purposes, including treating people with respect and supporting their
agency, as well as explaining some manifestations of oppression that impact
people through their sense of self and the norms that they internalise (see
Chapter 6). However, oppression also has a lot to do with how other people
treat us and how we are positioned within social structures, and this might
proceed in ways that don't line up with a person's gender identity. Indeed, in a
society that is cissexist as well as patriarchal (see §4.4), this situation is unfortunately not at all uncommon. Therefore, if we want to explain oppression in
ways that help us to oppose it, we need to appeal to gender kinds other than
gender identity kinds (such as hegemonic gender kinds and interpersonal
gender kinds) some of the time.[12] For some of these kinds, trans people will
be members of gender kinds that do not align with their gender identity, because of the ways in which they are routinely misgendered in this cissexist society. If I am right, then the Ontology-First approach funnels proponents of
trans-inclusive social practices towards trying to defend a claim that is false.

Even if I am *not* right—that is, even if there are ways in which my arguments
about the explanatory value of different varieties of gender kinds could successfully be countered—I have at least established that there is plenty of room
to doubt the claim that gender identity kinds can do all of the explanatory

[11] I have encountered a range of different examples in the context of this kind of conversational
move; some involve healthcare settings, others involve biological reproduction, and others involve
the workings of oppression. In each case, the point is supposed to be that distinguishing between
people according to their gender identity will not help us make sense of what is going on.
[12] We may also need to appeal to biological kinds some of the time. As I noted in §4.1, my pluralist
account of social kinds is compatible with also recognising biological kinds.

work that we've historically asked 'gender' to do for us. This alone is sufficient to make that claim a very poor foundation for justifying trans-inclusive social practices, because doing so means that all the reasons to doubt that claim come to count as reasons to doubt the appropriateness of trans-inclusive social practices. It seems to me that a situation in which trans people's ability to navigate social spaces according to their self-declared gender identity is placed in prolonged doubt is an oppressive situation *even if* there is a prospect of trans-inclusive social practices ultimately being defended from objections (for exploration of a related claim, see Ahmed 2016). Thus, even if the claim that gender identity kinds can do all of the explanatory work that we've historically asked 'gender' to do for us can ultimately be defended, using it as a foundation for justifying trans-inclusive social practices is nevertheless liable to cause harm to trans people because mounting such a defence is a complicated and difficult task. Tying the justification of trans-inclusive social practices to that task therefore makes those practices appear complicated and difficult to justify.

The upshot of all of this is that the Ontology-First approach is liable to entrench the oppression of trans people *even when it is being used by those who support trans-inclusive social practices.* Let me be clear that this is a tendency, not an inevitability; what I've sketched here is the path of least resistance for a proponent of trans-inclusive social practices within the Ontology-First approach, and there are various possible exits from this path that may not carry the same likelihood of harm. For example, one might accept the Ontology-First approach but adopt a different view of what the ontology of gender is about, one that sets aside considerations of explanatory power in favour of prioritising some other factor. This would remove the need to claim that gender identity kinds can do the explanatory work that we've historically asked 'gender' to do for us, because the ontology of kinds would no longer be bound up with the explanatory work that they do. I am not claiming that such an argument would be untenable, nor do I propose to explore this avenue further here. The important point for my purposes is that the Ontology-First approach *funnels* proponents of trans-inclusive social practices *towards* the position of having to defend the claim that gender identity kinds can do the explanatory work that we've historically asked 'gender' to do for us—and that this is a highly undesirable position in which to end up.

Another way of putting my point here is to say that the arguments often made against trans-inclusive social practices are in the vicinity of some true and important points. There *is* a complicated debate to be had about the correct ontology of gender kinds. There *are* some good reasons to think that aspects of gender other than gender identity do important explanatory work in relation to feminist aims. The problem with the Ontology-First approach is that it ties these true and important points to questions about gender recognition in a way that makes it seem as though justifying trans-inclusive social practices requires us to rebut these points, when, in fact, it requires no such thing. On the contrary, we can hold that the ontology of gender kinds is complex and that some gender kinds other than gender identity kinds are vital for understanding gendered oppression, whilst still being firmly committed to trans-inclusive social practices.

8.3.3. Rejecting the Ontology-First Approach

Having introduced the Ontology-First approach and identified some of its drawbacks, I'm now in a position to show how my account of ontic injustice, defended in Chapter 1, entails the rejection of that approach. This implication is very straightforward. Indeed, in demonstrating it, I am in the fortunate position of being able to rely on an argument put forward by Dembroff (2018), which covers more or less the same ground whilst making use of slightly different conceptual resources. I will outline Dembroff's argument, showing as I go along how it applies in the present case.

Dembroff argues against what they call 'the "Real Gender" assumption' (2018, 22). This is the assumption that someone should be classified as a member of a certain gender if and only if they meet the membership conditions for being a member of that gender. The Real Gender assumption and the Ontology-First approach are closely related, but the Ontology-First approach is stronger than the Real Gender assumption: whereas the Real Gender assumption only tells us that gendered social practices and the facts about the ontology of gender should be aligned, the Ontology-First approach also tells us about how these should be investigated (first establish the ontology, and then infer from it the correct social practices). This is not the only approach to investigating the ontology of gender and the best way to organise gendered social practices that is compatible with the Real Gender assumption. An alternative approach that is equally compatible with the Real Gender assumption is to first establish what social practices we should adopt and then treat this as revealing the correct ontology of gender. Thus, the Real Gender assumption simply ties social practices to the ontology of social kinds, whereas the Ontology-First approach also builds in a sequence in which we are meant to investigate these.

I think that the sequential aspect of the Ontology-First approach is illuminating in relation to the dynamics of public discussions, and especially with regard to the ideological distortions relating to the "objective versus subjective" framing. However, for the purposes at hand, the differences between the Ontology-First approach and the Real Gender assumption do not matter: since the Ontology-First approach includes the Real Gender assumption, Dembroff's argument against the Real Gender assumption also applies to the Ontology-First approach.

Dembroff's argument trades on their concept of 'ontological oppression' (2018, 24–29), which is closely related to the concepts of ontic injustice and ontic oppression presented in Chapter 1 and Chapter 2. The precise similarities and differences between these three concepts are set out in §2.5.2, but they are not relevant to the argument under consideration. That argument is straightforward: recognising the possibility of ontological oppression renders the Real Gender assumption untenable, because if a social kind is oppressive, we ought not to defer to it unthinkingly in arranging our social practices (Dembroff 2018, 28–29). Indeed, the main step in Dembroff's argument, as I see it, is to outline and defend a concept of ontological oppression, because once this concept is on the table, the step to rejecting the Real Gender assumption is a small and rather obvious one. I will work through the reasoning here using the concept of ontic injustice, since that is the concept to which I am committed and which I have defended in this book and since it does the same work as the concept of ontological oppression in the context of this argument.

In Chapter 1, I argued that there is an implicit consensus among different accounts of social ontology that what it is to be a member of a certain social kind is, at least in part, to fall under certain social constraints and enablements. What it is to be a member of a certain social kinds—to be a judge, for example—is to be enabled to do certain things (e.g., to pass sentences) and constrained from doing others (e.g., having certain sorts of business interests). I then argued that the very fact that an individual is constructed as a member of a social kind can be wrongful, because the constraints and enablements that partly constitute kind membership can fall short of what is morally owed to the individual who is subjected to them. When this happens, the person suffers ontic injustice. In Chapter 2, I defined ontic oppression as a particular species of ontic injustice that is useful in the context of emancipatory theory; but for the purposes at hand, the broader concept of ontic injustice can do the necessary work, and so I will focus just on that.

As Dembroff (2018, 28–29) points out in relation to ontological oppression, considering the possibility of ontic injustice fatally undermines the Real Gender assumption and, with it, the Ontology-First approach. When an existing social kind is ontically unjust, why should we consider ourselves bound to defer to it in arranging our social practices? In arranging our social practices, without further consideration, so as to track the distinction between people who are members of the kind and people who are not, we run the risk of perpetuating the pattern of unjust constraints and enablements that constitute the kind.

To be clear, I am not claiming (nor is Dembroff) that we should *never* arrange our social practices so that they track ontically unjust kinds. We might need to respond differently to kind members and non-kind-members precisely in order to mitigate the effects of oppression. But the mere possibility that we might want to organise our social practices in ways that do *not* track existing social kinds is enough to undermine the Ontology-First approach, because of the way that approach assumes that social practices should *always* track existent kinds. As soon as we switch to a view on which social practices should *sometimes* track existing kinds and *sometimes* depart from them, we have rejected the Ontology-First approach. Overall, then, recognising the possibility of ontic oppression shows that the Ontology-First approach is unjustified.

Of course, one does not *need* the concept of ontic injustice, or Dembroff's concept of ontological oppression, in order to reject the Ontology-First approach. Plenty of people in public discussions of gender recognition have called for less emphasis on questions like 'What makes someone a woman?' and more emphasis on the practical upshots of different policies, especially their impact on trans people's equality and dignity. One example is video essayist Natalie Wynn (creator of the YouTube channel ContraPoints), who observes that slogans such as 'Sex is real' are used to present 'the trans debate' 'as an intellectual conflict about the metaphysics of gender, instead of what it really is, which is a political conflict about the social equality of transgender people'. Wynn advocates a move away from the slogan 'Trans women are women' and favours instead 'Trans liberation now'. (I'm very sympathetic to this suggestion.) Perhaps most interestingly, in what can potentially be read as a subversion of the 'Choose Reality' slogan, Wynn observes that focusing on trans people's struggle for equality rather than on the metaphysics or semantics of gender actually serves to 'bring reality back into focus', by directing our attention to 'a concrete political project' (ContraPoints 2021).[13]

All of these points are cogent and can be articulated without reference to ontic injustice or anything like it. However, in virtue of the ways in which the Ontology-First approach is intertwined with the "objective versus subjective" framing, the move to reject it carries some danger, as I shall show, and I believe appealing to a philosophical concept such as ontic injustice can be of some use in mitigating that danger. The danger in question relates to the two framings of discussions that currently feature prominently in public discussions about gender recognition identified earlier in this chapter: the "objective versus subjective" framing and the "conflict of interest" framing.

Rejecting the Ontology-First approach undercuts the "subjective versus objective" framing of disagreements about gender recognition by making clear that the status of certain claims about reality as "subjective" or "objective" is orthogonal to questions of gender recognition. If facts about the ontology of gender are not decisive in determining how we should organise social practices to do with gender, then claiming to have identified the "objective" facts no longer provides support for one's preferred mode of organising social practices. Although someone could still claim that the aspect of gender on which they prefer to focus is the "objective truth" of gender, without the Ontology-First approach, this does not constitute a case for organising gendered social practices around that aspect of gender. Therefore, recognising and rejecting the Ontology-First approach undercuts the force of the "objective versus subjective" framing of discussions about gender recognition.

The danger, however, is that appeals to shift the emphasis of discussions of gender recognition away from facts about the ontology of gender kinds may be picked up on as further evidence of a wilful disregard for "reality", "objective truth", "the facts", and so on. This danger is significant, because the tactic of presenting trans-inclusive practices as requiring a "denial of reality", as seen in the Fair Play For Women advert, is a popular one, and I think it can be very rhetorically effective. The advocate of the shift in emphasis may therefore be presented as abandoning clear-headed investigation of the facts in favour of generating a convenient fiction to suit their preferred social

---

[13] See also the discussion in Faye 2021, 8–16, which directs attention firmly to the material realities of trans people's lives, although it does not explicitly direct attention away from ontological questions about gender.

practices, leading to further entrenchment of the "objective versus subjective" framing rather than its abandonment.

Using a philosophical tool such as the concept of ontic injustice or of ontological oppression to undermine the Ontology-First approach is helpful in pushing back against these kinds of hostile responses. This approach makes it clear that rejecting the Ontology-First approach does not amount to a "denial of reality" in the pejorative sense implied by the 'Choose Reality' slogan and similar rhetorical devices. Rather, the claim is that the way that social reality has been constructed can be wrongful and that given this possibility, we should not uncritically align our social practices with the current reality of social kinds. This approach enables us to keep open the option of actively intervening in an oppressive situation with the aim of creating a different, better social reality. This is something that feminists have always done and, indeed, something that members of any anti-oppressive social movement must do.

8.4. Gender Pluralism and Gender Recognition Reconsidered

8.4.1. Displacing "Objective versus Subjective" and "Conflict of Interest"

So far, I've shown that the Ontology-First approach generates significant obstacles to defending trans-inclusive social practices, and I've also shown how recognising that ontic injustice is possible entails the rejection of the Ontology-First approach. In this section, I build upon these points to respond to the worry that putting forward a view that acknowledges the existence of some gender kinds that do not align with people's gender identities is likely to have political effects that run counter to trans liberation in the current social context. I argue that on the contrary, in the current social and political context, the most likely implications of articulating my account are conducive to trans liberation. I do not want to overstate the benefits of my account, however; I am certainly not claiming that it is a panacea for the intense and troubling manifestations of transphobia that we have seen in this chapter. Nor do I think that it is straightforward to predict how philosophical arguments are likely to play out when they come into contact with public discussions (though I think it's important to think about this all the same).

My claim is much more modest: I think there is more reason to be optimistic about the likely impacts of my account of gender kinds than there is to be pessimistic, such that the worry I am considering in this chapter is not a genuine objection to my account.

My pluralist account of gender kinds includes the claim that many gender kinds are ontically oppressive (where ontic oppression, as explained in Chapter 2, is a particular species of ontic injustice). The account therefore has a rejection of the Ontology-First approach built in. By contrast, the thought that it is imperative to develop an account of the ontology of gender according to which the only gender kinds that exist are those that correspond to how people self-identify seems to derive its force *from* the Ontology-First approach. It is based on the assumption that any approach that does not deliver the resources needed to mount a defence of trans-inclusive social practices *within* the Ontology-First approach is antithetical to trans liberation. Accordingly, if I am right that the Ontology-First approach is counterproductive when it comes to advocating trans-inclusive approaches to gendered social practices, then this tells against the worry I am considering.

To put the point another way, the supposed drawback of my account, in terms of its likely interaction with public discussions of gender recognition, is that it would undercut our ability to argue for trans-inclusive social practices. If this only applies on the assumption that we are working within the Ontology-First approach, and if we have independent reasons to reject the Ontology-First approach, then the worry loses its force. Correspondingly, since my account includes resources for rejecting the Ontology-First approach, then if such a rejection would place those advocating for trans-inclusive social practices in a better position, this is a positive implication of articulating my account in the present social and political context.

So far, what I have said relates to the fact that my account includes a commitment to recognising some gender kinds as ontically oppressive. However, the specifically pluralist aspects of the account also have likely implications that are conducive to trans liberation, as I shall now show. This is because the pluralist nature of the account offers helpful resources for disrupting the two problematic framings of discussions of gender recognition that we encountered in §8.2.2 and §8.2.3: the "objective versus subjective" framing and the "conflict of interest" framing.

In the previous section, I showed how recognising the possibility of ontic injustice helps to disrupt the "objective versus subjective" framing. In addition, as we saw in §8.2.2, the "objective versus subjective" framing includes an anti-pluralist assumption: gender is *one thing* (and we just have to work out what this thing *really is*, then use it to organise *all* gendered social practices). Merely rejecting the Ontology-First approach does not challenge the anti-pluralist assumption embedded in the "objective versus subjective" framing. However, my pluralist account of gender kinds *does* challenge it. On this account, various different varieties of gender kinds have explanatory value for different tasks within an emancipatory project. These kinds include hegemonic gender kinds, which are (roughly) sex-based hierarchical social roles; interpersonal gender kinds, which are based on the ways in which people respond to each other in specific social contexts; and gender identity kinds, which are based on a person's sense of self. Our ontological picture, I argued, should include each of these types of gender kinds, as well as resources for systematising the relations between them, which I offered in the shape of the CEF elaborated in Chapter 3.

My pluralist account of gender kinds therefore undermines the claim that we must make an either/or choice between conceptualising gender as an identity and conceptualising it as a sex-based social role, as the "objective versus subjective" framing suggests we must. If I am right, we can think of gender as both of these things, and as more besides, and we can do so without losing the ability to use gender kinds to do explanatory work in the service of emancipatory endeavours. On this view, it is not the case that we face one single question about gender recognition, such that all gendered social practices must be organised around a single variety of gender kinds. Rather, we can allow that different gendered social practices can be organised around different varieties of gender kinds. Accordingly, rather than facing one single question about gender recognition, we face lots of different questions about various gendered social practices, where these questions may well have different answers from one another.

This disposes fully of the "objective versus subjective" framing. What about the "conflict of interest" framing? The thought behind the "conflict of interest" framing is that it is in cis women's interests for gendered social practices to be based on (supposedly "objective") sex-based social roles and that it is in trans people's interests for gendered social practices to be based on (supposedly "subjective") gender identity. Rejecting the "objective versus subjective" framing makes it harder to tie the two "sides" of the supposed conflict of interest to this contrast. However, the "conflict of interest" framing could simply be adapted to drop the reliance on the supposed objective/

subjective contrast. Thus, rejecting the Ontology-First approach does not directly undermine the "conflict of interest" framing.

Nevertheless, we can use my pluralist account of gender kinds to undermine this framing as well. The "conflict of interest" framing relies on three claims:

(1) We face an either/or choice between basing gendered social practices on gender identity or basing them on sex-based social roles.
(2) Basing gendered social practices on gender identity primarily benefits trans people.
(3) Basing gendered social practices on sex-based social roles primarily benefits cis women.

Together, these are taken to entail that there is a conflict of interest between trans people and cis women.

I have already shown how my pluralist account contradicts (1). Since there are many different varieties of gender kinds, we could very well base different gendered social practices on different gender kinds. Rejecting (1) is enough to undermine the conclusion, since if there is no need to make an either/or choice, then there need be no conflict of interest, even if (2) and (3) are true. However, I also think my account gives us reasons to be doubtful about (2) and (3). A full assessment of the best way to organise gendered social practices, which would be required to conclusively reject (2) and (3), is beyond the scope of this chapter. Nevertheless, the "conflict of interest" framing is often mobilised in ways that suggest the following revised versions of (2) and (3):

(2*) *Thinking of gender* in terms of gender identity primarily benefits trans people.
(3*) *Thinking of gender* in terms of sex-based social roles primarily benefits cis women.

Recall, for example, the claim from Women's Liberation Front that '[t]he redefinition of the word "sex" to mean "gender identity" would have myriad harmful effects on women and girls' (Burns 2019).

I think *these* claims—that is, (2*) and (3*)—*are* decisively undermined by my pluralist account of gender kinds.

Regarding (2*), on the account of gender identity I elaborated in Chapter 6—and on most other accounts as well, for that matter—gender identity isn't the sole preserve of trans people; most cis people have a gender identity, too. I also argued there that gender identity matters for emancipatory purposes *not only* because of its necessity in avoiding misgendering and its associated harms but *also* because it plays a role in emancipatory social change more broadly. Following Zheng (2018), I argued that such change will come about in part through people inhabiting gendered social roles in resistant ways, which is to say, taking up certain sorts of gender identities. If this is right, then cis women have an interest in using the concept of gender identity, because doing so helps to resist gendered oppression, and cis women suffer gendered oppression. Taken together, then, these two points show that we should reject the claim that attending to gender identity kinds is beneficial mainly to trans people.

My pluralist account of gender kinds also undermines (3*)—the claim that thinking of gender in terms of sex-based social roles primarily benefits cis women—in a similar way. In Chapter 4, I outlined a variety of gender kinds that I termed 'hegemonic gender kinds', which (more or less) amount to coercively imposed and hierarchical social roles that are based on perceived sex. I argued that the social processes and practices involved in constructing and maintaining hegemonic gender kinds harm trans people enormously. On my account, many trans people, including some trans women, some trans men, and some non-binary people, are subordinated via being hegemonically gendered as women, and many other trans people are subordinated via being hegemonically gendered as gender 'others'. All of these people have experiences of oppression that are illuminated by investigating hegemonic gender kinds, meaning that we should reject the claim that attending to hegemonic gender kinds is beneficial mainly to cis women.

This is not to say that on my view there can never be conflicts of interest between different groups regarding which type of gender kind to use in a particular explanatory project. As I argued in §3.2.3, there is no guarantee of harmony among the overlapping patchwork of inquiries that make up the overarching project of understanding oppression with an emancipatory interest. Different kinds may be useful for different sorts of investigation or may be illuminating in different ways, and this might benefit different groups of people who are differently situated within an oppressive society. Rather, what I take myself to have rejected is the idea that there is a conflict of interest about how to understand gender kinds in general *that falls neatly along a line between trans people and cis women.* If my arguments in this book are correct, there is no such conflict of interest.

To conclude, recall the three claims that make up the "conflict of interest" framing:

(1) We face an either/or choice between basing gendered social practices on gender identity or basing them on sex-based social roles.

(2) Basing gendered social practices on gender identity primarily benefits trans people.

(3) Basing gendered social practices on sex-based social roles primarily benefits cis women.

Although I cannot here offer the kind of assessment of all the different options for organising gendered social practices that would be needed in order to conclusively reject (2) and (3), their association with (2*) and (3*), which my account does show to be false, suggests that the association of different types of gender kind with the interests of trans people and cis women cannot be maintained. However, my pluralist account of gender kinds does entail the rejection of (1), which is sufficient to undermine the "conflict of interest" framing overall.

Thus, as well as entailing the rejection of the Ontology-First approach, my pluralist account of gender kinds supports the rejection of the "objective versus subjective" framing and the "conflict of interest" framing of discussions about gender recognition. Given that these framings are counterproductive when it comes to advocating for trans-inclusive ways of organising gendered social practices, this is a further indication that my pluralist account of gender kinds is likely to have positive implications in the current social and political context.

8.4.2. Reframing Gender Recognition

What I have said so far about the likely implications of my account mostly concerns how it might disrupt some of the ways that public discussions about gender recognition are currently proceeding. However, it is also relevant to think about alternative and more constructive directions these discussions might take. Rejecting the Ontology-First approach tells us how *not* to try to settle questions about gender recognition: we ought not to appeal to the ontology of gender kinds as decisively determining how we should arrange gendered social practices. But the question remains: how *should* we approach discussions of gender recognition? If disrupting the problematic framings that I have identified left us with no better alternatives, then this would cast doubt on the idea that in helping to disrupt them, my account has positive implications. Accordingly, in this subsection, I will sketch an alternative way of approaching discussions about gender recognition, one that is compatible with my account and offers an attractive alternative to the Ontology-First approach.

I have already shown how my account implies a pluralist approach to gendered social practices. Rather than thinking that all gendered social practices should be organised in exactly the same way, we should allow that different social practices may call for the use of different varieties of gender kinds. Building on this, I want to suggest that discussions of gender recognition could helpfully be framed as primarily *practical* and *normative* rather than primarily *metaphysical*. Whereas the Ontology-First approach directs us to focus on establishing the correct ontology of gender kinds and to choose social practices that reflect these ontological facts, I suggest that we should instead view questions of gender recognition as requiring us to consider the consequences of adopting one or another kind of social practices and to choose the practices that are most conducive to emancipatory efforts in the context in which we are situated.

I will illustrate this approach by considering the example of social practices concerning the use of gender-separated toilets. Jones and Slater (2020) show that contestations around toilet access are at present often shaped by an impetus to delegitimate trans people and assert narrow definitions of womanhood and femaleness. This speaks to a framing of the issue in terms of "figuring out who is really a woman", which is to say, the Ontology-First approach. On the alternative approach I am suggesting, toilet access would be conceptually uncoupled from questions about what gender *is*, meaning that these sorts of considerations would be ruled out from the start. Instead, we would proceed by considering the consequences of the different options. In modelling this approach, I will, for the sake of simplicity, restrict my focus to options that hold fixed the current *provision* of toilet spaces, demarcated by gender, and consider two possible ways of organising social practices: what happens if trans people are able to use the gender-differentiated toilets that most closely match their gender identity (as they have been doing, perfectly legally, for many decades in the United Kingdom and many other countries), and what happens if they are not?[14]

I'll begin by considering the consequences of trans-exclusive social practices in this regard, which is to say, of preventing trans people from using the toilets that best match their gender identity. First, policing toilet access on the basis of perceived gender results in people being subject to denial of access, verbal harassment, and physical assault (Herman 2013). These risks generate stress and effectively prevent some people from using those toilets, which in turn prevents them from accessing a wide range of public spaces; depending on people's circumstances, it may severely limit their ability to leave their homes at all (Jones and Slater 2020).

These negative effects are widespread and well documented. The report of the 2015 US Transgender Survey, which surveyed more than 27,000 trans people in the United States, found that in the past year, 24 percent of respondents had been questioned or challenged over their presence in a toilet (restroom); 12 percent had been verbally harassed, physically attacked, or sexually assaulted when accessing or using a toilet in the past year; and 9 percent had been denied access to a toilet in the past year. More than half (59 percent) had avoided using a public toilet due to fear of such problems— either sometimes (48 percent) or always (11 percent)—and, related to this, almost a third (32 percent) limited the amount they ate or drank in order to avoid using the toilet, while 8 percent reported having a urinary tract infection, kidney infection, or another kidney-related problem as a result of avoiding toilets (James et al. 2016, 224–30).

Toilet policing also encourages the scrutinising of gendered bodies in light of culturally dominant stereotypes of femininity and masculinity. This negatively impacts many cis people as well as trans people, with particular implications for those with non-normative gender presentations and, given the intertwinement of perceptions of gender and race, for people of colour (Jones and Slater 2020, 844). It is clear, then, that trans-exclusionary approaches to toilet access undermine trans people's safety, dignity, and ability to participate in society and reinforce oppressive gender stereotypes that impact on everyone.

On the other hand, there are no credibly evidenced negative effects of enabling trans people to use toilets that match their gender identity.

---

[14] A more thorough exploration would also consider different ways of providing toilet spaces, such as individual, self-contained, non-gendered toilets, but I cannot undertake such an exploration here for reasons of space.

Peer-reviewed studies have assessed whether there is evidence that trans-inclusive policies lead to a rise in sexual offences (Barnett, Nesbit, and Sorrentino 2018) or safety and privacy violations more broadly (Hasenbush, Flores, and Herman 2019) and found that there is not.

One might reasonably think that this is sufficient to establish the lack of negative effects of trans-inclusive policies regarding toilet use. However, those who oppose trans-inclusive practices regarding toilet use often make a further argument in support of their position. This kind of argument relies on the broader claim that trans women either are *in fact* cis men or that they are *similar* to cis men in respects that justify their exclusion from women's spaces such as toilets. For example, a pamphlet entitled 'Not Our Sisters', distributed at a feminist march in London in 2014, claimed that trans women, who were described as 'male transgenders', commit violence against women 'at exactly the same rates as non-transgender males' (cited in Ahmed 2016). Similarly, a statement on the website of the organisation nia, which delivers services for women, girls, and children who have experienced sexual and domestic violence, asserts, 'A gender recognition certificate, whether through self-identification or a verification process, does not change a person's sex; it does not undo years or decades of sex-role socialisation and it will not stop an abusive man from being abusive' (nia 2020).

The claim that trans women should not access women's spaces such as women's toilets because they are in fact men clearly amounts to an appeal to the Ontology-First approach, which is explicitly contrary to the approach I am proposing here. Accordingly, this approach directs that such claims should be treated as totally irrelevant to deciding questions about the organisation of gendered social practices. However, the claim that trans women should not access such spaces because they are *similar* to cis men in relevant respects cannot be dealt with in this way but requires further examination.[15] This is because, at least on the surface, it is a claim about the practical consequences of organising gendered social spaces in trans-inclusive ways.

Those who make such claims, such as the two instances cited earlier, do not typically appeal to evidence that specifically assesses rates of violence against women committed by trans women, and I am not aware of any academic studies that offer specific evidence on this point. Rather, those who

---

[15] The examination that follows draws on an essay I co-wrote with Lorna Finlayson and Rosie Worsdale about the Gender Recognition Act consultation (Finlayson, Jenkins, and Worsdale 2018). My sincere thanks to them both.

make such claims seem to rely on an argument that goes something like the following. First, it is claimed that men pose a heightened risk of violence to women, compared with other women. I do not dispute this claim. The next move is to assert that this heightened risk is due to features that trans women, or many of them, share with cis men: namely, their 'sex' (in this context, I take this to mean something like having a penis, testes, and higher levels of testosterone) and having a certain history of 'sex-role socialisation'. From this, it is concluded that trans women pose the *same* risk of violence to women as cis men.

Although the terms in which these claims are phrased are ones I would wish to interrogate, it is certainly the case that some trans women—those who have not undertaken hormone therapy or genital surgery—do have the bodily features in question. It is also clearly the case—virtually by definition, in fact—that trans women are people who have been socially classified as male and treated in a way that reflects this classification for some part of their lives. I do not dispute either of these claims. What I do dispute is the claim that these features—either singly or in conjunction—are the correct basis for determining the risk that an individual poses in terms of violence against women. Although we do have overwhelming evidence that men commit violence against women at much higher rates than women commit violence against either women or men, this evidence does not establish that the basis of this heightened risk is a universal or widely shared "male biology" and/or a universal or widely shared "male socialisation". That is to say, while it may be reasonable to think that biological and social factors jointly exhaust the possible explanations that can be given for gendered violence—indeed, it's not clear what other factors there might be that could come into the picture here—it is *not* reasonable to assume that either biology or socialisation operates along sharply divided gender lines in the way that would be required to support this argument.

But do we need specific evidence for this? The pattern of violence is, after all, gendered, and some people might think it obvious that bodily difference, such as genitals and hormones, is the most likely candidate for being the basis of the differential risk of violence between men and women. There are, however, good feminist reasons for not taking this for granted. Many feminists have argued, successfully in my view, that people in sexist societies are often very bad at distinguishing between differences that are the result of bodily features and differences that are produced by social factors (Fine 2011). More specifically, the idea that men's violence against women is largely underpinned by male biology has also long functioned as a way of 'naturalising' this violence, depicting it as something brute-like and pre-programmed, even inevitable. Radical feminist Andrea Dworkin cautioned strongly against the belief that women are 'biologically good' compared with men, calling it an instance of 'the world's most dangerous and deadly idea', biological superiority (Dworkin 1989).

For this reason, many feminists have preferred to emphasise the role of social factors in making men violent. Indeed, as Sara Ahmed notes, arguments in this area often involve a shifting target: an argument may start out by appealing to 'traditional biology', but 'if we start engaging with arguments on these terms, the target will move', and '[t]rans women will become not women because they were socialized as boys and men, or for some other reason that has yet to be invented' (Ahmed 2016, 30). Despite this propensity for shiftiness, since the argument under consideration also alludes to the socialisation that those classed as male receive, it may seem as though all bases are covered: whatever the interplay between the social and the biological, some combination of the two is giving us men who are violent against women.

However, this overlooks the fact that trans women *are* different from cis men, because they have a female gender identity.[16] If we consider socialisation, for example, there is clearly a difference between the experience of a child who is treated by others in ways that are characteristic of boys and also identifies as a boy, on the one hand, and a child who is treated by others in ways that are characteristic of boys whilst identifying as a girl, on the other. It is, to say the very least, not obvious that gender identity makes no difference to the way in which biological and social factors manifest themselves.

It's important to be clear here. My claim is not that neither biology nor socialisation makes a difference to a person's propensity to commit violence or to commit violence against women in particular. Rather, it is that all sorts of variables combine and interact with the factors of having a certain anatomy and being classified as a certain gender on account of that anatomy, affecting—potentially profoundly—the way in which those factors shape us. Gender identity is among the factors that could, quite plausibly, make a difference. Because most studies and statistics concerning violence against

---

[16] Another thing that is also being overlooked here is the intersectional nature of experiences of gendered social structures: there is no single 'socialisation' that even all cis men can be said to undergo, because of the ways in which other aspects of identity and social position—race, class, sexuality, and disability among them—impact on people's experiences. However, exploring this point would take me too far afield from my present argument.

women do not draw clear distinctions between cis men, trans men, and trans women, there is little empirical evidence on this point, and I am aware of none that rules out this hypothesis. In light of this, thosemaking the kinds of purportedly feminist claims we encountered previously are not justified in assuming that all or some trans women share with cis men the features in virtue of which the latter pose a higher risk of violence to women.

At this point, one option for a proponent of those claims is to fall back on the sentiment "Better to be safe than sorry!" In other words, "We're pretty confident about the relative risks of violence against women from cis men and cis women, respectively; trans women are an unknown quantity; so better to play safe". But safe for whom? When keeping women's spaces for cis women only is held to be safest for cis women, or "females", the tacit assumption behind this exhortation to "play it safe" seems to be that trans women are not ("really") women. Indeed, this *must* be the assumption, since if we think of trans women as one among many groups within the larger group *women*, then it becomes unclear how their exclusion from women's spaces could be justified *even if* there were compelling evidence that they were more prone to violence than cis women are (which, to be clear, there is not).

To elaborate on this point, those who advocate for the exclusion of trans women from women's spaces such as toilets would, I think, be reluctant to advocate the same for other groups of women among whom cis women are included, in the event of there being similar evidence of higher statistical likelihood of violence in their case. For example, if it was shown that White women are more likely than women in general to commit violence against women of colour or that straight women are more likely than women in general to commit violence against queer women, I think the proponents of trans-exclusionary policies for toilet access would be unlikely to advocate excluding White women or straight women from women's toilets. I think this shows that it is because those making these arguments do not consider trans women to be "really women" that they are so willing to exclude trans women from women's spaces "just in case". Thus, behind the appeals to safety, which on the surface may look like the sort of consequence-based consideration that I am encouraging us to focus on, we find, once again, a tacit reliance on the Ontology-First approach.

What other possible negative consequences might result from enabling people to use the toilets that best match their gender identity? One point that is sometimes raised is the discomfort some cis women may feel at such an arrangement. I am in agreement with Brian Barnett, Ariana Nesbit, and Renée Sorrentino's assessment of this point:

> The discomfort that some cis individuals who encounter an obviously transgender individual in the restroom may feel is a minor harm that pales in comparison to the results of the discrimination that transgender individuals may experiences as a result of the denial of access. (2018, 237)

Moreover, once again, I would question whether those who wish to rely on this point would be equally willing to use some White women's discomfort at sharing spaces with women of colour, for example, as a reason, even a *pro tanto* reason, to exclude women of colour from women's spaces. A possible response here would be to claim that only racists would think that some White women's discomfort at sharing spaces with women of colour were well founded, and they would be wrong, whereas discomfort experienced by cis women in relation to trans women is founded on legitimate and reasonable fears for safety; thus, the two cases are different. However, this point returns us to the assessment of safety risks already discussed, which, as we have seen, does not play out in a way that supports the claims of the proponent of trans-exclusionary practices.

What is more, I very much doubt whether those making this argument would be willing to use some *trans* women's discomfort at sharing space with *cis* women as a reason to exclude *cis* women from women's spaces—and yet, given the evidence we have seen about violence experienced by trans people in toilets, discomfort of this sort seems like it would be well founded on legitimate and reasonable fears for safety. There seems to be an asymmetric treatment of trans women and cis women at work here, one that would only start to make sense on the assumption that trans women are "not really" women. Yet again, we encounter lingering traces of the Ontology-First approach, ruling this consideration irrelevant on the approach I am proposing.

Thus, within the approach I am advocating, the question of how to organise access to gender-differentiated toilets has a very obvious answer: people should be able to use the toilet that best fits their gender identity (assuming that we are holding fixed current provision of toilet spaces). Now, I'm not claiming that *all* decisions about how to organise gendered social practices necessarily have equally easy resolutions. The point is rather that it is much easier to point to evidence about the practical effects of different policies for toilet access than it is to answer ontological or metaphysical questions such as 'What makes someone a woman?'. I am further suggesting that the same move will have a similarly simplifying and helpful effect for other decisions about gender recognition as well, even if in some cases there is more left over to discuss after this move has been made.[17]

Furthermore, on the approach I am suggesting, presenting questions about ontology as relevant to determining how we should organise gendered social practices can be clearly reframed as derailing. This will help to prevent the fairly straightforward conclusions we can draw about how to arrange particular social practices from being (either deliberately or inadvertently) obscured. Protecting against this will still be a significant task; as we have seen, the Ontology-First approach has become deeply embedded in discussions that may appear on the surface to be about consequences, such that weeding it out thoroughly is a rather wearisome task. It is, however, a task worth doing.

To sum up, I take myself to have shown that when my account of gender pluralism, which includes an analysis of ontic oppression, comes into contact with current discussions of gender recognition, it is more likely to have effects that are conducive to trans liberation than effects that are antithetical to trans liberation. One reason for this is that the account challenges the Ontology-First approach, and the Ontology-First approach is counterproductive from the point of view of trans liberation. Another reason is that my account helps to displace the problematic framings that are currently applied to discussions of gender recognition. A third reason is that my account opens up space for an alternative and more productive way of thinking about gender recognition, which focuses on practical and normative considerations instead of metaphysical ones.

None of this is to say that my position is a perfect remedy for all that's toxic in public discussions about gender recognition or that it will win over people who are staunchly committed to trans-exclusionary social practices. But it is enough, I think, to disarm the worry that putting forward a view that acknowledges the existence of some gender kinds that do not align with people's gender identities is likely to have political effects that run counter to trans liberation in the current social context.

---

[17] For an illuminating discussion in this vein of four detailed case studies (identity documents, bathrooms, educational institutions, and sports), see Davis 2017.

8.5. A Note on "Transracialism"

My main aim in this chapter has been to respond to a worry that specifically focused on my account of *gender* kinds. However, I have also offered a pluralist account of *race* kinds. And whilst I do not propose to discuss all the possible implications of that account for public discussions of race and racism, I do want to briefly comment on a particular way in which race is brought into public discussions about gender recognition. This happens via the idea of "transracialism", a term used to refer to a certain sort of experience of racial identity that has been much discussed in the last few years.[18] In this final section, I will briefly examine how "transracialism" has been brought into public discussions about gender recognition, highlight a particular manifestation of the Ontology-First approach in this context, and show why it should be rejected here as well as in the contexts considered previously.

"Transracialism" is typically understood as the experience of having and expressing a racial identity that is different from the way in which one is categorised with regard to race by dominant frameworks, as modelled by way of an analogy with the experience of being trans(gender). Discussions of "transracialism" have often exhibited a heavy reliance on the case of Nkechi Amare Diallo, previously known as Rachel Dolezal (Brubaker 2016; Tuvel 2017; for discussion, see Borck 2017). Diallo is an American woman whose (non-adoptive) parents are both White and who identifies as Black. She presented herself as Black for several years, including acting as president for her local chapter of the NAACP, until her history was made public in 2015, leading to a media controversy.

Although Diallo rejects the term 'transracial' (McGreal 2015), it has been widely applied to her, and her name has been linked with that of Caitlyn Jenner, a celebrity who had recently come out as a trans woman at the time when Diallo's history was made public. This link was made especially strongly as part of a narrative promoted by right-wing news sources that aimed to undermine recognition of trans people as members of their identified genders.[19] As one news article at the time described this narrative:

---

[18] I use this term in scare quotes as I am suspicious of the assumptions it builds in, for reasons that will become clear by the end of the section.

[19] This linking was strengthened by news and comment pieces that aimed to debunk the claim that an equivalence could be drawn between these cases: the proliferation of pieces with titles such as 'Why Comparing [Nkechi Amare Diallo] to Caitlyn Jenner Is Detrimental to Both Trans and Racial Progress' (Blay 2015) further entrenched the connection between these names in the popular imagination. In time, these disagreements found an outlet in academic scholarship as well as public discussion (Brubaker 2016; Borck 2017; Tuvel 2017; Botts 2018).

The right's argument about [Diallo] answered a society that, more or less, had just welcomed Jenner's transformation with a much-lauded Diane Sawyer interview and a *Vanity Fair* cover. There is an objective truth, the line goes. Jenner is a man; [Diallo] is white. How can one be criticized while the other is praised? (Moyer 2015)

This narrative mobilises the language of 'objective truth' in relation to questions about criticism and praise to imply that the facts about social kind membership should determine how we respond to people. The thought is that if someone "really is" a member of one category and claims to be a member of another category, then we should respond to that claim with a negative moral appraisal because it is at odds with the "objective facts". This is an instance of the "objective versus subjective" framing that we encountered in public discussions of gender recognition (see §8.2.2).

Discussions about gender recognition and "transracialism" thus share this "objective versus subjective" framing. They also, however, exhibit a *distinctive* framing, which relates to the suggestion of an equivalence between gender and race that is conveyed by the linking of Diallo and Jenner. Many people seem to think that we ought to adopt different approaches when it comes to recognising people's claims about their identities. Nevertheless, discussions of gender recognition and "transracialism" often rely on the idea that such an asymmetric treatment of race and gender *stands in need of explanation and justification*—in other words, that race and gender should be treated as equivalent in this respect *unless and until* we identify a firm reason to do otherwise. I have frequently encountered this view in conversations, for example, with both philosophy undergraduate students and non-philosophers. Similarly, Camisha Russell describes a student in one of her philosophy classes strongly advocating the equivalence of trans(gender) and "transracial" identities in a classroom discussion, to the frustration of Black women students in the group (the speaker was a Black man) (2019, 178–79). I think this idea is widely held, including by those who do want to adopt different practices of recognition for race and for gender. Call this framing of discussions of gender recognition and "transracialism" the "presumption of equivalence" framing.

I think that the line of thought underpinning the "presumption of equivalence" framing goes something like the following. First, an ontological equivalence is assumed: race and gender kinds exist in the same way as each other; to recall the quote about Diallo and Jenner, they are equivalent as a matter of 'objective truth' (note the link here to the "objective versus subjective" framing). Second, this ontological equivalence is presumed to entail a first-personal ethical equivalence: since race and gender exist in the same way, having and expressing a racial identity that is at odds with how one would usually be categorised with regard to race has the same moral status as having and expressing a gender identity that is at odds with how one would usually be categorised with regard to gender. Finally, this first-personal ethical equivalence is presumed to entail a third-personal ethical equivalence: we ought (morally speaking) to respond in the same way to other people who express racial and gender identities that are ethically equivalent to one another.

This progression of thought establishes a default presumption in favour of treating race and gender in the same way when it comes to deciding how we respond in cases in which someone identifies with a category that does not match the way they would be categorised by dominant conventions. In other words, the "presumption of equivalence" framing relies on the idea that we should follow through from an ontological similarity ("race and gender are both socially constructed") to a first-personal ethical similarity ("if it's fine to be transgender, then it's fine to be transracial") and then finally to a third-personal ethical equivalence ("if we praise Jenner for saying she is a woman, then we ought to praise Diallo for saying she is Black")—unless, of course, we locate a good reason to stop somewhere along this route.

The "presumption of equivalence" framing is thoroughly undermined by the arguments presented in this chapter, together with the pluralist account of race and gender kinds developed in the earlier chapters. First, let's consider the overall move that the framing makes, from ontological equivalence to third-personal ethical equivalence. In making this move, the "presumption of equivalence" framing relies on the Ontology-First approach: it presents questions about what social practices we ought to adopt as being ultimately decided by facts about the ontology of social kinds.[20] I argued in §8.3.3 that we should reject the Ontology-First approach. This targets the overall move made by the "presumption of equivalence" framing, from ontological similarity (step 1) to third-personal ethical similarity (step 3).

In addition, my account also offers resources for targeting the intermediate moves from ontological similarity to first-personal ethical similarity

---

[20] Much of the discussion revolved around whether we should describe people as 'a woman' or 'Black'; I take linguistic choices about the application of terms such as 'woman' and 'Black' to be instances of social practices, since such choices are underdetermined by the meaning of the relevant terms.

(step 1 to step 2) and from first-personal ethical similarity to third-personal ethical similarity (step 2 to step 3). Regarding the first of these, the move from ontological similarity to first-personal ethical similarity, my account of race and gender kinds in relation to ontic oppression should give us pause for thought. In Chapters 4, 5, and 6, I have argued that some race and gender kinds are ontically oppressive, while others are not. Recognising the phenomenon of ontic oppression means that we cannot draw ethical conclusions about kinds simply from knowing about their ontology. Two kinds might be ontologically similar in the sense of being constituted by very similar sorts of constraints and enablements, but nevertheless one may be ontically oppressive and the other may not, because the normative status of those constraints and enablements may be different. Given this possibility, we cannot simply assume that ontological similarity entails a similarity in terms of the ethics of identifying with a kind. Still less can we infer this sort of ethical similarity between two kinds from the mere fact that they are both socially constructed.

Finally, let's consider the move from first-personal ethical similarity to third-personal ethical similarity. In §8.4.2, I advocated an approach to organising gendered social practices that is based on practical and normative considerations. When such an approach is extended to racialised social practices, we should expect the complex histories of racialised and gender oppression to make a difference to the outcomes of various options for organising social practices. Just because organising explicitly gendered social practices around a certain sort of gender kind has consequences that are conducive to emancipatory aims, it does not follow that the equivalent way of organising explicitly racialised social practices will similarly have positive consequences. The complexities of the practical and normative considerations at play—which concern the intermeshed but varied histories of racialised and gendered oppression—mean that we are not justified in assuming that the answers will come out the same for (single-moniker) race kinds as they do for (single-moniker) gender kinds.

Thus, the overall step made by the "presumption of equivalence" framing and the two intermediate steps this involves are all undermined by the arguments presented in this book. It is not reasonable to assume that whatever response people have towards trans people in general or Jenner in particular, they should have the same response to "transracial" people in general or to Diallo in particular, unless they can offer a specific justification for responding differently. Rather than framing questions of gender recognition as precisely parallel to questions of racial recognition, we should reject that framing as unfounded and unhelpful, whilst recognising that it is often employed cynically to undermine trans-inclusive ways of organising gendered social practices in conjunction with the equally dubious "objective versus subjective" framing. To the extent that the very term "transracialism" builds in a comparison with experiences of being trans(gender), it should be rejected along with the "presumption of equivalence" framing.

Doing justice to questions about people's complicated experiences of racial identity that are at odds with their membership in hegemonic and interpersonal race kinds requires a different approach, one that engages these experiences in their own right and not as an offshoot of discussions about gender recognition. Such a treatment is beyond the scope of this chapter, though I am hopeful that the pluralist account of race kinds offered in Chapters 4, 5, and 6 may provide some useful resources for an investigation of this sort. However, merely rejecting the problematic and unwarranted "presumption of equivalence" framing, as my pluralist account of race and gender kinds helps us to do, is a step in the right direction.

8.6. Conclusion

In this chapter, I have offered a response to the concern that putting forward a view that acknowledges the existence of some gender kinds that do not align with people's gender identities is likely to have political effects that run counter to trans liberation in the current social context. I approached this task by exploring how the account of gender kinds and ontic oppression developed in the rest of the book is likely to interact with public discussions of gender recognition that are currently taking place in the United Kingdom and other places. I showed how these discussions are marked by a number of problematic framings and how they often exhibit what I have called the Ontology-First approach, which holds that we should first aim to settle questions about the current ontology of gender kinds and then treat this as automatically determining what shape our gendered social practices ought to take. I argued that the Ontology-First approach is counterproductive from the perspective of trans liberation: it fuels disagreements about gender recognition and contributes to the perpetuation and amplification of transphobia.

I further showed how the account of ontic injustice presented in the first chapter of this book entails the rejection the Ontology-First approach—and given the drawbacks of that approach, I take this to be a positive result for my account. Recognising the possibility of ontic injustice undermines the idea that claims about the ontology of gender kinds should be treated as straightforwardly resolving questions about gender recognition: given the ways in which social reality can be unjust, the fact that certain social practices track facts about the ontology of gender kinds is not a compelling reason to adopt them. I then demonstrated some additional positive effects my account can reasonably be expected to have on discussions of gender recognition: it has the potential to disrupt various problematic framings, and it paves the way for an alternative approach to gender recognition, based on practical and normative considerations, that I believe is more conducive to trans liberation. Finally, I offered some thoughts on the ways in which considerations of racial identity are sometimes recruited into discussions of gender recognition and suggested that my account also offers useful resources in this regard.

At the risk of repeating myself, I will stress one last time that I am not claiming that my pluralist account of gender kinds offers any kind of complete solution for the many distortions and other dispiriting features that characterise current public discussions about gender recognition. I also want to acknowledge that it is difficult to predict in advance what the effects will be of articulating a particular philosophical position in a given social and political context. My claim, then, is simply that there is cause for optimism about the likely implications of my account in the present context—sufficiently so to alleviate the concern that was considered in this chapter.

Andrea Dworkin was once asked in an interview how she would like her work to be remembered. She is said to have replied, 'In a museum, when male supremacy is dead'.[21] I feel similarly about this chapter: I hope it ages badly, in the sense that I hope the dynamics of public discussions about gender recognition shift in ways that make my arguments here seem like curios from a bygone age. Despite this hope, it was very important to me to include this chapter in the book, for two reasons.

The first reason is that, as outlined in the Introduction, I am approaching philosophy in the spirit of emancipatory theory. On this approach, a success condition of the theory is that it should feed back into its social situation in a way that fosters emancipatory social change. The worry addressed in this chapter was that on the contrary, my account of ontic oppression and gender pluralism was likely to feed back into its social situation in a way that

---

[21] I have not been able to find the original interview, but the remark is quoted in the obituary for Dworkin in the *Guardian*, where it is described as having been made in an interview for that newspaper (Bindel 2005).

hindered emancipatory social change. If this worry turned out to be well founded, it would, according to my approach, have shown that my account was defective as a philosophical theory. So this chapter was important in relation to the success of my overall arguments in the book, given the success conditions I endorse for my philosophical work.

The second reason relates to a sense of responsibility. The vast majority of the people making arguments against trans-inclusive social practices in these discussions are cis people, and many of those making the versions of the arguments that I have focused on here are cis women who explicitly present themselves as feminists and who explicitly present their arguments as based on feminist considerations.[22] Moreover, although I have not focused on these aspects of discussions in this chapter, rejecting trans-inclusive social practices is often presented as being particularly in the interests of cis women who are lesbian or bisexual and of cis women who are survivors of sexual violence.[23] As a cis woman who is a feminist (who, indeed, currently makes a living from teaching and researching feminist philosophy), who is bisexual, and who is a survivor of sexual violence, I felt a particular responsibility to contribute to countering these arguments as one way of saying: *not in my name.*

---

[22] For example, Murray 2017 begins the opinion piece discussed in §8.3.1 by describing herself as a feminist.

[23] For example, the organisation LGB Alliance claims that there is a 'conflict between trans rights and the rights of LGB [lesbian, gay, and bisexual] people' (LGB Alliance 2020). The organisation nia, which delivers services for women, girls, and children who have experienced sexual and domestic violence, claims that excluding trans women from women's refuges 'keeps women safer' and 'can help create an environment in which women can recover' (nia 2020).

Conclusion

My main aims in this book have been to introduce the concept of ontic injustice and to illustrate it by exploring its application to race and gender kinds. I fulfilled the first aim in Chapter 1, and the rest of the book was devoted to the pursuit of the second aim. In service of this aim, I supplied the accompanying normative and ontological commitments needed to apply the concept of ontic injustice to race and gender kinds. On the normative side (Chapter 2), this took the form of the concept of ontic oppression, and on the ontological side, it took the form of the constraints and enablements framework (CEF) for theorizing human social kinds in general (Chapter 3). Using these resources, I have argued (Chapters 4, 5, and 6) that some race and gender kinds are ontically oppressive, though others are not, and some even serve an emancipatory function. Overall, I argued (Chapter 7), this pluralist account has many benefits and can be defended from several objections. Finally, in Chapter 8, I responded to the worry that my account of gender pluralism and ontic oppression would have negative consequences for trans liberation when articulated in the current social and political context, arguing that on the contrary, there are grounds for optimism on this point.

There are many more questions about my main aims that might have been considered as part of this book and that would have extended the discussion in useful ways. It would also have been informative to explore connections between the concepts of ontic injustice and ontic oppression and other areas of philosophy beyond social ontology. In particular, I think it would be interesting to consider the relationship between ontic injustice/oppression and epistemic injustice/oppression, and I also think that much could be learned from considering ontic injustice/oppression alongside the literature on recognition and misrecognition. Although I was not able to explore these connections here, they offer inviting avenues for further study.

One question that is quite deliberately excluded from the scope of my project, however, is the question of what we should *do* about ontic injustice

Ontology and Oppression. Katharine Jenkins, Oxford University Press. © Katharine Jenkins 2023.
DOI: 10.1093/oso/9780197666777.003.0010

and ontic oppression. My choice to focus on conceptualizing and identifying these wrongs rather than trying to offer a solution to them is based on my conviction that combating ontic injustice and ontic oppression is an endeavour best pursued as part of broader efforts to oppose various forms of injustice and oppression. Ontic injustice, including ontic oppression, does not show up alone; rather, it is the product of social arrangements that almost always give rise to other dimensions of injustice and oppression. Accordingly, I think that the task of working out how to combat ontic injustice is best undertaken as part of inquiries into particular forms of injustice and oppression, with close reference to the material conditions in a particular time and place, and not as part of a more general study of ontic injustice such as the one I have been engaged in here.

Beyond introducing the concepts of ontic injustice and ontic oppression as tools that I hope others will take up and use, the main upshots of my exploration come in the form of two cautions. The first caution is against an all-or-nothing approach to applying the concept of ontic oppression to race and gender. I have argued that we should be pluralists about race and gender kinds. Doing so, I argued, is justified because there are multiple race and gender kinds that do important explanatory work from the perspective of emancipatory theory. Being pluralists also helps us to make sense of the intersectional nature of race and gender categories. The pluralist picture is messy, but it is a warranted messiness that helps us understand the messy world we live in, and I have offered conceptual resources, in the form of the CEF, to help keep the messiness manageable. On my pluralist account, we cannot make the blanket claim that race and gender kinds such as *Black* or *woman* are ontically oppressive. It depends on which kind we have in mind. Some race and gender kinds, I argued, *are* ontically oppressive, but others are not, and some even serve an emancipatory social function. While I think it is important and illuminating to note the oppressive nature of some race and gender kinds, as many other theorists have done, it is misleading and counterproductive to frame this as a general claim about race and/or gender as such.

The second caution, developed in relation to current discussions about gender recognition, is a caution against a way of approaching social ontology that I think overlooks the possibility and the implications of ontic oppression and that I take to be a hindrance to working for emancipation even though it may initially appeal to emancipatory theorists. This approach to social ontology aims to vindicate social practices that are conducive to emancipation by showing that such practices align with existing social kinds. It therefore commits us to identifying social kinds with contours that support the sorts of social practices that will be effective in reducing oppression. However, given that social kinds can be ontically oppressive, there is no guarantee of our finding any such kinds. Sometimes we may find them, and sometimes we may not. Even when we find them, there may be other, oppressive social kinds in their vicinity, and it may not be straightforward or even possible to show that the emancipatory kinds are more significant for our explanatory purposes as emancipatory social theorists than the oppressive kinds.

Instead of trying to locate existing social kinds that serve emancipatory aims, I think we should organise our social practices in ways that are conducive to emancipation regardless of whether this aligns with existing social kinds. At the same time, I think we should be willing to envision and to craft the social kinds we would like to see. In an award acceptance speech given in 2014, the science fiction and fantasy writer Ursula K. Le Guin said:

> Hard times are coming, when we'll be wanting the voices of writers who can see alternatives to how we live now, can see through our fear-stricken society and its obsessive technologies to other ways of being, and even imagine real grounds for hope. We'll need writers who can remember freedom—poets, visionaries—realists of a larger reality. (Le Guin 2014)

Although I think philosophy may have a much smaller part to play in galvanizing resistance and change than many philosophers would like to think, I nevertheless believe that those of us who approach the study of social ontology with an emancipatory interest must aim to be 'realists of a larger reality' in Le Guin's sense. Yes, we should seek to understand how oppressive social realities work and, most important, where we can take aim at them so that they begin to fall apart—but we should resist the temptation to try to read the liberation we seek into the way the social world currently exists. That way lie various forms of confusion that have the potential to undermine our emancipatory aims. Instead, we should remember that our work does not stop at describing the current state of social reality but extends to envisioning ways in which it might be refashioned in the interests of freedom.

That second step, although it should not be collapsed into the first, is vital. To pursue it, we should reject without equivocation the promptings of those who, out of fear, demand that we narrow our vision to deal only with the way social reality currently is and not the ways it could be. The people who urge us to take up a defensive position around oppressive social kinds and protect them from perceived intruders, rather than trying to figure out social practices that would have the effect of alleviating oppression, are either not interested in emancipatory social change or are confused about how to achieve it. Working to bring a better social reality into being is a crucial part of what it means to pursue emancipation. It always has been, and it always will.

Bibliography

Ahmed, Sara. 2016. 'An Affinity of Hammers'. *TSQ: Transgender Studies Quarterly* 3 (1–2): 22–34.

Alcoff, Linda Martín. 2006. *Visible Identities: Race, Gender, and the Self*. Studies in Feminist Philosophy. New York: Oxford University Press.

Alexander, Michelle. 2012. *The New Jim Crow: Mass Incarceration in the Age of Colourblindness*. Rev. ed. New York: The New Press.

Anderson, Elizabeth. 2012. 'Epistemic Justice as a Virtue of Social Institutions'. *Social Epistemology* 26 (2): 163–73.

Andreasen, Robin. 2004. 'The Cladistic Race Concept: A Defense'. *Biology and Philosophy* 19 (3): 425–42.

Andreasen, Robin. 2005. 'The Meaning of "Race": Folk Conceptions and the New Biology of Race'. *Journal of Philosophy* 102 (February): 94–106.

Appiah, K. Anthony. 1996. 'Reconstructing Racial Identities'. *Research in African Literatures* 27 (3): 68–72.

Ashley, Florence. 2022. '"Trans" Is My Gender Modality: A Modest Terminological Proposal'. In *Trans Bodies, Trans Selves*, edited by Laura Erikson-Schroth, 22. 2nd ed. Oxford, New York: Oxford University Press.

Ásta. 2018. *Categories We Live By: The Construction of Sex, Gender, Race, and Other Social Categories*. New York: Oxford University Press.

Ásta. 2019. 'Response to Critics'. *Journal of Social Ontology* 5 (2): 273–83.

Bach, Theodore. 2012. 'Gender Is a Natural Kind with a Historical Essence'. *Ethics* 122 (2): 231–72.

Bailey, Louis, Sonja J. Ellis, and Jay McNeil. 2014. 'Suicide Risk in the UK Trans Population and the Role of Gender Transition in Decreasing Suicidal Ideation and Suicide Attempt'. *Mental Health Review Journal* 19 (4): 209–20.

Barnes, Elizabeth. 2020. 'Gender and Gender Terms'. *Noûs* 54 (3): 704–30.

Barnes, Elizabeth, and Matthew Andler. 2020. 'Categories We Live By: The Construction of Sex, Gender, Race, and Other Social Categories, by Ásta'. *Mind* 129 (515): 939–47.

Barnett, Brian, Ariana Nesbit, and Renée Sorrentino. 2018. 'The Transgender Bathroom Debate at the Intersection of Politics, Law, Ethics, and Science'. *Journal of the American Academy of Psychiatry and the Law* 46 (June): 232–41.

Bartky, Sandra. 1991. 'On Psychological Oppression'. In *Femininity and Domination: Studies in the Phenomenology of Oppression*, by Sandra Bartky, 22–32. Abingdon: Oxon; New York: Routledge.

Bell, Rowan. 2022. 'Gender Norms and Gendered Traits'. PhD diss., Syracuse University.

Bernstein, Sara. 2020. 'The Metaphysics of Intersectionality'. *Philosophical Studies* 177 (2): 321–35.

Bettcher, Talia Mae. 2007. 'Evil Deceivers and Make-Believers: On Transphobic Violence and the Politics of Illusion'. *Hypatia* 22 (3): 43–65.

Bettcher, Talia Mae. 2009. 'Trans Identities and First-Person Authority'. In *You've Changed: Sex Reassignment and Personal Identity*, edited by Laurie Shrage, 98–120. New York: Oxford University Press.

Bettcher, Talia Mae. 2013. 'Trans Women and the Meaning of "Woman"'. In *Philosophy of Sex: Contemporary Readings*, edited by R. Halwani, N. Power, and A. Soble, 233–50. 6th ed. Lanham, MD: Rowman & Littlefield.

Bettcher, Talia Mae. 2017. 'Getting "Naked" in the Colonial/Modern Gender System: A Preliminary Transfeminist Analysis'. In *Beyond Speech: Pornography and Analytic Feminist Philosophy*, edited by Mari Mikkola, 157–76. New York: Oxford University Press.

Bettcher, Talia Mae. 2018. '"When Tables Speak": On the Existence of Trans Philosophy'. *Daily Nous*, 30 May. https://dailynous.com/2018/05/30/tables-speak-existence-trans-philosophy-guest-talia-mae-bettcher/.

Bey, Marquis. 2017. 'The Trans*-Ness of Blackness, the Blackness of Trans*-Ness'. *Transgender Studies Quarterly* 4 (2): 275–95.

Bierria, Alisa. 2014. 'Missing in Action: Violence, Power, and Discerning Agency'. *Hypatia* 29 (1): 129–45.

Bindel, Julie. 2005. 'Obituary: Andrea Dworkin'. *Guardian*, 12 April. http://www.theguardian.com/news/2005/apr/12/guardianobituaries.gender.

Blay, Zeba. 2015. 'Why Comparing Rachel Dolezal To Caitlyn Jenner Is Detrimental to Both Trans and Racial Progress'. HuffPost, 12 June. https://www.huffpost.com/entry/rachel-dolezal-caitlyn-jenner_n_7569160.

Borck, C. Ray. 2017. 'Negligent Analogies'. *Transgender Studies Quarterly* 4 (3–4): 679–84.

Botts, Tina F. 2018. 'Race and Method: The Tuvel Affair'. *Philosophy Today* 62 (1): 51-72.

Boyd, Richard. 1999. 'Homeostasis, Species, and Higher Taxa'. In *Species: New Interdisciplinary Essays*, edited by R. A. Wilson, 141–85. Cambridge, MA: MIT Press.

Brännmark, Johan. 2019. 'Contested Institutional Facts'. *Erkenntnis* 84 (5): 1047–64.

Brännmark, Johan. 2021. 'Social Positions and Institutional Privilege as Matters of Justice'. *European Journal of Political Theory* 20 (3): 510–28.

Brison, Susan J. 2003. *Aftermath: Violence and the Remaking of a Self*. Princeton, NJ: Princeton University Press.

Brubaker, Rogers. 2016. *Trans: Gender and Race in an Age of Unsettled Identities*. Princeton, NJ: Princeton University Press.

Burman, Åsa. 2007. *Power and Social Ontology*. Lund: Bokbox.

Burman, Åsa. 2019. 'Categories We Do Not Know We Live By'. *Journal of Social Ontology* 5 (2): 235–43.

Burns, Katelyn. 2019. 'The Rise of Anti-Trans "Radical" Feminists, Explained'. Vox, 5 September. https://www.vox.com/identities/2019/9/5/20840101/terfs-radical-feminists-gender-critical.

Butler, Judith. 1990. *Gender Trouble: Feminism and the Subversion of Identity*. New York: Routledge.

Butler, Judith. 1993. *Bodies That Matter: On the Discursive Limits of Sex*. New York: Routledge.

Calvert, Randall L. 1998. 'Rational Actors, Equilibrium, and Social Insitutions'. In *Explaining Social Institutions*, edited by Jack Knight and Itai Sened, 57–93. Ann Arbor: University of Michigan Press.

Carastathis, Anna. 2014. 'The Concept of Intersectionality in Feminist Theory'. *Philosophy Compass* 9 (5): 304–14.

Card, Claudia. 1991. 'Rape as a Terrorist Institution'. In *Violence, Terrorism, and Justice*, edited by Raymond Gillespie Frey and Christopher W. Morris, 296–319. Cambridge: Cambridge University Press.

Celikates, Robin. 2006. 'From Critical Social Theory to a Social Theory of Critique: On the Critique of Ideology after the Pragmatic Turn'. *Constellations* 13 (1): 21–40.

Cho, Sumi, Kimberlé Williams Crenshaw, and Leslie McCall. 2013. 'Toward a Field of Intersectionality Studies: Theory, Applications, and Praxis'. *Signs: Journal of Women in Culture and Society* 38 (4): 785–810.

Coates, Ta-Nehisi. 2015. *Between the World and Me*. New York: Spiegel & Grau.

Collins, Patricia Hill. 2000. *Black Feminist Thought: Knowledge, Consciousness, and the Politics of Empowerment*. 2nd ed. New York: Routledge.

Combahee River Collective. 1978. 'A Black Feminist Statement'. In *Capitalist Patriarchy and the Case for Socialist Feminism*, edited by Zillah R. Eisenstein, 362–72. New York: Monthly Review.

Connell, R. W. 1987. *Gender and Power*. Sydney: Allen and Unwin.

Connell, R. W., and James W. Messerschmidt. 2005. 'Hegemonic Masculinity: Rethinking the Concept'. *Gender and Society* 19 (6): 829–59.

ContraPoints. 2021. 'J. K. Rowling'. https://www.youtube.com/watch?v=7gDKbT_l2us.

Cooper, Davina. 2019. 'A Very Binary Drama: The Conceptual Struggle for Gender's Future'. *Feminists@law* 9 (1). https://doi.org/10.22024/UniKent/03/fal.655

Corredor, Elizabeth S. 2019. 'Unpacking "Gender Ideology" and the Global Right's Antigender Countermovement'. *Signs: Journal of Women in Culture and Society* 44 (3): 613–38.

Crenshaw, Kimberlé. 1989. 'Demarginalizing the Intersection of Race and Sex: A Black Feminist Critique of Antidiscrimination Doctrine, Feminist Theory and Antiracist Politics'. *University of Chicago Legal Forum* 1989 (1): 139–167.

Crenshaw, Kimberlé. 1991. 'Mapping the Margins: Intersectionality, Identity Politics, and Violence against Women of Color'. *Stanford Law Review* 43 (6): 1241–99.

Crenshaw, Kimberlé. 2010. 'Close Encounters of Three Kinds: On Teaching Dominance Feminism and Intersectionality'. *Tulsa Law Review* 46 (1): 151–90.

Cross, William E. 1991. *Shades of Black: Diversity in African-American Identity*. Philadelphia: Temple University Press.

Cudd, Ann E. 1994. 'Oppression by Choice'. *Journal of Social Philosophy* 25 (1): 22–44.

Cudd, Ann E. 2006. *Analyzing Oppression*. New York: Oxford University Press.

Cull, Matthew J. 2019. 'Against Abolition'. *Feminist Philosophy Quarterly* 5 (3). DOI: https://doi.org/10.5206/fpq/2019.3.5898

Curry, Tommy J. 2017. *The Man-Not: Race, Class, Genre, and the Dilemmas of Black Manhood*. Philadelphia: Temple University Press.

Darwall, Stephen L. 1977. 'Two Kinds of Respect'. *Ethics* 88 (1): 36–49.

Darwall, Stephen. 2004. 'Respect and the Second-Person Standpoint'. *Proceedings and Addresses of the American Philosophical Association* 78 (2): 43–59.

Davis, Heath Fogg. 2017. *Beyond Trans: Does Gender Matter?* New York: New York University Press.

Dembroff, Robin. 2017. 'Categories We (Aim to) Live By'. PhD diss., Princeton University.

Dembroff, Robin. 2018. 'Real Talk on the Metaphysics of Gender'. *Philosophical Topics* 46 (2): 21–50.

Dembroff, Robin. 2020a. 'Beyond Binary: Genderqueer as Critical Gender Kind'. *Philosopher's Imprint* 20 (9): 1–23.

Dembroff, Robin. 2020b. 'Cisgender Commonsense and Philosophy's Transgender Trouble'. *TSQ: Transgender Studies Quarterly* 7 (3): 399–406.

Dembroff, Robin, and Catharine Saint-Croix. '"Yep, I'm Gay": Understanding Agential Identity'. *Ergo* 6 (20). https://doi.org/10.3998/ergo.12405314.0006.020

Dotson, Kristie. 2011. 'Tracking Epistemic Violence, Tracking Practices of Silencing'. *Hypatia* 26 (2): 236–57.

Dotson, Kristie. 2013. 'How Is This Paper Philosophy?' *Comparative Philosophy* 3 (1): 3–29.

DuBois, W.E.B. 1997 [1903]. *The Souls of Black Folk,* edited by David W. Blight and Robert Gooding-Williams. Boston: Bedford Books.

Dupré, John. 1995. *The Disorder of Things: Metaphysical /Foundations of the Disunity of Science*. Cambridge, MA: Harvard University Press.

Dworkin, Andrea. 1974. *Woman Hating*. New York: Penguin.

Dworkin, Andrea. 1989. 'Biological Supremacy: The World's Most Dangerous and Deadly Idea'. In *Letters from a War Zone: Writings, 1976–1989*, by Andrea Dworkin, 110–16. New York: E. P. Dutton.

Eadie, Jo. 1993. 'Activating Bisexuality: Toward a Bi/Sexual Politics'. In *Activating Theory: Lesbian, Gay, Bisexual Politics*, edited by Joseph Bristow and Angelia R. Wilson, 139–70. London: Lawrence & Wishart.

El-Enany, Nadine. 2019. 'Before Grenfell: British Immigration Law and the Production of Colonial Spaces'. In *After Grenfell: Violence, Resistance and Response*, edited by Dan Bulley, Jenny Edkins, and Nadine El-Enany, 50–61. London: Pluto.

El-Enany, Nadine. 2020. *Bordering Britain: Law, Race and Empire*. Manchester: Manchester University Press.

Epstein, Brian. 2015. *The Ant Trap: Rebuilding the Foundations of the Social Sciences*. Oxford: Oxford University Press.

Equality and Human Rights Commission. 2011. 'Equality Act 2010 Statutory Code of Practice: Services, Public Functions and Associations'. https://www.equalityhumanrig hts.com/sites/default/files/servicescode_0.pdf.

Fanon, Frantz. 2008 [1952]. *Black Skin, White Masks*. Translated by Charles Lam Markmann. London: Pluto.

Faye, Shon. 2021. *The Transgender Issue: An Argument for Justice*. London: Allen Lane.

Ferguson, Stephen C. II, and John H. McClendon III. 2013. 'Indignity and Death: Philosophical Commentary on White Terror, Black Death, and the Trayvon Martin Tragedy'. In *Pursuing Trayvon Martin: Historical Contexts and Contemporary Manifestations of Racial Dynamics*, edited by George Yancy and Janine Jones, 41–58. Lanham, MD: Lexington.

Fine, Cordelia. 2011. *Delusions of Gender: The Real Science behind Sex Differences*. London: Icon.

Finlayson, Lorna, Katharine Jenkins, and Rosie Worsdale. 2018. '"I'm Not Transphobic, But . . .": A Feminist Case against the Feminist Case against Trans Inclusivity'. Versobooks.com. 17 October. https://www.versobooks.com/blogs/4090-i-m-not-tran sphobic-but-a-feminist-case-against-the-feminist-case-against-trans-inclusivity.

Foster, Dawn. 2017. 'Would a White British Community Have Burned in Grenfell Tower?'. *The New York Times*, 20 June. https://www.nytimes.com/2017/06/20/opinion/lon don-tower-grenfell-fire.html

Fraser, Nancy. 2014. *Justice Interruptus: Critical Reflections on the 'Postsocialist' Condition*. New York: Routledge.

Fricker, Miranda. 2007. *Epistemic Injustice: Power and the Ethics of Knowing*. Oxford: Oxford University Press.

Frye, Marilyn. 1983. 'Oppression'. In *The Politics of Reality*, by Marilyn Frye, 1–16. Berkeley, CA: Crossing.

Gadsby, Hannah, Jon Olb, and Madeleine Parry. 2018. *Hannah Gadsby: Nanette*. Netflix.

Garry, Ann. 2011. 'Intersectionality, Metaphors, and the Multiplicity of Gender'. *Hypatia* 26 (4): 826–50.

Geuss, Raymond. 1981. *The Idea of a Critical Theory: Habermas and the Frankfurt School*. Cambridge: Cambridge University Press.

Gill-Peterson, Jules (Published as Gill-Peterson, Julian). 2018. *Histories of the Transgender Child*. 3rd ed. Minneapolis: University of Minnesota Press.

Glasgow, Joshua. 2007. 'Three Things Realist Constructionism about Race—or Anything Else—Can Do'. *Journal of Social Philosophy* 38 (November): 554–68.

Glasgow, Joshua, Sally Haslanger, Chike Jeffers, and Quayshawn Spencer. 2019. *What Is Race? Four Philosophical Views*. New York: Oxford University Press.

Glasgow, Joshua, and Jonathan M. Woodward. 2015. 'Basic Racial Realism'. *Journal of the American Philosophical Association* 1 (3): 449–66.

Golden, Timothy Joseph. 2013. 'Two Forms of Transcendence: Justice and the Problem of Knowledge'. In *Pursuing Trayvon Martin: Historical Contexts and Contemporary Manifestations of Racial Dynamics*, edited by George Yancy and Janine Jones, 73–84. Lanham, MD: Lexington.

Greif, Avner, and Christopher Kingston. 2011. 'Institutions: Rules or Equilibria?' In *Political Economy of Institutions, Democracy and Voting*, edited by Norman Schofield and Gonzalo Caballero, 13–43. Berlin: Springer.

Griffith, Aaron M. 2019. 'Individualistic and Structural Explanations in Ásta's Categories We Live By'. *Journal of Social Ontology* 5 (2): 251–60.

Groff, Ruth. 2012. *Ontology Revisited: Metaphysics in Social and Political Philosophy*. London: Routledge.

Guala, Francesco, and Frank Hindriks. 2015. 'A Unified Social Ontology'. *Philosophical Quarterly* 65 (259): 177–201.

Guardian. 2020. 'Family judges could get training after row over comments on rape'. *The Guardian* 23 January. https://www.theguardian.com/society/2020/jan/23/outdated-views-rape-judges-training-appeal

Gunnarsson, Lena. 2017. 'Why We Keep Separating the "Inseparable": Dialecticizing Intersectionality'. *European Journal of Women's Studies* 24 (2): 114–27.

Hacking, Ian. 1990. 'Making Up People'. In *Forms of Desire: Sexual Orientation and the Social Constructionist Controversy*, edited by Edward Stein, 69–88. London: Routledge.

Hampton, Jean. 1991. 'Correcting Harms versus Righting Wrongs: The Goal of Retribution'. *UCLA Law Review* 39: 1659–1702.

Harding, Sandra, ed. 2004a. *The Feminist Standpoint Theory Reader: Intellectual and Political Controversies*. 1st ed. New York: Routledge.

Harding, Sandra. 2004b. 'Introduction: Standpoint Theory as a Site of Political, Philosophical, and Scientific Debate'. In *The Feminist Standpoint Theory Reader: Intellectual and Political Controversies*, edited by Sandra Harding, 1–16. New York: Routledge.

Harris, Joshua Lee. 2021. 'Why Critical Social Ontologists Shouldn't Be Univocalists'. *Ergo* 8 (1). https://doi.org/10.3998/ergo.1138

Hartman, Saidiya V. 2007. *Lose Your Mother: A Journey along the Atlantic Slave Route*. New York: Farrar, Straus and Giroux.

Hasenbush, Amira, Andrew R. Flores, and Jody L. Herman. 2019. 'Gender Identity Nondiscrimination Laws in Public Accommodations: A Review of Evidence Regarding Safety and Privacy in Public Restrooms, Locker Rooms, and Changing Rooms'. *Sexuality Research and Social Policy* 16 (1): 70–83.

Haslanger, Sally. 2005. 'What Are We Talking About? The Semantics and Politics of Social Kinds'. *Hypatia* 20 (4): 10–26.

Haslanger, Sally. 2012a [2000]. 'Gender and Race: (What) Are They? (What) Do We Want Them to Be?' In *Resisting Reality: Social Construction and Social Critique*, by Sally Haslanger, 221–47. New York: Oxford University Press.

Haslanger, Sally. 2012b [1995]. 'Ontology and Social Construction'. In *Resisting Reality: Social Construction and Social Critique*, by Sally Haslanger, 83–112. New York: Oxford University Press.

Haslanger, Sally. 2012c. *Resisting Reality: Social Construction and Social Critique*. New York: Oxford University Press.

Haslanger, Sally. 2012d. 'Social Construction: Myth and Reality'. In *Resisting Reality: Social Construction and Social Critique*, by Sally Haslanger, 183–219. New York: Oxford University Press.

Haslanger, Sally. 2012e [2005]. 'You Mixed? Racial Identity Without Racial Biology'. In *Resisting Reality: Social Construction and Social Critique*, by Sally Hanslanger, 273–97. New York: Oxford University Press.

Haslanger, Sally. 2014. 'Race, Intersectionality, and Method: A Reply to Critics'. *Philosophical Studies* 171 (1): 109–19.

Haslanger, Sally. 2015. 'Social Structure, Narrative and Explanation'. *Canadian Journal of Philosophy* 45 (1): 1–15.

Haslanger, Sally. 2016a. 'Theorizing with a Purpose: The Many Kinds of Sex'. In *Natural Kinds and Classification in Scientific Practice*, edited by Catherine Kendig, 129–44. London: Routledge.

Haslanger, Sally. 2016b. 'What Is a (Social) Structural Explanation?' *Philosophical Studies* 173 (1): 113–30.

Haslanger, Sally. 2017a. 'Culture and Critique'. *Aristotelian Society Supplementary Volume* 91 (1): 149–73.

Haslanger, Sally. 2017b. 'Racism, Ideology, and Social Movements'. *Res Philosophica* 94: 1–22.

Hawley, Katherine. 2019. 'Comments on Brian Epstein's The Ant Trap'. *Inquiry* 62 (2): 217–29.

Hayward, Eva S. 2017. 'Don't Exist'. *TSQ: Transgender Studies Quarterly* 4 (2): 191–94.

Herman, Jody L. 2013. 'Gendered Restrooms and Minority Stress: The Public Regulation of Gender and Its Impact on Transgender People's Lives'. *Social Policy* 16: 65–80.

Honneth, Axel. 1996. *Struggle for Recognition: The Moral Grammar of Social Conflicts*. Translated by Joel Anderson. Cambridge: Polity.

hooks, bell. 1982. *Ain't I a Woman: Black Women and Feminism*. Boston: South End.

hooks, bell. 1984. *Feminist Theory: From Margin to Center*. Boston: South End.

Horkheimer, Max. 1972. 'Traditional and Critical Theory'. In *Critical Theory: Selected Essays*, translated by Matthew J. O'Connell, 188–243. New York: Herder & Herder.

Hull, Gloria T., Patricia Bell Scott, and Barbara Smith. 1982. *But Some of Us Are Brave: Black Women's Studies*. Old Westbury, NY: The Feminist Press.

Jaeggi, Rahel. 2009. 'Rethinking Ideology'. In *New Waves in Political Philosophy*, edited by Boudewijn de Bruin and Christopher F. Zurn, 63–86. London: Palgrave Macmillan.

James, Sandy E., Jody. L. Herman, Susan Rankin, Mara Keisling, Lisa Mottet, and Ma'ayan Anafi. 2016. 'The Report of the 2015 U.S. Transgender Survey'. National Center for Transgender Equality. https://transequality.org/sites/default/files/docs/usts/USTS-Full-Report-Dec17.pdf

Jeffers, Chike. 2013. 'The Cultural Theory of Race: Yet Another Look at Du Bois's "The Conservation of Races"'. *Ethics* 123 (3): 403–26.

Jenkins, Katharine. 2014. '"That's Not Philosophy": Feminism, Academia and the Double Bind'. *Journal of Gender Studies* 23 (3): 262–74.

Jenkins, Katharine. 2016a. 'Amelioration and Inclusion: Gender Identity and the Concept of Woman'. *Ethics* 126 (2): 394–421.

Jenkins, Katharine. 2016b. 'Ontic Injustice'. PhD diss., University of Sheffield. https://ethe ses.whiterose.ac.uk/13453/.

Jenkins, Katharine. 2018a. 'Toward an Account of Gender Identity'. *Ergo* 5. https://doi. org/10.3998/ergo.12405314.0005.027

Jenkins, Katharine. 2018b. 'The Wrong of Injustice, by Mari Mikkola'. *Mind* 127 (506): 618–27.

Jenkins, Katharine. 2019. 'Two Routes to Radical Racial Pluralism'. *Aristotelian Society Supplementary Volume* 93 (1): 49–68.

Jenkins, Katharine. 2020a. 'Conferralism and Intersectionality: A Response to Ásta's Categories We Live By'. *Journal of Social Ontology* 5 (2): 261–72.

Jenkins, Katharine. 2020b. 'Ontic Injustice'. *Journal of the American Philosophical Association* 6 (2): 188–205.

Jones, Charlotte, and Jen Slater. 2020. 'The Toilet Debate: Stalling Trans Possibilities and Defending "Women's Protected Spaces"'. *Sociological Review* 68 (4): 834–51.

Jones, Karen. 2014. 'Intersectionality and Ameliorative Analyses of Race and Gender'. *Philosophical Studies* 171 (1): 99–107.

Jorba, Marta, and Maria Rodó-Zárate. 2019. 'Beyond Mutual Constitution: The Properties Framework for Intersectionality Studies'. *Signs: Journal of Women in Culture and Society* 45 (1): 175–200.

Kaplan, Jonathan Michael. 2010. 'When Socially Determined Categories Make Biological Realities: Undertanding Black/White Health Disparities in the U.S.'. *The Monist* 93 (2): 283–99.

Kapusta, Stephanie Julia. 2016. 'Misgendering and Its Moral Contestability'. *Hypatia* 31 (3): 502–19.

Khalidi, Muhammad Ali. 2015. 'Three Kinds of Social Kinds'. *Philosophy and Phenomenological Research* 90 (1): 90–112.

Kitcher, Philip. 2007. 'Does "Race" Have a Future?' *Philosophy & Public Affairs* 35 (4): 293–317.

Kukla, Rebecca. 2014. 'Performative Force, Convention, and Discursive Injustice'. *Hypatia* 29 (2): 440–57.

Lamont, Tom. 2021. 'Nish Kumar: "Do They Just Hate My Jokes?"' *Guardian*, 16 May. http://www.theguardian.com/culture/2021/may/16/nish-kumar-standup-comed ian-do-they-just-hate-my-jokes.

Langton, Rae. 1993. 'Speech Acts and Unspeakable Acts'. *Philosophy & Public Affairs* 22 (4): 293–330.

Le Guin, Ursula K. 2014. 'Ursula K Le Guin's Speech at National Book Awards: "Books Aren't Just Commodities"'. *Guardian*, 20 November. http://www.theguardian.com/books/2014/nov/20/ursula-k-le-guin-national-book-awards-speech.

Lewis, David. 2002. *Convention: A Philosophical Study*. Oxford: Blackwell.

LGB Alliance. 2020. 'LGB Alliance Statement on Reports That the UK Government Plans to Drop Its Previous Proposals to Reform the GRA'. https://web.archive.org/web/20210228135226/https://lgballiance.org.uk/gra/. Accessed 28 February 2021.

Ludwig, David. 2016. 'Overlapping Ontologies and Indigenous Knowledge: From Integration to Ontological Self-Determination'. *Studies in History and Philosophy of Science Part A* 59 (October): 36–45.

Ludwig, David. 2017. 'Letting Go of "Natural Kind": Toward a Multidimensional Framework of Nonarbitrary Classification'. *Philosophy of Science* 85 (1): 31–52.

Ludwig, David, and Daniel A. Weiskopf. 2019. 'Ethnoontology: Ways of World-Building across Cultures'. *Philosophy Compass* 14 (9): e12621.

Lugones, María. 2003. *Pilgrimages/Peregrinajes: Theorizing Coalition against Multiple Oppressions*. Lanham, MD: Rowman & Littlefield.

Lugones, María. 2007. 'Heterosexualism and the Colonial/Modern Gender System'. *Hypatia* 22 (1): 186–209.

Lugones, María. 2010. 'Toward a Decolonial Feminism'. *Hypatia* 25 (4): 742–59.MacKinnon, Catharine A. 1989. *Toward a Feminist Theory of the State*. Cambridge, MA: Harvard University Press.

MacKinnon, Catharine A. 2005 [1991]. 'From Practice to Theory, or What Is a White Woman Anyway?' In *Women's Lives, Men's Laws*, by Catharine A. MacKinnon, 22–31. Cambridge, MA: Harvard University Press.

Mallon, Ron. 2004. 'Passing, Traveling and Reality: Social Constructionism and the Metaphysics of Race'. *Noûs* 38 (4): 644–73.

Mallon, Ron. 2016. *The Construction of Human Kinds*. New York: Oxford University Press.

Mason, Rebecca. 2020. 'Rejecting the "Implicit Consensus": A Reply to Jenkins'. *Thought: A Journal of Philosophy* 9 (2): 140–47. https://doi.org/10.1002/tht3.447.

Massimi, Michela. 2022. 'Perspectival Ontology: Between Situated Knowledge and Multiculturalism'. *The Monist* 105 (2): 214–28. https://doi.org/10.1093/monist/onab032.

McGowan, Mary Kate. 2019. *Just Words: On Speech and Hidden Harm*. Oxford: Oxford University Press.

McGreal, Chris. 2015. 'Rachel Dolezal: "I Wasn't Identifying as Black to Upset People. I Was Being Me"'. *Guardian*, 13 December. http://www.theguardian.com/us-news/2015/dec/13/rachel-dolezal-i-wasnt-identifying-as-black-to-upset-people-i-was-being-me.

Medina, José. 2013. *The Epistemology of Resistance: Gender and Racial Oppression, Epistemic Injustice, and the Social Imagination*. New York: Oxford University Press.

Mikkola, Mari. 2009. 'Gender Concepts and Intuitions'. *Canadian Journal of Philosophy* 39 (4): 559–83.

Mikkola, Mari. 2016. *The Wrong of Injustice: Dehumanization and Its Role in Feminist Philosophy*. New York: Oxford University Press.

Mikkola, Mari. 2019. 'Grounding and Anchoring: On the Structure of Epstein's Social Ontology'. *Inquiry* 62 (2): 198–216.

Mills, Charles W. 1999. *The Racial Contract*. Ithaca, NY: Cornell University Press.

Mills, Charles W. 2005. ' "Ideal Theory" as Ideology'. *Hypatia* 20 (3): 165–83.

Ministry of Justice. 2013. 'An Overview of Sexual Offending in England and Wales: Statistics Bulletin'. Ministry of Justice, Home Office, and the Office for National Statistics.   https://www.gov.uk/government/statistics/an-overview-of-sexual-offend ing-in-england-and-wales

Moraga, Cherríe, and Gloria Anzaldúa, eds. 2015. *This Bridge Called My Back: Writings by Radical Women of Color*. 4th ed. Albany: State University of New York Press.

Moyer, Justin Wm. 2015. 'The Surprising Ways Caitlyn Jenner and Rachel Dolezal Are Now Linked'. *Washington Post*, 15 June. https://www.washingtonpost.com/news/morn ing-mix/wp/2015/06/15/the-surprising-ways-caitlyn-jenner-and-rachel-dolezal-are-now-linked/.

Murray, Jenni. 2017. 'Be Trans, Be Proud—but Don't Call Yourself a "Real Woman"'. *Sunday Times*, 3 May. https://www.thetimes.co.uk/article/be-trans-be-proud-but-dont-call-yourself-a-real-woman-frtld7q5c.

nia. 2020. 'Self-ID Dropped'. 22 September. https://niaendingviolence.org.uk/self-id-dropped/.

O'Donnell, Katherine. 2019. 'The Theological Basis for Trans-Exclusionary Radical Feminist Positions'. In *Lesbian Feminism: Essays Opposing the Global Heteropatriarchy*, edited by Niharika Banerjea, Kath Browne, Eduarda Ferreira, Marta Olasik, and Julie Podmore, 81–102. London: Zed.

Olufemi, Lola. 2020. *Feminism, Interrupted: Disrupting Power*. London: Pluto.

Oyěwùmí, Oyèrónkẹ́. 1997. *Invention of Women: Making an African Sense of Western Gender Discourses*. Minneapolis: University of Minnesota Press.

Pearce, Ruth. 2018. *Understanding Trans Health: Discourse, Power and Possibility*. Bristol, UK: Policy.

Pearce, Ruth, Sonja Erikainen, and Ben Vincent. 2020. 'TERF Wars: An Introduction'. *Sociological Review* 68 (4): 677–98.

Pettit, Philip. 1996. 'Freedom as Antipower'. *Ethics* 106 (3): 576–604.

Piper, Adrian. 1992. 'Passing for White, Passing for Black'. *Transition* 58: 4–32.

Renault, Emmanuel. 2016. 'Critical Theory and Processual Social Ontology'. *Journal of Social Ontology* 2 (1): 17–32.

Ritchie, Katherine. 2017. 'Ron Mallon: The Construction of Human Kinds'. *Ethics* 128 (2): 478–82.

Ritchie, Katherine. 2020. 'Social Structures and the Ontology of Social Groups'. *Philosophy and Phenomenological Research* 100 (2): 402–24.

Root, Michael. 2000. 'How We Divide the World'. *Philosophy of Science* 67: S628–39.

Rothstein, Richard. 2017. *The Color of Law: A Forgotten History of How Our Government Segregated America*. New York: Liveright.

Russell, Camisha. 2019. 'On Black Women, "In Defense of Transracialism", and Imperial Harm'. *Hypatia* 34 (2): 176–94.

Searle, John. 1996. *The Construction of Social Reality*. London: Penguin.

Searle, John. 2011. *Making the Social World*. Oxford: Oxford University Press.

Serano, Julia. 2013. *Excluded: Making Feminist and Queer Movements More Inclusive*. Berkeley, CA: Seal.

Serano, Julia. 2016. *Whipping Girl: A Transsexual Woman on Sexism and the Scapegoating of Femininity*. 2nd ed. Emeryville, CA: Seal.

Sharpe, Christina. 2016. *In the Wake: On Blackness and Being*. Durham, NC: Duke University Press.

Snorton, C. Riley. 2017. *Black on Both Sides: A Racial History of Trans Identity*. 3rd ed. Minneapolis: University of Minnesota Press.

Soon, Valerie. 2021. 'Social Structural Explanation'. *Philosophy Compass* 16 (10): e12782.

Spelman, Elizabeth V. 1990. *Inessential Woman*. Boston: Beacon.

Spencer, Quayshawn. 2014. 'A Radical Solution to the Race Problem'. *Philosophy of Science* 81 (5): 1025–38.

Spencer, Quayshawn. 2018. 'A Racial Classification for Medical Genetics'. *Philosophical Studies* 175 (5): 1013–37.

Spencer, Quayshawn. 2019. 'A More Radical Solution to the Race Problem'. *Proceedings of the Aristotelian Society Supplementary Volume* 93 (1): 25–48.

Spillers, Hortense J. 1987. 'Mama's Baby, Papa's Maybe: An American Grammar Book'. *Diacritics* 17 (2): 65–81.

Stein, Rachel. 2017. 'Trans Women Are Women'. Stonewall, 5 March. https://www.stonewall.org.uk/node/45364.

Stone, Alison. 2007. *An Introduction to Feminist Philosophy*. Cambridge: Polity.

Stryker, Susan. 1994. 'My Words to Victor Frankenstein above the Village of Chamounix: Performing Transgender Rage'. *GLQ: A Journal of Lesbian and Gay Studies* 1 (3): 237–54.

Sundstrom, Ronald R. 2002a. 'Race as a Human Kind'. *Philosophy & Social Criticism* 28 (1): 91–115.

Sundstrom, Ronald R. 2002b. '"Racial" Nominalism'. *Journal of Social Philosophy* 33 (2): 193–210.

Sundstrom, Ronald R. 2003. 'Race and Place: Social Space in the Production of Human Kinds'. *Philosophy & Geography* 6 (1): 83–95.

Táíwò, Olúfẹ́mi O. 2020. 'Being-in-the-Room Privilege: Elite Capture and Epistemic Deference'. *The Philosopher*. https://www.thephilosopher1923.org/essay-taiwo.

Tanesini, Alessandra. 2016. '"Calm Down, Dear": Intellectual Arrogance, Silencing and Ignorance'. *Aristotelian Society Supplementary Volume* 90 (1): 71–92.

Tanesini, Alessandra. 2018. 'Intellectual Servility and Timidity'. *Journal of Philosophical Research* 43 (October): 21–41.

Tanesini, Alessandra, and Mark Norris Lance. 2000. 'Identity Judgements, Queer Politics'. *Radical Philosophy* 100: 42–51.

Thomasson, Amie. 2003. 'Foundations for a Social Ontology'. *Protosociology* 18: 269–290.

Thompson, Michael J. 2017. 'Social Ontology and Social Critique: Toward a New Paradigm for Critical Theory'. In *The Social Ontology of Capitalism*, edited by Daniel Krier and Mark P. Worrell, 15–45. New York: Palgrave Macmillan.

Truss, Elizabeth, and Government Equalities Office. 2020. 'Written Ministerial Statement: Response to Gender Recognition Act (2004) Consultation'. https://www.gov.uk/government/speeches/response-to-gender-recognition-act-2004-consultation.

Tuvel, Rebecca. 2017. 'In Defense of Transracialism'. *Hypatia* 32 (2): 263–78.

Van Fraassen, Bas C. 1980. *The Scientific Image*. Oxford: Clarendon; New York: Oxford University Press.

Waldron, Jeremy. 2014. *The Harm in Hate Speech*. Cambridge, MA: Harvard University Press.

Watson, Lori. 2016. 'The Woman Question'. *Transgender Studies Quarterly* 3 (1–2): 246–53.

White, Joy. 2020. *Terraformed: Young Black Lives in the Inner City*. London: Repeater.

Wilchins, Riki. 2017. *Burn the Binary! Selected Writings on the Politics of Trans, Genderqueer and Nonbinary*. Riverdale, NY: Riverdale Avenue.

Williams, Pete. 2020. 'In Landmark Case, Supreme Court Rules LGBTQ Workers Are Protected from Job Discrimination'. NBC News, 15 June. https://www.nbcnews.com/politics/supreme-court/supreme-court-rules-existing-civil-rights-law-protects-gay-lesbian-n1231018.

Wills, Vanessa. 2013. ' "What Are You Doing around Here?": Trayvon Martin and the Logic of Black Guilt'. In *Pursuing Trayvon Martin: Historical Contexts and Contemporary Manifestations of Racial Dynamics*, edited by George Yancy and Janine Jones, 225–36. Lanham, MD: Lexington.

Witt, Charlotte. 2011. *The Metaphysics of Gender*. New York: Oxford University Press.

Wittig, Monique. 1996. 'The Category of Sex'. In *Sex in Question: French Materialist Feminism*, edited by Diana Leonard and Lisa Adkins, 25–30. London: Taylor & Francis.

Women and Equalities Committee. 2021. 'Reform of the Gender Recognition Act: Third Report of Session 2021–22'. House of Commons. https://committees.parliament.uk/publications/8329/documents/84728/default/.

Yancy, George. 2016. *Black Bodies, White Gazes: The Continuing Significance of Race in America*. 2nd ed. Lanham, MD: Rowman & Littlefield.

Young, Iris Marion. 1980. 'Throwing Like a Girl: A Phenomenology of Feminine Body Comportment Motility and Spatiality'. *Human Studies* 3 (1): 137–56.

Young, Iris Marion. 2011. *Justice and the Politics of Difference*. Princeton, NJ: Princeton University Press.

Zheng, Robin. 2018. 'What Is My Role in Changing the System? A New Model of Responsibility for Structural Injustice'. *Ethical Theory and Moral Practice* 21 (4): 869–85.

Index

For the benefit of digital users, indexed terms that span two pages (e.g., 52–53) may, on occasion, appear on only one of those pages.